The Act
of Writing

The Act of Writing

Eric Gould
University of Denver

Robert DiYanni
Pace University, Pleasantville

William Smith
Virginia Commonwealth University

Random House New York

First Edition
987654321
Copyright © 1989 by Random House, Inc.

Library of Congress Cataloging in Publication Data
Gould, Eric, 1943–
The act of writing.

Includes index.
1. English language—Rhetoric. 2. College readers.
I. DiYanni, Robert, 1947– II. Smith, William, 1947–
III. Title.
PE1417.G59 1988 808'.042 88-26450
ISBN 0-394-35502-4

Cover Painting: Janie Paul

Cover Design: Karin Batten

Text acknowledgments appear on pp. 307–311.

Manufactured in the United States of America

Preface for Teachers

The Act of Writing, like its companion text, *The Art of Reading*, aims to involve students directly and immediately in the process of intellectual inquiry. Where our earlier book demonstrated an approach to reading, this one presents an approach to writing. In our view the two acts are reciprocal. Both reading and writing are essentially revisionary processes that involve repeated attempts to make sense in, with, and through language. Both require the expression and evocation of feeling along with the initiation and development of thought. Mutually supportive, reading and writing depend on one another, stimulate one another, engender one another. Both are personal, individual acts that are nonetheless rife with social implications since they depend on a shared understanding of language and culture.

These are the assumptions that underlie our book.

We have organized *The Act of Writing* to accentuate the dynamic, interactive character of the writing process. We begin by encouraging students to consider how dialogue empowers writers to engage readers. In our opening chapter, "Creating Dialogue," we invite students to enter boldly into the experience of reading and writing dialogic texts. From here we turn in our second chapter, "Writing from Reading," to ways writers make sense of texts for themselves and for others through writing. We invite students to explore how writing aids reading and how writing flows naturally from it. We provide opportunities here for students to do three kinds of writing: (1) writing to understand texts; (2) writing to explain texts; and (3) writing to evaluate texts.

Chapters 3 and 4, on "Writing and Thinking" and on "Writing and Form," offer a combination of traditional and fresh approaches to invention and arrangement. Invention is treated from the perspective that writing is a form of thinking, that generating and sifting ideas is a natural, inevitable part of the process. Arrangement is approached first as a set of macroscopic rhetorical patterns of expression and second as a way of heightening students' perception of form. We try to show how arrangement is more than a matter of providing an organizational framework, how it also involves developing an appreciation of how form orders life as well as language. We explore style in our final chapter, "Writing and Revising," in which we attend to small-scale stylistic considerations at the level of sentence and word. Our emphasis on style is on the effect linguistic choices and patterns have on readers.

Chapter 5, "The Persuasive Voice," focuses on developing a credible and persuasive voice in writing. It also attends to the converse of this: how readers are persuaded by a writer's credibility. Although our discussion of persuasion is positioned near the end of the book, it shares affinities with the opening chapter on dialogue. Persuasion, of course, is the ultimate aim of all writing, whatever its mode or form. Our approach to persuasion allows room for feeling and aesthetic pleasure as well as logical argument and rational conviction.

Throughout *The Act of Writing* we stress the dynamic, fluid, interactive dimension of writing. We repeatedly place acts of writing in the context of varied situations. Moreover, we try to suggest the revisionary nature of writing by including references to revising throughout the book. And in an attempt to make the book both accessible and pedagogically viable, we include student writing, literary and nonliterary texts, visual texts, and many invitations to compose. Finally, we also try to keep the book's temper amiable.

In working on the book we received assistance from the following reviewers, whose sound advice helped us very much: Joseph Comprone, University of Louisville; Jan Cooper, Oberlin College; Diana George, Michigan Technological University; Richard K. Harmston, University of Michigan; Richard Jenseth, Pacific Lutheran University; Bruce N. Leland, Western Illinois University; Robert B. Lyons, Queens College; Susan Miller, University of Utah; and Jeffrey Sommers, Miami University of Ohio.

For bringing us together to work on *The Act of Writing* (and *The Art of Reading* as well) and for supporting our efforts so generously and graciously, we thank Steve Pensinger. Thanks also to his associates at Random House, who expertly guided the book through the stages of production: Tom Holton, David Morris, Safra Nimrod, Susan Phillips, and Harold Vaughn.

Preface for Students

Writing is a creative act. None of our writing is simply a translation of completed thoughts into words on a page. Even if we are only presenting a list of facts, we have to choose from among the evidence and decide how to present it. The act of writing is creative because it requires us to interpret or make sense of something: an experience, a text, an event. We write largely in order to understand and not just to express ourselves. In fact, most of our writing in college and the world of work aims both to reach an understanding and to share that understanding with other people.

In doing this, we often begin with, or at least pass through, stages of confusion and doubt. We rarely know, for example, exactly what we will write before we start writing. We don't really know what we want to say until we have finished writing, which usually means going through several drafts. Of course, we usually have *some* idea of what we want to say, and our opening sentences may be transcriptions of key ideas. As we continue writing, however, we may run out of inspiration. Or we may discover other ideas that we didn't know we had.

The more we write, the clearer it becomes that writing is a way of finding out what our ideas, and even our intentions really are. And those discoveries involve a good deal of rereading and rewriting. We state and restate our ideas, revising our texts, until we are at least reasonably satisfied that "this is what we want to say."

Thus writing is always a discovery *process;* it is not a mechanical act of saying what we already know. It is a *process,* a series of interdependent steps toward an end. The "end" in this case is the text we create, a text that we feel satisfied with. The steps we take to produce such texts are what this book is about.

We will consider writing as a series of related text-making activities: generating, arranging, and developing ideas in sentences; drafting, shaping, and rereading the texts we make; and editing and revising them. This is why we call writing a process rather than a procedure. Procedure suggests that there is a necessary order to the activities of writing, or a set of rules for producing good writing. There is not. We occasionally suggest that you follow a *progressive* set of activities in producing your written texts. But such progressions can be developed in many ways. You are encouraged to develop your own habits of writing and not to follow any formula. Above all you are encouraged to see writing as a social act.

Although writing requires us to think and interpret independently, to describe and invent, to explain and argue from our own points of view, even to change our minds in unexpected ways, it is nonetheless more than a lonely act of struggling with words. That description does not do justice to the other side of writing: that we write for others, for readers outside ourselves. For the meanings we make in our writing must be completed by another—a reader. It is this reader who brings our text to life.

In short, writing is not private; it is always *a form of social dialogue,* a way of talking to someone. And that is true not just because it is pleasant to have conversations with people, or because it is good to be friendly with readers in order to win them over to our ways of seeing things. The reader is essential to complete the meaning of anything we write.

The message the reader receives is actually the message the reader puts together. The writer directs the reader's thoughts, limiting the range of information on paper. But the reader selects the most important information to focus on, for hardly any of us can absorb everything on a page, especially not in a single reading. Furthermore, although a writer can tell the reader exactly what he or she is thinking, the reader has to decide what the writer's intentions "really" are, based on the evidence of what is said. Readers adapt what they read to their own experience; they build it on to what they already know. That is the only way any of us can make sense of anything.

There is no single "ideal" reading of any text and there is no ideal expression of a thought. We have many texts, readers, and thoughts—and many shared readings. The best writing and reading draws readers in and lets them participate in making its meaning. It keeps readers reading on, making them think about what is happening and encouraging them to develop their own insights in response to what the writer is saying.

You may think that such reading experience is true only of literary texts, but it is not. It is true of business reports that set out information clearly and make strong arguments. It is true of a good university handbook that makes you feel that you are an important part of an educated community and not merely another body in class. It is true of every text that values a reader's involvement. And we do not enjoy reading texts unless they *do* try to keep our attention.

So we have two main aims in this book. We want to show you that *writing is a discovery process,* a way of finding out what you are thinking and what you want to say in particular situations. Second, we want you to develop your writing as something said to readers, as *a form of social dialogue,* a way of talking to people. You are invited to begin doing just that by turning to the opening chapter.

Contents

An insert of color photographs can be found following p. 174.

CHAPTER 4 *Writing and Form 135*

CHAPTER 6 *Writing and Revising* *259*

CHAPTER **1**

Creating Dialogue

DIALOGUE

DORIS: . . .Are you all right, honey?

GEORGE: I'm fine.

DORIS: You sure there's not something bothering you?

GEORGE: Yes—you. Do you always go around dressed like a bad finger painting?

DORIS: *(Grinning.)* No. I have to admit that today I am a little—well—visually overstated.

GEORGE: Why?

DORIS: I guess I wanted to make sure you knew you were dealing with the "new me." Sort of "show and tell."

GEORGE: You look like a refugee from Sunset Strip.

DORIS: Berkeley. I went back to school.

GEORGE: *(Bewildered.)* What for?

DORIS: *(Grins.)* You mean what do I want to be when I grow up?

GEORGE: Well, you have to admit it's a bit strange becoming a schoolgirl at your age.

DORIS: Are you kidding? Listen, it's not easy being the only one in the class with clear skin.
(She moves to get her duffel bag, unpacks it through the following.)

GEORGE: *(Sitting.)* What made you do it?

1

DORIS: It was a dinner party that finally pushed me into it. Harry's boss invited us for dinner and I panicked.

GEORGE: Why?

DORIS: I'd spent so much time with kids, I didn't know if I was capable of carrying on an intelligent conversation with anyone over five who wasn't a supermarket checkout clerk. Anyway, I went and was seated next to *the* boss. Well, I surprised myself. He talked—then I talked— you know, just a real conversation. I was feeling real cool until I noticed him looking at me in a weird way. I looked down and realized that all the time we'd been talking I'd been cutting up the meat on his plate. At that moment I *knew* I had to get out of the house.

GEORGE: But why school?

(She stretches out on the bed.)

DORIS: It's hard to explain. I felt restless and—undirected and I thought an education might give me some answers.

GEORGE: What sort of answers?

DORIS: *(Shrugs.)* To find out where it's really at.

GEORGE: *(Gets up.)* Jesus.

DORIS: What's the matter?

GEORGE: That expression.

DORIS: Okay. To find out who the hell I was.

GEORGE: You don't get those sort of answers from a classroom.

DORIS: I'm not in the classroom all the time. The demonstrations are a learning experience in themselves.

GEORGE: Demonstrations against what?

DORIS: The war of course. Didn't you hear about it? It was in all the papers.

GEORGE: *(Curtly.)* Demonstrations aren't going to stop the war.

DORIS: You have a better idea?

GEORGE: Look, I didn't come up here to discuss politics.

DORIS: Well, so far you've turned down sex and politics. You want to try religion?

GEORGE: I think I'll try a Librium.

(She watches him as he takes pill out and moves to take it with a glass of water from the drink tray.)

Here is some background to the situation just dramatized: George and Doris are lovers in *Same Time, Next Year,* a play by Bernard Slade. They meet every year at the same time and place, an inn near Mendocino, north of San Francisco. This extract, from the second act of the play, occurs fourteen years after their first meeting, in 1965, when George is forty-one and Doris is thirty-eight. The student demonstrations referred to are those at Berkeley against the Vietnam War. George, according to the staging notes, "is wearing an expensive conservative suit, his hair is gray and is worn unfashionably short . . . he looks and acts older than his years." Doris "is wearing a brightly colored granny gown, beads, sandals, and her hair is long and flowing. She is carrying a decal-decorated duffel bag."

Consider the following questions:

1. What is Doris trying to tell George about her life and why?

2. What clues can you find that George does or does not understand what she is saying? Does he approve or disapprove?

3. What problems do Doris and George have as they try to communicate with each other?

4. What, for you, are the broad social and moral implications of the encounter of George and Doris?

5. In what ways do you think this extract is like and unlike speech as it would be spoken in real life?

Dialogue and Monologue Dialogue is a conversation and exchange of ideas between two or more people that occurs for some *reason*. We talk to people in a social context: to transfer or gain information, to make connections, to explore similarities among and differences between ourselves, to express ourselves, and to discuss a topic. All dialogue, in fact, occurs in social situations.

A dialogue differs from a *monologue*, which is prolonged discourse by a single speaker. People may talk without interruption because they are anxious, in an expansive mood, merely self-centered, or because they believe their ideas are important.

But in both a monologue and a dialogue, to talk is to talk *to* someone. The difference is that in a dialogue, the specific interest is also in talking *with* someone, in trying to close a gap between ourselves and others, in trying to get the "other" involved in what we say. Beyond the transfer of information, we talk to become involved, to feel less marginal, to connect with others. In this chapter we deal with talking and writing as efforts to create real dialogue: to overcome isolation, to explore differences, to make connections. We discuss speech and writing together because they share closely these everyday functions of dialogue.

Let us return to the extract from *Same Time, Next Year* for a moment. Of course, it is not an exact transcription of how people talk to each other. It has been polished; all the pauses, "you knows," "ers," and "ums" have been removed. But it represents people trying to talk to one another. Let us consider further how this fictional conversation works.

Doris reaches out to George with "Are you all right, honey?" but George is put off by Doris's outfit and by her recent return to school. He retreats a little and we sense a barrier between them. He seems intimidated. He acts as though he does not understand why Doris wants to dress like a sixties "flower child" and why she wants to return to college. But perhaps he understands only too well and is resisting what he knows. What do you think?

Doris tries to explain her new outlook on life: the need to get out of the house and to find real conversation, to "find herself," and "to find out where it's really at." But George is not impressed with this language. It is too stale for him. (Or is it the idea of "finding oneself" or "being oneself" that he is resisting?) Why does he take a tranquilizer?

The passage seems to record an unsuccessful dialogue, one in which George and Doris have been having a kind of conversation, and information has changed hands, but they have not really exchanged ideas. Of course, they are *trying to*, and each realizes what the other wants to say. She especially is trying to get through to him, but he is resisting for some reason. Why? There is a distance growing between them; there are differences that somehow have to be resolved because *each can read the other's speech all too well.*

Exercises

Form pairs in which one person plays Doris and the other George. As a warm-up to getting into your character, read the extract out loud, taking your parts, then consider the questions asked in the text above.

1. Discuss the steps you think George and Doris have to take to create a real dialogue.

2. Continue the conversation between George and Doris that might *follow* from the extract to finally create a genuine dialogue between them. (The next few lines do not have to present a real breakthrough, but by the end of the conversation, try to have some kind of useful exchange of ideas between the two characters.) Ask yourself: What does Doris have to say to get through to George about her new life, to close the distance between them? What would you say next if you were Doris? Develop how you think George would respond to her until the two reach a mutual understanding.

Shortening Distances   The art of dialogue is the art of shortening the distance between yourself and a listener. There are any number of ways in which this can be done, but here are a few you will probably recognize:

- You can explore a topic objectively, noting facts that can be shared and agreed upon, trying to establish common perceptions and grounds for discussion.

- You can talk honestly—but not for too long—about your reactions to and feelings about the topic, trying to raise the listener's interest in and respect for your experiences.

- You can talk about the other person's reactions, showing that you understand the listener's position and appreciate it, and even agree with a part or all of what he or she is saying.

- You can ask the other person questions, trying to draw out comments, and making it clear that you are genuinely interested in learning about that person's ideas.

- You can be sensitive to differences that emerge as you talk, carefully exploring rather than accentuating them.

We all know from daily experience that most of our attempts at dialogue are not very artful. Distances do not always narrow easily between people in conversation. Sometimes goodwill is lacking; sometimes personal agendas are too radically opposed. Attempts at dialogue are rarely completely rational or objective. We bring to every discussion all our emotional needs and psychological uncertainties. We may have to take into account feelings we do not understand, or have not thought through, or cannot resist blurting out.

But in even the most stubbornly evasive efforts to communicate, as the English playwright Harold Pinter once said, our problem is not that we do not or cannot get through to each other, but that we communicate all too well and resist what is said. We talk *at* each other and *appear* not to be communicating at all, but we do; we just will not confront what the other person is saying. Do you find George and Doris doing that? Why or why not?

But a real dialogue can make us feel comfortable and allow us to open up to others. It can be remarkably intimate and not intimidating. We do not just reach out and touch someone, and we do not just find out something about the other person. Nor do we simply exchange information. We begin to find *ourselves* reflected in what the other person says, whether we like it or not. We become conscious of ourselves as part of the conversation, *in relationship to the other*. (What is the evidence that George and Doris find themselves in each other's words?) In fact, we actually learn what we are like from how others see us.

A dialogue, then, is not just an exchange of ideas. It is also an intimate exercise in self-revelation and self-understanding. A dialogue shortens distances between the self and the other, but it does *not* have to eradicate differences to do so. We do not have to make the other person agree with us in order to have a dialogue. Most often, in fact, dialogue grows out of, and preserves, differences even when our deepest secrets emerge.

At the end of the scene in which the extract from *Same Time, Next Year* is taken, Doris has discovered that George has some violent views about the Vietnam War, quite the opposite of how she feels. And as she criticizes him roughly for them, and he becomes very defensive, we find the two dramatically at odds. But then, strangely, the dialogue starts to grow.

DORIS: My God, how could you vote for a man like that [Goldwater]?

GEORGE: *(Moving toward her.)* Could we talk about this later?

DORIS: *(Pushing him away.)* No, we'll talk about it *now!* Why?

GEORGE: *(Frustrated—yelling.)* Because I have a son who wants to be a rock musician!!

DORIS: What kind of reason is *that?*

GEORGE: *(Sitting.)* The best reason I can come up with right now in my condition!

DORIS: Well, you're going to have to do a lot better!

GEORGE: Okay, he was going to end the war!

DORIS: By bombing the hell out of innocent people!

GEORGE: What innocent people? They're *Reds!*

DORIS: They just wanted their country back!

GEORGE: Oh, I'm sick of hearing all that liberal crap! We've got the H bomb. Why don't we use it!

DORIS: *Are you serious?*

GEORGE: Yes, I'm serious. Wipe the sons of bitches off the face of the earth!

(She stares at him for a moment.)

DORIS: *(Quietly, incredulous.)* My God, I don't know anything about you. What sort of a man are you?

GEORGE: Right now—very frustrated.

DORIS: All this time I thought you were a liberal Democrat. You told me you worked for Stevenson.

GEORGE: *(In a tired voice.)* That was years ago.

DORIS: What changed you? What happened to you?

GEORGE: *(Bitterly.)* I grew up.

DORIS: Yeah, well in my opinion you didn't turn out too well.

GEORGE: Let's forget it, huh?

DORIS: Forget it? How can I forget it? I mean being stuffy and—and old-fashioned is one thing but being a Fascist is another!

GEORGE: *(Flaring.)* I am not a Fascist!

DORIS: You're advocating mass murder!

GEORGE: Doris—drop it, okay! Just—drop it!

DORIS: How could you *do* this to me? Why, you stand for everything I'm against!

GEORGE: Then maybe you're against the wrong things!

DORIS: You used to think the same way I did.

GEORGE: I changed!

DORIS: *Why?*

GEORGE: Because Michael was killed! How the hell else did you expect me to feel!!

(There is a long pause as she stands transfixed, trying to absorb this.)

DORIS: *(Finally.)* Oh—dear—God. How?

GEORGE: He was trying to get a wounded man onto a Red Cross helicopter and a sniper killed him.

(Without a word she moves to him, starts to put her arms around him. He brushes her away, rises and moves to window and stares out.)

DORIS: *(Finally—almost in a whisper.)* When?
(There is a pause.)

GEORGE: *(Dispassionately.)* We heard in the middle of a big July 4th party. Helen went completely to pieces—I'll never forget it. I didn't feel a thing. I thought I was in shock and it would hit me later. *(He turns to face her.)* But you know something? It never did. The only emotion I can feel is blind anger. I didn't shed a tear.
(She doesn't say anything.)

Isn't that the darnedest thing? I can't cry over my own son's death. I loved him but—for the life of me—I can't seem to cry over him.
(She doesn't move as he crosses to shakily pour himself a drink.)

Doris, I'm sorry about—everything. Lately I've been a bit on edge and—
(The glass slips out of his hand, he tries to save it but it hits the dresser and smashes.)

Oh, great! Will you look at that—I've gone and cut myself. If it isn't—one—damn thing—after—
(He starts to sob. DORIS moves to him and puts her arms around him. He sinks into a chair, and buries his head into her chest as the curtain falls.)

Exercises

1.   Consider the following questions:

(a)   Why does George not want to tell Doris about his son?
(b)   Why do you think George has never been able to cry over his son's death until now?
(c)   Why *does* George cry now?
(d)   Do you think George and Doris have shortened the distance between them? Have they preserved or eradicated their differences? Explain your responses.
(e)   What do you think George learns about himself from his discussion with Doris? And what does Doris learn about herself?

2.   Re-form into pairs as you did for the exercise at the end of the preceding section.

(a)   Try out your answers to the above questions on your partner and see if you can reach agreement.
(b)   Compare and contrast the version of the dialogue after the first extract that you wrote with the one the playwright provides.

3.   Here is an exercise from John Gardner's *The Art of Fiction*.

(a)   Read it carefully and write the dialogue as requested, making sure you develop a contrast between the two voices.

(b)   Now imagine that you are either the man or the woman in the scene. Write a letter to a close friend describing the encounter with your husband or wife and explain what the secret is.

> Write a dialogue in which each of the two characters has a secret. Do not reveal the secret but make the reader intuit it. For example, the dialogue might be between a husband, who has just lost his job and hasn't worked up the courage to tell his wife, and his wife, who has a lover in the bedroom. Purpose: to give two characters individual ways of speaking, and to make dialogue crackle with feelings not directly expressed. Remember that in dialogue, as a general rule, every pause must somehow be shown, either by narration (for example, "she paused") or by some gesture or other break that shows the pause. And remember that gesture is a part of all real dialogue. Sometimes, for instance, we look away instead of answering.

The Listener in Mind   It is easy to idealize what "good communication" is, or to make up vast lists of characteristics of how we might communicate well. But dialogue is largely unpredictable, no matter how we try to control a situation. We relate to others in complex social situations, largely by learning how to *read* the other person and our own feelings by drawing on our experience of similar social situations. Dialogue is a *socially learned* activity.

More important, *we learn to say things with our listener in mind*, remembering previous conversations with him or her and with others. Whatever we say is conditioned not only by where we are and what we want to say, but by our *concept* of the person we are talking to.

No matter why or how we want to communicate with someone—in speech or in writing—one thing makes communication possible: We believe that in some way we can be understood by listeners and that we can understand them. Dialogue takes place *because* we want to make connections with someone and because we have developed honest strategies for doing so. This is even true when we try to communicate with people with whom we do not share a language, as we do when we are lost in a foreign city.

Dialogue is our way of taking chances with language, projecting ourselves into a world of *differences*—different people, different situations, different interpretations of life, even our own conflicting opinions. And we take chances in dialogue because we believe that we can make connections. That is where writing begins, not just in self-expression, but in making connections. Writing is always in some way an exploration of our ideas and an act of faith in telling others about them. We have to project ourselves out to an audience; we have to trust that they will pay attention; we make ourselves vulnerable; we ask the audience to listen and respond in part on our terms. But we do so knowing three things:

- Dialogue is always *possible* and we can help create it.
- Dialogue develops when we have a listener in mind.
- Dialogue explores but does not have to eradicate differences.

Here are three more speeches from three modern plays for you to consider.

No Man's Land
Harold Pinter

BRIGGS: We're old friends, Jack and myself. We met at a street corner. I should tell you he'll deny this account. His story will be different. I was standing at a street corner. A car drew up. It was him. He asked me the way to Bolsover street. I told him Bolsover street was in the middle of an intricate one-way system. It was a one-way system easy enough to get into. The only trouble was that, once in, you couldn't get out. I told him his best bet, if he really wanted to get to Bolsover street, was to take the first left, first right, second right, third on the left, keep his eye open for a hardware shop, go right round the square, keeping to the inside lane, take the second Mews on the right and then stop. He will find himself facing a very tall office block, with a crescent courtyard. He can take advantage of this office block. He can go round the crescent, come out the other way, follow the arrows, go past two sets of traffic lights and take the next left indicated by the first green filter he comes across. He's got the Post Office Tower in his vision the whole time. All he's got to do is to reverse into the underground car park, change gear, go straight on, and he'll find himself in Bolsover street with no trouble at all. I did warn him, though, that he'll still be faced with the problem, having found Bolsover street, of losing it. I told him I knew one or two people who'd been wandering up and down Bolsover street for years. They'd wasted their bloody youth there. The people who live there, their faces are grey, they're in a state of despair, but nobody pays any attention, you see. All people are worried about is their illgotten gains. I wrote to The Times about it. Life At A Dead End, I called it. Went for nothing. Anyway, I told him that probably the best thing he could do was to forget the whole idea of getting to Bolsover street. I remember saying to him: This trip you've got in mind, drop it, it could prove fatal. But he said he had to deliver a parcel. Anyway, I took all this trouble with him because he had a nice open face.

Twirler*
"Jane Martin"

A young woman stands center stage. She is dressed in a spangled, single-piece swimsuit, the kind that is specially made for baton twirlers. She holds a shining, silver baton in her hand.

APRIL: I started when I was six. Momma sawed off a broom handle, and Uncle Carbo slapped some sort of silver paint, well, grey really, on it and I went down in the basement and twirled. Later on, Momma hit the daily double on horses named Spin Dry and Silver Revolver and she said that was a sign so she gave me lessons at the Dainty Deb Dance studio where the lady, Miss Aurelia, taught some twirling on the side.

   I won the Ohio Juniors title when I was six and the Midwest Young Adult Division three years later and then in High School I finished fourth in the nationals. Momma and I wore look-alike Statue of Liberty costumes that she had to send clear to Nebraska to get, and Daddy was there in a T-shirt with my name, April . . . my first name is April and my last name is March. There were four thousand people there, and when they yelled my name, golden balloons fell out of the ceiling. Nobody—not even Charlene Ann Morrison—ever finished fourth at my age.

   Oh, I've flown high and known tragedy both. My daddy says it's put spirit in my soul and steel in my heart. My left hand was crushed in a riding accident by a horse named Big Blood Red, and though I came back to twirl, I couldn't do it at the highest level. That

*See cautionary note, p. 307.

was denied me by Big Blood Red who clipped my wings. You mustn't pity me though. Oh, by no means! Being denied showed me the way, showed me the glory that sits inside life where you can't see it.

People think you're a twit if you twirl. It's a prejudice of the unknowing. Twirlers are the niggers of a white University. Yes, they are. One time I was doing fire batons at a night game, and all of a sudden I see this guy walk out of the stands. I was doing triples and he walks right out past the half time marshalls, comes up to me . . . he had this blue bead head band, I can still see it. Walks right up, and when I come front after a back reverse, he spits in my face. That's the only, single time I ever dropped a baton. Dropped 'em both in front of sixty thousand people, and he smiles see, and he says this thing I won't repeat. He called me a bodily part in front of half of Ohio. It was like being raped. It shows that beauty inspires hate and that hating beauty is Satan.

You haven't twirled, have you? I can see that by your hands. Would you like to hold my silver baton? Here, hold it.

You can't imagine what it feels like to have that baton up in the air. I used to twirl with this girl who called it blue-collar zen. The "tons" catch the sun when they're up, and when they go up, you go up too. You can't twirl if you're not *inside* the "ton." When you've got 'em up over twenty feet it's like flying or gliding. Your hands are still down, but your insides spin and rise and leave the ground. Only a twirler knows that, so we're not niggers.

The secret for a twirler is the light. You live or die with the light. It's your fate. The best is a February sky clouded right over in the late afternoon. It's all background then, and what happens is that the "tons" leave tracks, traces, they etch the air, and if you're hot, if your hands have it, you can draw on the sky.

Charlene Ann Morrison . . . God, Charlene Ann! She was inspired by something beyond man. She won the nationals nine years in a row. Unparalleled and unrepeatable. The last two years she had leukemia and at the end you could see through her hands when she twirled. Charlene Ann died with a "ton" thirty feet up, her momma swears on that. I did speed with Charlene at a regional in Fargo and she may be fibben' but she says there was a day when her "tons" erased while they turned. Like the sky was a sheet of rain and the "tons" were car wipers and when she had erased this certain part of the sky, you could see the face of the Lord God Jesus, and his hair was all rhinestones and he was doing this incredible singing like the sound of a piccolo. The people who said Charlene was crazy probably never twirled a day in their life.

Twirling is the physical parallel of revelation. You can't know that. Twirling is the throwing of yourself up to God. It's a pure gift, hidden from Satan because it is wrapped and disguised in the midst of football. It is God throwing, spirit fire, and very few come to it. You have to grow eyes in your heart to understand its message, and when it opens to you, it becomes your path to suffer ridicule, to be crucified by misunderstanding, and to be spit upon. I need my baton now.

There is one twirling no one sees. At the winter solstice we go to a meadow God showed us just outside of Green Bay. The God throwers come there on December twenty-first. There's snow, sometimes deep snow and our clothes fall away and we stand unprotected while acolytes bring the "tons." They are ebony "tons" with razors set all along the shaft. They are three feet long. One by one the twirlers throw, two "tons" each, thirty feet up, and as they fall back, they cut your hands. The razors arch into the air and find God and then fly down to take your blood in a crucifixion, and the red drops draw God on the ground and if you are up with the batons you can look down and see him revealed. Red on white. Red on white. You can't imagine. You can't imagine how wonderful it is!

I started twirling when I was six, but I never really twirled until my hand was crushed by the horse named Big Blood Red. I have seen God's face from thirty feet up in the air and I know him.

Listen. I will leave my silver baton here for you. Lying here as if I forgot it and when the people file out you can wait back and pick it up, it can be yours . . . it can be your burden. It is the eye of the needle. I leave it for you.

(The lights fade.)

The Taking of Miss Janie
Ed Bullins

SHARON: And we were married . . . Len and I. At the First Unitarian Church. It was a dull wedding. But my mother was happy and cried. And my sister didn't act too snobbish. Even lots of my old beaus came. And it all turned out lots better than I thought it would. I was glad, in fact. And Len and I settled down in an apartment close to City College where Len was in his fifth year, even though it's a two-year school. And we started getting used to each other. Which was easier said than done. In fact, it was hell. You know, it took us over five years before we really sorta ironed out our difficulties. But the times we had, my

God! We gave a million parties. And I momentarily fell back into my bad habits with men. But it wasn't serious, so Len and I discussed it and decided it was merely an aspect of my neurosis. And we moved at least a dozen times. Sometimes trying to get away from each other. And I tried to break away from Len when he wasn't trying to put me down or in my place or in the kitchen and it was pretty terrible for a while. We even broke up a number of times. But that's history now. We're back together and are making it. We have a pretty large son now who is spoiled bad as hell and looks just like Len. Len's got his own business now. I kid him about his Marxist days now that he's a working capitalist, but he reminds me that he's really an intellectual. We're one of the lucky couples. We made it. But it took a lot of doing. And let me tell you, it's not easy being married to a Blackman . . . even if he's an intellectual or not. But we're making it.

Exercises

For each of the three speeches:

1. Explain what you think the speaker is like.

2. Describe what kind of listener you think the speaker has in mind and what the speaker thinks that listener might be thinking about the topic in question.

3. Write down your personal responses to the speeches: how they affect you; what they bring to mind.

4. Read over your answers so far, then invent and describe a social situation in which the speech could take place. You do not have to know what the original situation is in the play from which the speech is taken.

5. Describe how you would try to set up a dialogue with the speaker in that social situation.

6. Write down your reply to the speaker in an effort to set up a dialogue with him or her.

Conflicting Voices   When we attempt to create a dialogue with someone we listen to what he or she has to say. And we have certain expectations: We want to be able to understand what is said and to learn something new. We listen carefully to the voices we hear because we know that what someone says is very much a matter of *how* it is said.

The "how it is said" determines *voice*. Voice, of course, is audible: various sounds we make when we speak, sounds that can be described in musical and scientific ways. But voice is not just the pitch, range, or timbre of the noise that comes out of our mouths. It represents to others our power of expression and our power to command attention. It represents our distinctive way of saying things in order to be heard. Some of the qualities most often valued in voice, for example, are authenticity, honesty, clarity, subtlety, liveliness, originality, spareness, wit, commitment, sensitivity, and persuasive power.

None of us always speaks in the same voice. Sometimes we will be direct, sometimes ironic, sometimes flippant, and so on; sometimes we are lively and sometimes dull. But by and large, we are each identified by the characteristic ability or power of our verbal expression.

As special as we think our voices are, though, we actually learn them from our social interactions. We internalize the voices we hear and read. We may even consciously imitate the voices of our parents, teachers, friends, politicians, writers, favorite television characters and personalities, and so on. We are not born speaking or writing beautifully. We have to learn to do so, and we learn by assimilation—by listening, reading, absorbing—and also by experiment. Even our thoughts are a kind of inner speech, voices in our mind's ear that we have heard elsewhere and learned to speak in our heads.

The following "vision of America" is by Dick Jackman, director of corporate communications for the Sun Company. Mr. Jackman gave this after-dinner speech at the twenty-seventh annual awards dinner of the National Football Foundation and Hall of Fame in 1984.

Thank you. Sorry I'm so late getting up here. It's about a $2 cab ride from the back row. All of us back there in the cheap seats admire these young athletes, and some of us remarked that we have underwear older than they are.

I'm pleased to be here to share this moment. I look at the logistics here on the dais—Doug Flutie seated alongside Joe Greene. That's like parking a Volkswagen alongside a school bus. And for those of you sitting under the chandelier, you should be aware that it was installed by the low bidder some time ago.

O.K. A football team seems to do best when it produces a combination of leadership and teamwork, and America seems to do best when it produces that same combination. Teamwork being that special quality that helps us look at life not from the standpoint of what's in it for us but from the standpoint of what we can do to help, and leadership being that special quality that helps an awful lot of people in and out of this room stand up on their tiptoes and look over the horizon and lead people there.

You cannot possibly leave this hotel tonight without a great deal of optimism about the future of not only football but America, because there's so much of it in here, and optimism is not meant to be stored. It's meant to be exported. You export it to other people. You make them determined to do that something extra in life that brings a response from others.

Let me mention the finest illustration I've ever heard of doing something extra. We had a teenage neighbor back home, a nice fellow. One day he got home at midnight. His mother said, "Where have you been?" He said, "I was out with my girl." His mother said, "I ought to give you a whipping for staying out so late, but you're being honest with me. I admire your honesty. Have some cookies and go to bed." The next night, the kid got home at 1:00 A.M. His mother said, "Where were you tonight?" He said, "Same place. Out with my girl." His mother said "I ought to give you the whipping of your life, but since you're being honest with me, have some more cookies and go to bed." The next night, he came home at 2:00 A.M. His father was waiting up for him. The kid walked into the house. The father picked up a huge frying pan and turned to face him. The mother leaped to her feet and screamed, "Please don't hit him!" The father said, "Who's going to hit him? I'm going to fry him some eggs. He can't keep this up on cookies." So, good people, if you sometimes have difficulty keeping up the pace and the love and the concern for other people on cookies, then let me encourage you to fry some eggs.

By this time we've all learned that, aerodynamically, the bumblebee shouldn't be able to fly. The body is too large. The wings are too small. Every time it takes off it should plunge back to the earth. But fortunately, the bumblebee does not understand its engineering limitations. And it's a good thing it doesn't, or we'd be living in a world of plastic flowers and putting mustard on our pancakes. It's a good thing that Scott Hamilton, at 5'3" and 115 pounds, did not realize that he could not possibly become the world's greatest ice skater, and that Mary Lou Retton, at 4'10", and Doug Flutie, who is here with us tonight, about a foot taller than that, did not realize that they could not possibly become the best at what they do, and that Shakespeare, whose mother could not read or write, did not realize that he couldn't possibly become the world's most honored writer.

And perhaps it's a great thing that 208 years ago, Betsy Ross took out her needle and thread. She did not realize that she could not possibly be sewing together an emblem that would one day umbrella the greatest experiment in human opportunity ever tried on this planet.

Let us not look at our limitations tomorrow morning. Let us pursue our possibilities.

On our track team at the University of Iowa we had a cross-eyed javelin thrower. He didn't win any medals, but he certainly kept the crowd alert. Perhaps part of our mission tonight and all the nights and days to follow is to keep the crowd in our homes, in our schools, and in our country alert to their possibilities and not their limitations.

That's far enough. Have an exciting life. Good night. □

Exercises

1. Describe the voice presenting this speech in as much detail as you can. Do you find more than one voice?

2. What are your reactions to this speech?

3. What strategies do you think the speaker is using to impress his audience? Are you impressed? Do you agree with all the sentiments expressed? Give a detailed answer.

4. Write your own after-dinner speech to be made at the annual dinner of some club or organization that you belong to (or would want to belong to).

Even the most straightforward speech, like this light, humorous piece, allows for considerable *interpretation*. When we interpret something we try to reach an understanding of it; we make meaning out of it. And we can interpret any verbal or written text not only by what we find in it but by what it leaves out.

Jackman's talk is a collection of amusing anecdotes held

together by the general theme of optimism in America. The references to teamwork and leadership, to doing "something extra," to valuing honesty, to being oneself, to achieving greatness, to loving America the land of opportunity, and to staying alert to our possibilities and not limitations are all part of this theme. The witty voice telling jokes also tells us to dare to be great and to have an exciting life. And that is in turn linked to the patriotic voice which wants us to realize that this land is indeed the land of opportunity. It all seems so upbeat, and simple, and funny, and short. It seems appropriate for an after-dinner speech at the National Football Foundation Hall of Fame. Only a party-pooper would complain that it's simple-minded, too obviously patriotic, too evasive of reality. Do you agree? Why or why not?

So we can take this speech for what it is in its social situation and still examine what sentiments have had to be suppressed for such an easy statement as "have an exciting life" to be made. Can we indeed just go out and have an exciting life? What about those people who cannot have exciting lives? What about those who do not make $7 million a year out of college as a quarterback in the NFL? What about those parents who do not make their children fried eggs when they come in at 2 A.M. after a date? Should all parents do that? And so on. Of course the speech is entertaining, but if you listen hard, you can hear other voices, too, voices that say to you that life is not quite so simple.

In fact, it has been said that every speaker or writer is really a lot of different people trying hard to be one person, a lot of voices trying to be one voice. Mr. Jackman has made it look easy, but in fact, one of the hardest things to do is to find out what we *really* think or what we really believe.

Every dialogue is made up of conflicting voices. Every act of speech or writing begins with options that must be taken or discarded. We can have more than one opinion, or contradictory opinions, or unrelated ideas. Try as hard as we can to speak with a single voice, we cannot suppress some of the other voices we use or deliberately do not use. They are there, though, conspicuous in their absence, as in Mr. Jackman's speech, or peeping through when we let out our real feelings.

Indeed speaking—and writing, as you will see—is a process of coming into consciousness about what we really believe, contradictions and all. And we are capable of playing more than one role as a speaker and writer; we can suggest more than one thing at once.

So acknowledge your complexity and changing views and experiment with different voices, different ideas, before you commit yourself. And then once you have committed yourself, remember that the listener may very well hear more than one voice anyway.

Here is another "vision of America." This one is an extract from a long, single-spaced, mimeographed letter handed out to passers-by at Grand Central Station in New York. Both this passage and the speech above were originally published together in *Harper's Magazine* in March 1985. Read the passage carefully.

Upon returning to New York in 1977 I began looking for a place to live. I looked at around ten apartments and called to inquire about several others. Since the secret police had already selected and prepared an apartment for me, this proved to be a futile endeavor. I signed a two-year lease for an apartment on East Eleventh Street and moved into the building in November. The apartment provides me with a place to live, but it also provides the secret police with an environment they can control. The building where I live, the surrounding buldings, and the neighborhood serve as a theatrical set; the "tenants" of my building, various neighborhood characters, and the intelligence agents stage theatrical productions.

The number of "tenants" seems to change every few months, but approximately fourteen people pretend to live in the building. Sometimes I encounter someone in the halls: a mad-looking bag lady, a sleeping derelict, a sleeping teenage boy, a fifty-year-old woman wearing only white panties, a man waving a knife, one of the "tenants." I believe I am the only person who lives in the building. Among the things the secret police do to make the building seem "real" and inhabited are putting phony mail in the mailboxes, collecting garbage from elsewhere to fill the building's trash cans, and placing people in various apartments to make noises as I pass by.

Since the secret police operations began in 1977 I have been woken up a few hundred times. Sometimes I am allowed to sleep undisturbed for a week; at other times I am woken up once, twice, or three times for several nights in a row. A few times the provocation succeeded in making me sufficiently angry that I could not get back to sleep. During one five-day period I was woken up ten times. Between March 19, 1982, and July 10, 1982, I recorded wake-up incidents on 55 out of 125 nights.

Most of the time I am woken up by loud, argumentative conversations, yelling, or noises coming from apartment twenty-three. Other nighttime noises are hammering; barking dogs; blaring radios and televisions that are repeatedly turned off and on or left on for hours; a tape recording of the blips, bleeps, and wrroooooips of a video game; sirens; and lead-footed walking on the roof directly over my bed.

The wake-up incidents are designed to generate hostility and to create tension and weariness through sleep deprivation. This serves to increase my vulnerability to the intensive game-playing of the secret police.

When I descend the stairs from my building I usually meet some of the "tenants" trying hard to look as if they lived there, or staging a scene for me to observe. Frequently groups of men are standing or sitting on the stoop, sometimes blocking the steps so that I have to ask them to move. On days when it is felt some special intimidation is needed, a police car will drive by as I go out and again as I come home.

When I go out I almost always head west and walk through the intersection of Eleventh Street and Avenue B. Since I might then head in any of three directions, this is the only place where the secret police can be fairly certain that I will enter into their staged scene. The operations at this intersection are usually more elaborately choreographed than they are elsewhere, and it is likely that there are hidden cameras. As I approach the intersection a signal is given, and people start crossing from every direction: people walking on the sidewalks, boys riding bikes, people driving cars.

Over 200 secret police agents and collaborators have participated in efforts to induce me to use drugs that might have led to psychological or physiological addiction. I believe one of the major reasons the secret police set up an apartment for me on the Lower East Side was that the area is the center of New York's illegal drug trade. The secret police have used their techniques of street theater to make sure I know that drugs are readily available and where they can be purchased. Within the first two months after moving into the neighborhood at least forty people offered to sell me drugs as I walked to and from my apartment.

At 3:24 P.M. on Wednesday, September 9, 1981, a short-circuited transformer in a Con Ed generator at East Fourteenth Street and Avenue C resulted in a power failure in lower Manhattan. I believe the blackout was a result of an act of sabotage committed by individuals employed by American intelligence agents. All of the details I am about to recount could be considered circumstantial evidence, but as I hope the rest of this letter demonstrates, the secret police so thoroughly involve themselves in every detail of my life that what for other people would be a series of unrelated incidents and random coincidences are for me parts of a complex and carefully planned operation.

On Tuesday, September 8, I left my apartment around 3:30, intending to pay my Con Ed bill. As I walked to the Con Ed office at 4 Irving Place I counted sixteen collaborators engaged in street theater. When I got to the office I looked in the window; it was unusually crowded and the bill-paying line was suspiciously long. I was apprehensive about entering a trap, so I decided to come back the next day. I left my apartment around 3:05 P.M. on Wednesday. As I walked across Fourteenth Street, I looked at every newsstand for a copy of the *New York Times*; I wanted to have something to read while waiting on line. Over a two-year period I frequently bought or saw the *Times* late in the afternoon at the various newsstands on Fourteenth Street; it is highly unlikely the paper would have been sold out. I believe intelligence agents asked the newsstand dealers to hide the papers so I would have nothing to do while waiting except observe the operation.

Inside the main-floor customer service area, the agents had placed at least twenty-five people, and it seemed as if all the employees had been given some sort of briefing and were participating in the operation. The operation was obvious. Seven young men presented themselves to be looked at, and a man and a woman each walked by me twice, staring holes through me. I believe intelligence agents chose to stage this scene to elicit an angry outburst that could be used as "proof" that, through paranormal powers, I had somehow triggered the transformer malfunction and the resulting blackout. I was in the Con Ed office about ten minutes, from approximately 3:20 to 3:30; the power failure began at 3:24. I believe intelligence agents committed an act of sabotage to coincide with the secret police operation being staged.

The blackout left a large section of Manhattan without power for around five hours. According to one press account, 3.5 million people were affected.

To most Americans, it probably seems beyond the realm of possibility that men working for an American intelligence agency, acting with the authority and probably the knowledge of the president, would commit such a brazen terrorist act. The standards of sanity and morality by which our society judges individuals are not being applied to the many people who participate in or are responsible for secret police operations. Because these people act with the authority of or in the name of the federal government, they seem to be exempt not only from the nation's laws but from internationally recognized standards of civilized behavior. Three words—"protecting national security"—now have the magical power to transform craziness into sanity, evil into good, and authoritarian and fascist methods of political control into legitimate means of governing a democratic nation. The collective madness of secret police operations has become an official policy of the United States Government. □

Exercises

1. Divide into small groups and discuss the following questions:

   (a) How would you characterize the voice(s) in this text?
   (b) Which of the two "visions of America"—this one and Mr. Jackman's—is in your opinion a more realistic American voice, and why? If they are both equally realistic, explain that too.

2. Read the following short essay, "Only the Fearful Know Television," by Walter Karp, taken from the journal *Channels of Communications,* and answer the questions that follow it.

   Abysmally inane though it often is, prime-time television holds some 100 million Americans in its grip every night. This is almost half the entire population. Yet the reason for TV's strong and enduring appeal has never puzzled anybody very much. The inanity seems to account for the appeal quite adequately. Between a tasteless, boorish mass audience and its nightly dose of witless jokes, Punch-and-Judy antics, comic-strip drama, and mind-numbing ads there seems to be an obvious and powerful affinity. So, at any rate, I had assumed until recently, when the true secret of television's appeal came to me in a surprising revelation.

   It flashed upon me while I was suffering from a spell of middle-age panic. The fleetness of time, a precarious income, and a generally snuffed-out feeling had combined to produce a powerful inclination to go to bed early and switch on the TV. What met my first anxious glance was an ad about "Miller Time." The spectacle by now is doubtless familiar. A band of hearty oil-riggers, stockmen, or construction workers barrel into a bar at the end of the workday and order their favorite beer. Hitherto mildly irksome, the ad this time displayed an astonishing power to please. The honest outdoor labor, the joyous good fellowship, the well-earned refreshment—how extraordinarily enviable they had become! I had been through "Miller Time" a score of times before, yet never had I felt its vivid charms. It was as though a black-and-white movie had suddenly turned into Technicolor. Was it possible that I had been seeing television for thirty-five years the way the colorblind see the world, missing the whole rich spectrum of hues?

That, as it turned out during the next few days, was exactly the case. Failure and fear, like a special set of lenses, brought out powers and charms and colors I never knew television possessed. The stalest clichés of advertising brimmed with moral vitality. Repellent Rosie, who sops up spilt coffee with "the quicker picker-upper," became a figure of strength, oddly reassuring. An endless stream of smiling faces, grinning jackasses I had always thought them, now peopled a neighborly world of kindly store managers and happy young families with nice front lawns.

The most banal prime-time shows shared in the transformation wrought by an anxious spirit. The unblemished bliss of the rich, loving Harts brought surprisingly intense delight, undiminished by a tenth-rate mystery plot. Smashing through shrubbery in a souped-up jalopy, the *Dukes of Hazzard* and their moronic activity brought the joy of reckless abandon. I was in prime time's grip for sure. When the sleek white *Love Boat* sailed off on a sun-dappled sea, I actually felt a surge of excitement. In television's kindly little havens, where everyone knows one another and decency always triumphs—a diner, a bar, a slack police station—I found heart's ease by the hour, at least for a while.

But the keen delights and sweet consolations that made television so richly alive lasted only as long as my panic did. When the spell passed, the vitality of television vanished. All that was left behind was the old gray succession of deadly clichés and half-witted jokes. These, I now realize, form the outer shell of television, a mere container for potent charms not visible to everyone. Perhaps only the lost and the fearful know television truly. For them, I suspect, it is chiefly designed. The affinity between television and its nightly mass audience is no trifling matter after all. It is a powerful bond fashioned by television's profound understanding of America's careworn, lonely, and failure-ridden people and of their surprisingly innocent yearnings. □

(a)   Describe the qualities of the voice you hear speaking in this essay.
(b)   What does this voice tell you about the writer's frame of mind (a) when he was watching television and (b) when he wrote the essay?
(c)   What does this voice tell you about the state of contemporary television?
(d)   You are going to write a short essay explaining the impact of an evening's television on you, commercials and all.

>   (i)   Jot down your impressions while you watch TV for an hour or two. Then underline the impressions and ideas you think are the most important. Choose the strongest and see if you can relate some of the others to it. This will give you a strong impression to start from.
>   (ii)   Write a paragraph describing the reader you are writing for.
>   (iii)   Write about two pages developing your strong impression as if you were writing or talking directly to a reader/listener.

Here are three short pieces on the significance of the Statue of Liberty in New York harbor. The pieces appeared in *The New York Times* just after the Statue was rededicated in a giant celebration in July 1986.

Confessions of a Lover
(Mobil advertisement)

Ah, that first meeting: Was it a sudden shipboard romance? A culmination of years of yearning from afar? Or just a youth's infatuation on an afternoon outing? No matter. This love lasts.

Through the decades spent together, times of bliss and sorrow, she never disappoints. She stirs deep passions. Bathed in moonlight, she is cool and soothing. Even in a crowd, she seems yours alone.

Yet, from the beginning, you knew you were not her first and would not be her last. Millions have fallen under her spell for a hundred years—all of them in her debt. Still, she never makes you jealous—too grand to let petty thoughts cheapen those to whom she promises her boundless favors.

And she keeps her promises. At first sight, she conjures up dreams of a home where nothing is impossible. She fires thoughts of heroic deeds, and offers the solace of compassion. You know she will be there for you, in good times and bad. And after you've known her for a lifetime, you realize it's all genuine: Under her influence you could, indeed, become all you strive to be. You could be proud to fight for her because you know she would be waiting.

And when you do return, she never makes you feel small. Though she can dwarf an armada of her lovers sailing past her island home, you somehow feel larger when you're close to her. And from afar, seen from the skyview of an airplane window, her stature is not diminished. She merely seems, for a moment, more embraceable.

She is a silent figure, yet based on eloquence. You know what she expects of you. Most of all, she wants you to be faithful—true to the ideals you shared when first you met. She requires you to grasp the opportunities she gives you—but not exploit them; rather, to make them work for all who might benefit. She wants you to be tolerant, knowing that she, like you or your forebears, came from foreign soil to share a home more abundant than any place on earth.

And she is patient if her lovers are imperfect. For all these years she has gazed indulgently on our passing follies. She has watched us submit to noble experiments and swallow goldfish . . . idolize the worthy and the unworthy . . . flirt with cults and pursue trivia.

As a century whipped salty breezes across her face, she defied age until those who love her could restore her radiance. Now, ever young, she is still the center of excitement—with the dance of ships below and the burst of fireworks above, as her lovers throw a gigantic birthday party in her honor.

She is 100. And she is a special part of all of us who love her and everything she stands for. ☐

Miss L. and Rambo

Flora Lewis

Because it's her 100th birthday, Miss Liberty is called upon more than ever this year to symbolize Independence Day and the nation. A combination of the calendar, French-American politics, commerce and the enduring importance of dreams is transforming the annual celebration into a gigantic spectacle.

The occasion has provoked all kinds of musings, from noble platitudes to blatant cynicism, all of them reasonably justified. In France, the editor of *Le Monde* was moved to deliver a front-page reflection titled "A Dream Become a Country."

He noted that nobody talks about a French dream, or a German, or Russian, or Chinese or Rumanian dream, because those countries simply are, and so accept themselves. But it seems right to talk about the "American dream" because the United States is a country that chose itself and its purposes, and almost all Americans are people or the descendants of people who chose to go there.

There's a point in all the contrasting observations, but the crux is the spectacle itself. The show does seem to have become the message, the fanfare overwhelms the hymn.

So the moment provokes thought more about what the techniques of communication have come to mean than about the underlying ideas, which need a quieter, more modest atmosphere to display their grace. It may be flippant, but it is irresistible to wonder how the other all-American symbol of the times measures up to Miss Liberty.

There isn't a monumental statue of Rambo with his fist raised staring across the harbor at the Lady with a torch. But he's just as real in the flickering imagination that has come to dominate the sense of events. It is becoming ever more difficult to separate entertainment and make-believe from the world that is, and so the image matters all the more.

This week's festivities are about brightness and joy, always welcome, but how do they mix with the other kind of proud patriotism, which seems to revel in scenes of gore and violence? Are they just different films, unrelated except by the flick of a dial or the chance of a program?

The columnist Pete Hamill wrote recently in *Mother Jones* magazine about "the bizarre militarism and nationalism that infect all levels of American life. This phenomenon is inaccurately labeled patriotism by the people, from Ronald Reagan down, who are spreading the virus. Safe, soft, well-paid American white men watch television and growl about the need to invade Nicaragua."

Maybe. People have been flocking to watch synthetic bellicosity and great pain. The question is why they enjoy it, what urge it satisfies among the same people who honor a stately matron offering haven from distress. One theory is the pleasure in being able to say, "Awful things may be happening out there, but they aren't happening to me. I'm safe."

Another may be the sublimation of deep human instinct, a recognition that civilized people cannot allow themselves to behave in such barbarous ways so the subconscious has to be satisfied with fantasy. Spectators know the actors will be back in another movie and that the tomato ketchup and red ink spilled didn't really involve suffering.

Scholars have shown that there has always been a conflict between the tribal spirit driven by hate and revenge and the social spirit, which accepts the need for law, for logic, for restraint. Imagery can articulate the destructive urge without the consequences, but the expression can also drive the deed.

In any case, it offers a sense of self, to compatriots and to the rest of the world, giving more importance to how the country looks than what it is, how the leader walks and smiles than what he says. There's probably no escape from it. Everybody sees the same pictures.

But there is a choice. Miss Liberty and Rambo do not make a happy pair. They need not be mated, they do not serve each other. There is something alarming when the contradiction in their meaning is blurred or brushed aside, when they seem to be presented as two sides of the same face, as inevitable, complementary aspects of America.

This is Miss Liberty's week. May her torch dispel the shadows cast on her by other, bad dreams. She does not need brass knuckles; a fond embrace will do. ☐

The Price of Liberty
Russell Baker

The following document is brought to you by E-Z Flow Tomato Ketchup, Achilles Tennis Shoes ("Tending more tenderly to tense, tired tendons"), Rub-a-Dub-Dub Hot Tubs and by Japasone, "The motorcycle that gets you there in one piece almost every time." And now, our sponsors proudly bring you a declaration:

"When, in the course of human events, it becomes necessary for one people to dissolve the political bands which have—"

Quickly now, because we only have a second left in this segment: What's the next word?

"—connected—"

Human events . . . connected . . . those are great ideas, ideas that built this country, but it takes more than great ideas to make a nation great. It takes a great beer like Suds, and great chewing gum like Cud's artificial-flavor-packed Ginger Mint ("never sticks even to loosest dentures, but adheres easily to the bedpost"). Suds and Cud's are proud to be bringing you this declaration, along with Mercutio Canned Pork and Beans, Glaze Shampoo, Father William Clerical Collars and Copperfield's Tick and Flea Powder. For over a century, when your dog cried out for fast relief from ticks and fleas, Copperfield's was there. Now back to our declaration:

"—them with another, and to assume, among the powers of the earth, the separate and equal station—"

Equal has never been good enough for Kafferdiddler's, the ice cream so superior, so expensive, yet so irresistible that paupers kill to get it. Rush right out and buy some Kafferdiddler's now, then rush right back in so you don't miss the next commercial break. While out there, also buy the P.D.Q. personal computer, the unbelievably erotic new eight-cylinder turbo-charged GXV with wire hubcaps at no extra cost, a set of Doctor Johnson's scientifically designed hip-caresser underpants and a complete set of Porpentine's Miniaturized Scissors, perfectly sized for getting at those hard-to-reach hairs in ears and nostrils. Meanwhile, back at the declaration:

"—to which the laws of nature and of nature's God—"

Ah, nature. It's a great American phenomenon, but sometimes it needs a little help, and fortunately Fin de Grouch, which is sponsoring this declaration, is always ready to make you thankful you live in the U.S.A. where, when irregularity strikes, you can do something about it instead of just feeling grouchy. Fin de Grouch. Buy some. Buy some Stench Enders, too. They're the socks chemically designed to end your fear of taking your shoes off in public. Buy Guzzle in the new giant Broken-Family size bottle. Now stay tuned; we'll be right back after these declarative words:

"—entitle them, a decent respect to the opinions of mankind requires that they—"

Respect! A great word, and respect is what you get when you buy Per Favore!, the underarm spray with the faint scent of oregano. Buy Sopsy Mopsy Paper Towels. Buy some Sit Tight Chair Spray for those hard-to-sit-up-straight-on chairs with vinyl seats. Spray lightly on chair seat and on back of trousers or skirt and your days of sliding embarrassingly off your chair will be over. Buy Mighty Oak toothpicks. Buy plenty of Call That Poetry? greeting cards. Buy the miraculous new Rembrandt Spray Painter, a machine so advanced you can now paint a 12-room house in 45 minutes. Now, back to our sentence:

"—should declare the causes which impel them—"

Impel is a powerful word, isn't it? That's why Jean-Louis de White Plains selected it to be the only word stitched on his world-famous blue jeans. Buy them and do some impelling of your own. While your checkbook is out, buy some incredibly cheap airline tickets to sexy Hawaii on Sky Slum Airline. Buy an incredibly expensive home copying machine from a company called "A Company Called." And think well of General Untaxables. That's right: as a Pentagon contractor, General Untaxables doesn't expect you to come in and buy one of its multibillion-dollar ultimate war machines for the pure pleasure of owning a stupendously overpriced ultimate war machine that doesn't work. All it asks, in return for helping bring you this great declaration, is that you think well of it even though it hasn't paid any taxes in five years. Now, back to our declaration:

"—to the separation. We hold these truths—"

I'm terribly sorry, but our time is up. Perhaps we can get the declaration to come back again some time because I'm sure we all want to hear more about those terrific truths. So long for now, folks, and remember, keep rushing right out and buying some right now. □

Exercise

In a short (two-page maximum) essay, compare the voices you hear in the three selections and explain which one you think captures best the significance of the statue and why.

WRITING AND DIALOGUE

Writing and Speech   As you can see from our discussion of spoken dialogue, we get involved in dialogues in social situations in which *we have to read conflicting voices and respond with a listener in mind.* We become increasingly conscious of the people we are talking *with* (and not just *to*) in a number of ways:

- We aim to avoid being misunderstood, but know that misunderstanding is possible.

- We talk with a developing concept of what the other person is like and how we can connect with him or her.

- We learn about what we are like from the other person's words and as we watch ourselves interact.

- We make dialogue in order to overcome isolation, to explore differences (but not necessarily to eradicate them), to question, and to make connections.

- We become conscious of having to resolve conflict in the voices we hear and in our own voices.

All this is part of the dynamics of good spoken dialogue. *It is also part of the dynamics of good writing.* When we write we can speak in many voices to show how we have read something—not only books, but events, feelings, ideas, and situations—and we always explain ourselves with a reader in mind. All writing, no less than speech, is written for readers.

Writing is an effort to create a dialogue with readers, and it involves exploring our relationships to our readers in much the same way that we explore our relationships to people we talk to.

But there are differences between writing and speech that have to be taken into account when we try creating a dialogue with a reader rather than a listener:

- When we talk to people, we know—or can find out—whom we are talking to. Much of our writing, though, is read by readers we do not know. Social conventions demand, then, that we *help create the reader we want to read our work,* or at least that we are conscious of trying to get readers involved in what we are saying. We also try to follow general agreements about *standard written American English.* Why? Because such conventions form a common expectation between readers and writers.

- Speech takes place in concrete social situations; *writing has to create its own social situation,* especially when we are writing for people we do not know. When we talk to people, our discussion takes place somewhere. The setting is part of the event. But the rooms in which we write, for example, are rarely part of the actual conversation we want to set up with a reader. Most of the time we are talking about something and somewhere else. We have to *invent* the social situation and ask the reader to be a participant in it. We cannot take too much for granted. There is no body language or gesturing to help give the message. We cannot change our minds from sentence to sentence and expect to impress a reader. The reader has to be given—in clear, concrete terms—a reason for wanting to read a written text and to enter the situation the writer is inventing.

- Writing can try to be a transcription of speech, or to sound "natural" and colloquial, like speech. When we read a novel with dialogue in it, for example, or a play, then we find deliberate representations of spoken language for special effects. But writing is not speech; it is a careful arrangement of words on a page which has its own idioms and format and does not transcribe the informalities of speech performance.

- Dialogue in speech goes back and forth between the participants with questions and answers, statements and counterstatements. Conversations develop readily. In writing, however, the writer alone talks, but the trick is to avoid simply writing a monologue, to always write with a reader in mind. Writers try, therefore, to *imagine readers:* what they are like, how they might respond to what we are saying, how we can be kind to them and make their reading easier, how we can meet their possible objections. And we talk to such imaginary readers, as you will see in this section. So the dialogue created in writing begins with the writer *speaking with a reader in mind,* even if the reader's answer is not readily available.

It helps to think of writing as the business of creating a dialogue with someone and not merely talking at them. And that effort requires certain skills that develop out of the skills of effective verbal dialogue. The next three selections—two speeches from an article called "Talking" by Bruce McCall, which appeared in the *New Yorker,* and a short extract from James Joyce's *Ulysses*—show these skills at work.

ETHEL MATTICE

She's not like most of the other people of America whose stories I've listened to, the soft-spoken folk with voices as faded and anonymous as their lives. Her voice is a bagpipe practicing to be a foghorn. The knickknacks on her mantelpiece jump and dance whenever she talks; I retreat out into the hall and just sort of edge the mike into the parlor doorway. This is what she says:

I started out in the Chin Musicians that was the kids' talking society ages about five to ten and oh goodness I don't think I could have been more than seven myself it was the year of the Columbian Exposition when I entered my first talking bee they had these talking bees out where I grew up in the Dakota Territory put on by the so-called talking societies every little town had its talking society there was let me think the Stephen Douglas and the William Jennings Bryan and of course the Garibaldis that was another one very snooty if you were in the Garibaldis you wore a big red sash and they even used those whatchamacallits those spray things yes atomizers that's the word to moisten their tonsils very la-di-da we used to say and wouldn't you know it one of the Garibaldis went on into the opera. *(Gasps)*

There was just this terrific emphasis on talking not just in my family in every family this came out of those long prairie winters out of the boredom of it being cooped up for months and months in your little sod hut talking was about the only way we knew to beat the blues things really closed in after Buffalo Day now Buffalo Day nobody remembers anymore but it was that day around the end of November when the wind finally got so strong it even blew the buffalo across the prairie I distinctly remember the night the buffalo hit our hut oh my what a commotion it busted Mama's ormolu vase into a million pieces but as I say talking real loud was the only way to drown out the howling of that awful wind. *(Gasps)*

So eventually somebody it was a farmer up Dilemma Falls way who claimed credit on the other hand he also said he invented the dog that man was not altogether reliable if you know what I mean but somebody decided to make it a public competition to buck up the spirits there was talking fastest and of course my specialty talking loudest and longest without taking a breath and then the novelty ones like talking while being tickled and talking with a mouthful of feathers for some reason only the Blackfoot Indians ever did that well and then talking in time with a grandfather clock we called it clocktalk and if you ask me clocktalk was even more boring than silence that was the specialty of a man name of Crowder he called himself the Human Metronome I'll tell you that man never got invited to dinner at the same house twice. *(Gasps)*

My brother Boone he left and went up Athabasca way the first day of spring after I took up the talking he was a patient soul but his nerves couldn't take the noise but my parents they did nothing but encourage me after dinner they'd go stand outside in the snow it got down to thirty below in January mind you just so I could practice what a grand thing it was I got to the All County finals and by age twelve there I was West Dakota Juvenile Champion in my category of talking loudest and longest without taking a breath and guess what I won I won a megaphone imagine that a megaphone. *(Gasps)* □

DUANE DIX

He keeps passing in and out of microphone range as he loops and swoops his skateboard around the living room, a figure skater gliding on cut pile. He just misses the coffee table and just misses the sleeping Irish setter. He just misses every object in the room, except the interviewer's casually outflung leg.

There was this one time I remember, this was real feeble, man, it was moron city . . . . . . my buddy Gary, from school? And some other guy from Evanston or someplace, a real konk . . . . this real sticky gray kind of tape, kind of industrial tape off a truck or something. Real retrograde, man . . . . . . they both go and seal up their whole face and mouth with this stuff, you know, this tape . . . . and they both wrap it around and around their heads like these mummies. It was so ultra-wonk, man . . . double depressing, you know, because . . . . like they couldn't talk or say nothing . . . . but like nobody even noticed and . . . . . hey, man, get out of my . . . . *(Inaudible)* □

PENELOPE

God of heaven theres nothing like nature the wild mountains then the sea and the waves rushing then the beautiful country with fields of oats and wheat and all kinds of things and all the fine cattle going about that would do your heart good to see rivers and lakes and flowers all sorts of shapes and smells and colours springing up even out of the ditches primroses and violets nature it is as for them saying theres no God I wouldnt give a snap of my two fingers for all their learning why dont they go and create something I often asked him atheists or whatever they call themselves go and wash the cobbles off themselves first then they go howling for the priest and they dying and why why because theyre afraid of hell on account of their bad conscience ah yes I know them well who was the first person in the universe before there was anybody that made it all who ah that they dont know neither do I so there you are they might as well try to stop the sun from rising tomorrow the sun shines for you he said the day we were lying among the rhododendrons on Howth head in the grey tweed suit and his straw hat the day I got him to propose to me yes first I gave him the bit of seedcake out of my mouth and it was leapyear like now yes 16 years ago my God after that long kiss I near lost my breath yes he said I was a flower of the mountain yes so we are flowers all a womans body yes that was one true thing he said in his life and the sun shines for you today yes that was why I liked him because I saw he understood or felt what a woman is and I knew I could always get round him and I gave him all the pleasure I could leading him on till he asked me to say yes and I wouldnt answer first only looked out over the sea and the sky I was thinking of so many things he didnt know of Mulvey and Mr Stanhope and Hester and father and old captain Groves and the sailors playing all birds fly and I say stoop and washing up dishes they called it on the pier and the sentry in front of the governors house with the thing round his white helmet poor devil half roasted and the Spanish girls laughing in their shawls and their tall combs and the auctions in the morning the Greeks and the jews and the Arabs and the devil knows who else from all the ends of Europe and Duke street and the fowl market all clucking outside Larby Sharons and the poor donkeys slipping half asleep and the vague fellows in the cloaks asleep in the shade on the steps and the big wheels of the carts of the bulls and the old castle thousands of years old yes and those handsome Moors all in white and turbans like kings asking you to sit down in their little bit of a shop and Ronda with the old windows of the posadas glancing eyes a lattice hid for her lover to kiss the iron and the wineshops half open at

night and the castanets and the night we missed the boat at Alge-
ciras the watchman going about serene with his lamp and O that
awful deepdown torrent O and the sea the sea crimson sometimes
like fire and the glorious sunsets and the figtrees in the Alameda
gardens yes and all the queer little streets and pink and blue and
yellow houses and the rosegardens and the jessamine and gerani-
ums and cactuses and Gibraltar as a girl where I was a Flower of the
mountain yes when I put the rose in my hair like the Andalusian
girls used or shall I wear a red yes and how he kissed me under the
Moorish wall and I thought well as well him as another and then I
asked him with my eyes to ask again yes and then he asked me
would I yes to say yes my mountain flower and first I put my arms
around him yes and drew him down to me so he could feel my
breasts all perfume yes and his heart was going like mad and yes I
said yes I will Yes. ☐

Exercises

Form small groups to discuss the preceding texts.

1. With each piece, describe what you think the person speaking is like.

2. Take turns to read parts of the different passages aloud. Compare how
    different readers give different intonations, different pacing, and have
    different rhythms of speech.

3. Describe the social context for the speech. It does not matter if you
    know the original texts from which these extracts are taken. Simply
    make up a situation based on the evidence in which these words
    could be spoken.

4. Assume that you are writing to a friend and reporting the speech to
    him or her. Summarize the gist of what is being said in your own
    words, shortening the passage where necessary but avoiding any
    special idiosyncrasies of the spoken English.

Who Is the Reader?   To write is to write for a reader, and a
reader, unlike someone who takes part in a conversation, cannot
interrupt the writer and join in the conversation. But that does not
stop a reader from participating in the dialogue set up by the writer.
Obviously it is hard to write for a reader unless you have some idea

of what he or she is like. If you know the reader, then you can focus on the reader's special interests or anticipate his or her reactions. But what if you do not?

In general, we write for readers we have to invent, and we do so by drawing on our experience. The reader may be anyone we know, like a friend, or colleague, or an authority figure (like a teacher, a parent, or the brainiest student in the class). It could be our idea of an "ideal" expert in the field that we are writing about. It could be some kind of generic reader we base on people we know, like writing for teachers, students, lawyers, the "average" reader, and so on.

Exercises

1. Write a short description of the reader you think is invented by "Penelope" in the text above.

2. You have been asked to write an article for your student newspaper on a pressing campus issue.

   (a)   State clearly what the issue is—refer to a current campus issue, or make one up.
   (b)   Describe carefully what you think the characteristics are of the "average" student reader at your university.
   (c)   Describe the tactics you would use in your article to set up a dialogue with that reader.
   (d)   How would such an audience and your tactics differ from that of the "average" professor on campus? And from your parents?

We can also develop a concept of an "ideal" reader in terms of what we know *any* reader does when he or she reads. And that is what we are going to concentrate on now.

We can always have some understanding of what our readers will do and feel as they read because we can draw on our *own* experience as readers. In short, we can learn to make a dialogue with a reader based on what we *need* to do when we read.

Reread the following passage a couple of times and then consider the exercises.

I'll Fight Jargon with Jargon
Janet Shilling

Recently, I've become aware that I'm missing a lot and that each day I'm falling further behind. It's not that I don't understand the issues under discussion and am therefore overwhelmed by the enormity of the problems facing the world. They are, after all, merely updated versions of the same old issues that have always been around: plague, pestilence, famine, war, sex, drugs and rock and roll.

It's not even that I'm a member of a group whose opinions are rarely sought by the public and am suffering from a larger dose of powerlessness than usual.

We, the middle-aged, middle-class housewives of America, were never in the vanguard of the movers and shakers.

But more and more lately, I don't understand words, because they are gradually being completely replaced by jargon. I am not referring to teenage slang, which changes almost daily. Nerd and grody are code words of a group that would, under any circumstances, ignore my existence.

I am referring to adults allegedly communicating information to other adults.

Jargon is proliferating at a scary rate. Next to money, jargon is the growth industry of the 80's. Jargon, the language by which in-groupies can communicate with other in-groupies while simultaneously excluding people deemed unworthy of groupie membership, is the gentrification of language. Jargon takes little slummy shacks of ideas and makes them seem like high-rise concepts.

Although they may be hostile to me, jargonists from one discipline are friendly with each other. They extend a form of professional courtesy to other jargonists, much like doctors and malpractice lawyers. Thus, people from different backgrounds can work together on committees from which a whole new unintelligible vocabulary will emerge.

It is not only that I feel ignorant, alienated and irrelevant, but I'm jealous as well. I hate watching others more fluent than I indulge their communications skills to the plaudits of their peers.

So I have solved the problem of being a silent member of a

jargonless, therefore voiceless, subculture. It is based on the law that "if you can't beat them, join them"—a statute never repealed, to my knowledge.

My solution is called Scwawrp. Of course, the word Scwawrp lacks the sparkle of CARE, NASA or SEATO, but it will have to do.

A catchy acronym is vital for getting new jargon off the ground. If pushed to the wall, I might claim that the letters stand for Senseless Contortion of Words and Abstractions Without Reason and Point. But that does not matter much. How many people remember, or can agree upon, what Yuppie stands for?

After one is launched on this course, however, the fear of sounding ridiculous is a stumbling block almost impossible to overcome. After all, as a middle-class, middle-aged housewife (Mcmah), reared in a simpler linguistic tradition, the Handy All-Purpose Reassuring Cliché (Harc) is more my métier. But it must be overcome. Under the new rules, the more obscure the nomenclature, the better.

Here is an example of how Scwawrp can be utilized to upscale even the most tedious of descriptions, the recitation of my morning activities.

First thing in the morning (Firam), I engage in preparing a comestiblation (Prepcom) or, alternatively, nutrient deprivation relief (Nudr) prior to detergentially reperfecticating the family's garmentic necessities. While the wash is in the machine, I open myself to megamedia saturation, inputting audio, video and print modes so I might better be prepared to group-share experiential data.

For lunch, in hopes of recycling some leftovers I attempt redemption of nutrients by liquefaction (Renl). If Renl fails, as it often does because a blender can't work miracles, I deecologize in my sanitational mode, especially on Tuesday when the Garbdept makes its rounds.

It sounds awful, doesn't it? But is it any worse than hearing that someone you love is booting up his DOS disk and formatting his bauds, bytes and modems?

I had a dream, a nonconscious ephemeral manifestation (Ncem): It was not as lofty as some, but then neither am I. I dreamed that I was asked an opinion about something more lasting than last night's dinner (Prevsup), and I gave that opinion in pure Scwawrp.

Where at first only bare civility and bored patience toward an undeserving Mcmah existed, suddenly attention was paid. Eyes sparkled. Note pads were produced and every meaningless syllable was recorded for an avid posterity (Futgen). I babbled abbreviations, bastardized words and synthesized never-before heard combinations of prefixes and suffixes.

My dream was replicated almost exactly on the 6 and 11 o'clock news but this time it starred three statesmen. Not every dream that does come true should come true. □

Exercises

1. What are your first reactions on reading this piece? Jot down your reading responses as they come to you, expressing your feelings directly in writing.

2. Describe what you think the speaker's voice is like. Do you hear more than one voice?

3. How do you think the writer is trying to get your attention and keep up your interest in this text? Is the writer successful?

4. As you were reading the essay, did you find yourself relating Shilling's examples of jargon to what you know of such uses of language? If so, briefly list those uses. If not, what were you thinking about? (For example, did you find yourself thinking of how your parents may have reacted in the past to teenage slang?)

6. Describe the social situation which this piece of writing deals with and tries to criticize. What does the final statement "Not every dream that does come true should come true" suggest to you about the social context?

Readers Make Meaning As you can see, reading is not a passive activity at all. Readers actually help make the meaning of texts. You read by reacting to a text and taking part in a dialogue that develops between you and the voices in the text. Like a listener in a conversation, you develop responses to what is being said—emotional responses, ideas, questions—in the process of reading. And these responses are the basis of the meaning you help to make.

Of course, the writer provides you with information and arranges it in such a way that your reading responses are to some extent controlled. So do speakers. But readers, like listeners, still have to select the most important information and *relate it to what they already know* and how they feel about the subject. All reading builds on previous experience; understanding depends on relating something new to something old.

What, then, does a reader want to do with a written text in order to enter a dialogue with it? Consider these points, for they are related to what you will do in your writing in order to attract and hold your own readers:

- Readers want to be able to enter the world of the text, to develop responses, and to get involved with the subject by having their curiosity aroused.

- Readers want to find information readily, to be able to follow a line of reasoning, or an argument, and to be able to locate the major points a writer is making.

- Readers want to be stimulated to think creatively *with* the text, perhaps identifying with characters and events, but in some way finding themselves or their needs and desires reflected in the text.

- Readers want to be able to make meaning with a text, to fill the gaps, to reach some kind of understanding of what is going on, to be able to *interpret* the text by placing it in a familiar social context.

When we talk about our reading, we are not just describing what a text is about, all on its own. We are describing what *we* think it is about. We describe how *we* have related to the text. We put it in *our* social contexts. We try to sort out the variety of voices *we* hear. We try to resolve conflict in our own reactions and make *our* responses coherent. We tell listeners, and other readers, what we think is important about the text based on our own judgments. Consider the following selection with this in mind.

Why Won't the Doctors Let Her Die?
Alvan R. Feinstein

Her chief complaint is that she wants to die and that the doctors will not let her.

She is 96 years old. She has attended the burial of her husband, two daughters-in-law, and all the people who were close friends throughout her lifetime. A woman of fierce and independent spirit, she never wanted to live with her children, to be supported by them or to be what she calls "a burden." After being widowed 24 years ago, she achieved those goals for a long time because she was in good health and her modest fiscal needs were met by the interest of the trust fund left by her husband.

Until 11 years ago, she lived alone and maintained her own apartment. She spent her time walking, talking with neighbors, reading, watching television, playing card games, attending religious services and traveling to visit children, grandchildren, and great-grandchildren in different cities. At age 85, however, she began to dislike shopping and cooking for herself; and she began to worry about living 60 miles away from her nearest relative. She moved, in a city where a son and grandchildren lived, into an apartment residence building that was the "congregate setting" of a geriatric center. The setting provided her with lunch, dinner, a social life and her own small apartment, in which she prepared her own breakfast.

On her 90th birthday, although in excellent mental and physical health, she began complaining that she had become too old. Her stated desire was to die in her sleep, preferably not on a night before she was scheduled to visit her great-grandchildren. When hospitalized with an episode of pneumonia that winter, she said, "My time has come." She bid a loving goodbye to each child, grandchild and great-grandchild who came to see her, and gave them a farewell blessing. When she recovered—thanks to intravenous fluids and antibiotics—she was surprised and somewhat dismayed, but she resumed her former life, remaining independent and perky.

During the next few years, she grew progressively more frail. She began having episodes of faintness, due to paroxysms of atrial fibrillation, but the episodes were brief, and the symptoms would vanish when she lay down briefly. She began walking with the aid of a cane. Although she would no longer travel long distances alone, her mind remained clear and her life independent. With each winter, however, she was rehospitalized with another bout of pneumonia. Each time she was sicker than before; each time she was prepared and wanted to die; and each time she received vigorous therapy and recovered.

During an episode three years ago, however, she had a spell of faintness while in the bathroom of her hospital room. Uncertain that she could successfully get back to her bed, she treated the symptom in her usual manner. She lay down calmly on the floor, closed her eyes and waited. In that position, and with a rapid irregular pulse, she was found by a nurse who promptly issued an emergency "Code" alarm. By the time the doctors and equipment arrived, she actually felt much better; but the excitement of the aggregated "team" convinced her she must be moribund. When she failed to die, she became angry and depressed. "I want to die, and I am ready to die," she said, "but the doctors won't let me."

After she returned to her small apartment, she became less depressed as she became persuaded that she needed to live at least another year to attend the religious confirmation of her youngest granddaughter. During that year, she became more frail, but her mind stayed clear and her spirits high. She traveled four hours in each direction by private car to go to the confirmation ceremony, and she took special pleasure in participating in it. During the trip, she laughed, sang, and joked, exchanging stories of the old days with a brother-in-law whom she seldom sees and who had come a long distance to ride with her to the ceremony.

Several days after her return home, she had a stroke. She became confused and disoriented. Although physically able to function, she could no longer take care of herself. She could not cook or successfully make her way alone to and from the dining room. When lucidity transiently drifted in, she would complain unhappily and bitterly about having a "companion," who had been hired to be with her during waking hours, and about having become "a burden."

About a week later, she re-entered the hospital with another, more severe stroke. She was conscious, seemed aware of her surroundings, and could state the names of her family visitors, but she made no other conversation. Moving her eyes toward the sky, she seemed to be pleading with God to take her at long last. When she developed anorexia, fever and pneumonia, her children asked the house staff to let her alone, but they and the attending physicians insisted that they could not "do nothing." Before one of her sons—a physician at a medical school in a distant city—could arrive to dispute the doctors' plan, she was given intravenous antibiotics, fluids and other vigorous support.

She recovered, left the hospital and now resides in a nursing home. She can still recognize her family visitors, say their names, and engage in trivial conversation, but her mind is substantially destroyed. She does not know where she is or how long she has been there. She cannot read, watch television, walk alone, use a telephone or play card games. She retains bladder and bowel continence, but she cannot dress herself, feed herself or transfer from bed to chair to bathroom.

She is no longer aware of her plight, and expresses no suggestion of despair, but everything she wanted to avoid has happened. In a semivegetating state, she has lost her functional and mental independence; and she is about to become a financial as well as a physical burden. Because she has the trust fund, the government will not pay for the costs of the nursing home; but the trust fund interest is not large enough to cover the charge of $80 a day. She had hoped to leave the trust-fund principal to her grandchildren, but now it will be gradually transferred to the nursing home.

As her visitors deal with the agony of her vegetation, they wonder why this problem has been created. Since the preservation of her life helps no one, and is desired neither by her nor by those who love her most dearly, why could her doctors not be content to let her die in peace and serenity? Why did they pursue a vigorous therapy that would benefit no one except their own satisfaction in thwarting death, regardless of the consequences?

I do not know the answers to these questions. But I, the physician son of this woman, weep for my mother and for what has happened to my profession. □

Main Point = where to draw the line. she wanted to die. classic case

Exercises

Form small groups to discuss the preceding text. Elect one member of the group as recorder.

1. Carefully note all the different readings the group members make of the text, specifically noting (a) what the main "message" of the text is, (b) its relevance to a student audience, and (c) how effectively the text draws and keeps the attention of the reader.

2. Within your group try to reach agreement on one "majority" reading, noting all disagreements and discussing the extent to which that reading is the product of the group and its social context as young adults still relating closely—in many cases—to parents. How do your other social assumptions affect your reading?

3. Ask a spokesperson from your class to discuss the interpretations from each group and whether one majority interpretation is possible.

4. Finally, as a class, discuss the nature of the reading *community* in your

class: what its values are, what it seems to look for in a text, and why, based on all your responses.

All these activities of reading are clues about what writing can and should do. Obviously, as writers we have to create texts that readers will want to read. We need to write texts readers can get involved with. When we say we have a reader in mind when we write, we do not just mean a reader who is like someone we approve of in terms of values and personality—though such readers are always in our imagination—but a reader who wants to be able to make meaning with a text.

The next two texts are student essays. Form small discussion groups and read one of the following essays.

Catch-22: Sanity and Insanity

In the novel *Catch-22* by Joseph Heller, sanity and insanity play a major role. Heller uses the concept of sanity and insanity to communicate his ideas about war and human nature. Heller also utilizes the question of sanity as a weapon to develop his characters and plot. Without the use of sanity and insanity the book would lose much of its content and meaning.

Sanity and insanity are the main aspects of Heller's characters. The characters' personalities revolve around the question of sanity. Heller does not come right out and say a character is insane. This decision is left to the reader to interpret. Heller only presents to the reader the actions and thoughts of his characters. Thus Heller leaves the real judgment of sanity to the reader. In the case of the main character, Yossarian, Heller presents a paradox. If one analyzes his actions the conclusion would be he is insane. But if you look at the morality behind his actions it is obvious he is the sanest person in the book. On the other hand the character of Milo presents an opposite paradox. Milo appears quite sane in his ability to monopolize trade and commerce in the area. But further investigation of his character reveals his obvious insanity. Heller attempts to show the judgment of sanity and insanity is a complex question.

Heller uses the sane and insane actions of his character to help build their personalities. Each of Heller's characters is symbolized by a particular action or quality. Hungry Joe's problems are symbolized by his constant nightmares whenever he has flown the required number of missions. Nately's character is symbolized by his love for the sleepy whore in Rome. Through this impossible love Heller shows the reader the gentle and naive personality of Nately. Havermeyer's insane bravery is expressed through his nightly slaughter of rats with his pistol. Yossarian's true nature is displayed by his compassionate and moral reaction to the deaths of his friends.

Heller uses the sanity and insanity of his characters and plot to express many of his views about war and life in general. The overall absurdity of the book characterizes Heller's idea of war. Heller finds war both sickening and absurd. Heller portrays this in several instances. The black humoristic episode in which the soldier has his legs cut off by the plane displays Heller's ideas of the uselessness of war. Heller's view of war as absurd is constant throughout the book. The characterization of the colonels and generals is an example of this. Throughout the novel Heller makes them appear everything from greedy to stupid. He portrays them as power-happy morons who feel no remorse at sending people to be killed. Heller also makes comments on human nature and society. In the dealings of Milo, Heller symbolizes the dealings of the American government. He pokes fun at the idea of us all owning a share of the wealth. He also shows the inadequacy of the government through Milo's buy-for-more and sell-for-less tactics.

Heller's style concerning sanity and insanity is the major force behind his story. Both his characters and plot rely on this style in their development. The personalities of his characters are symbolized by their sanity or insanity. Heller does not make the judgment of sanity himself but instead leaves this to reader interpretation. Through sanity and insanity Heller is able to comment on a wide variety of topics other than war. However the main reason for the use of sanity by Heller is to show the insanity of war in general. □

Polyester

It was a time of prosperity; petroleum based products were king. L. L. Bean was only a flickering in the imagination of an esoteric group of intellects. There was rayon, nylon, and orlon. When woven together, these fibers became a synthetic masterpiece. Everyone seemed contented with their world of simple synthetics. This was before the great explosion. It was before the world was turned upside down by the genesis of a new goddess—Polyester.

It all began on a steamy July day. It started out to be just like any other summer day; the sun was blistering and tempers flared. The workers at the Saran Wrap company began the day just as they had always done; before going into their plastic wrap paradise, the workers exchanged gossip with the employees of the adjacent thread factory. When the whistle sounded, the workers of both factories shuffled into their respective plants. Suddenly, a tremendous explosion erupted from the Saran Wrap factory. Flames were ubiquitous. A wave of molten plastic rushed out of the burning plastic factory toward the nearby thread plant. Screaming workers poured from both factories. Sirens blared. The molten plastic united with the spools of thread and a new fiber was born. Two workers were engulfed in this cascade of thread and plastic. Their names were Polly Smith and Esther Jones. Thus, this serendipity of fiber was called Polyester, in honor of these two pioneers.

The value of this product proved to be immeasurable. Billions of articles of clothing were produced. Everything from dresses to tresses. The utility of Polyester was proven; it didn't need to be ironed; if you normally wore a size sixteen, the Polyester product would stretch so that a size five would suffice, and Polyester never tore.

With the advent of Polyester, citizens began to ignore the altars of Cottona, the goddess of clothing. Cottona was enraged, so enraged that she sought revenge by turning the iron against Polyester, whose worst enemy was the heat and fire from which she was born. Cottona was so deranged with fury, that instead of melting Polyester, she scorched herself—a cloth suicide. The citizens rejoiced and Polyester was crowned the new goddess of clothing.

The people became oblivious to all fabrics except the treasured Polyester. They wore their multi-colored menageries with pride. Everything was printed on Polyester, from gaudy geometric patterns to jungle scenes. People were amazed at what could be printed on a shirt. Raincoats became obsolete; after all, Polyester was waterproof. Mothers extolled the virtues of Polyester; ironing was a no no. Washing became the exception rather than the rule; the dirt blended right into the pattern of the cloth and the sweat was repelled back into the armpits. Everything was wonderful. Generation after generation wore their Polyester with pride. Cotton was shredded at the altars of Polyester as a tribute. Great showcases for Polyester garments were opened, the most famous being Synthetics Unlimited where millions of test tube garments were produced (some historians claim that this was the actual oracle of Polyester). Thousands and thousands of Polyester garments hung from the racks of this Polyester haven. There were two hundred of every style, size, and color. Everyone from the bulging bimbo to the svelte secretary made Synthetics Unlimited their place to shop. It was said that if you couldn't find a Polyester dress at Synthetics Unlimited, then you couldn't find a Polyester dress. Everything seemed to be perfect, a veritable Polyester paradise. Polyester seemed destined to be the eternal fiber. Alas, this was not to be. Were these Polyester worshippers guilty of hubris?

There was trouble in Polyester paradise. Disaster struck from a foreign land. The celebrated Arab oil embargo lessened the thunder of the mighty Polyester. Petroleum prices soared and the once inexpensive manufacture of Polyester suddenly became costly. Polyester praisers began to notice all of its flaws. The high prices made them rationalize; after all, love is blind but shiny elbows are an eye-opener. The perils of Polyester became apparent: the pulls, the sheen of the "cloth" which became apparent after prolonged wear, the worn pattern on the elbows, and its most deadly flaw— extreme flammability. Cigarette smokers became enraged when a dropped ash turned into a volcanic crater on their Polyester print. Young children went up in flames. After toxic substances were found in the bloodstreams of many Polyester wearers, the deadly garments were recalled. Polyester lost its place under the sun; it couldn't stand the heat anyway.

Gradually, the word "bean" came to mean more than just a Saturday supper. A cotton renaissance evolved and the era of L. L. Bean began. Polyester worshippers began to melt the sacred cloth as sacrifices to Cottona. People begged her forgiveness. Polyester became enraged. In a drunken stupor, she melted herself and the people rejoiced. The king of the gods pitied these people and Cottona was reborn in the form of an Oxford shirt. Her realm became L. L. Bean, where cotton is king. The people were thankful and they vowed never to wear petroleum based products again. □

Exercises

1. Describe your experiences of reading the extract: its impact on your group and some reasons for that impact.

2. Describe what you think the writer is assuming about his or her reader.

3. Discuss how you would revise these essays to make them more effective, knowing what readers do when they read.

The power of writing—that is, the power of writing effectively—depends, as you have seen, on a writer catching a reader's interest and helping the reader to see some social situation afresh. Writers must dramatize an idea or event in such a way that the reader will want to get personally involved.

Here is a specific reading–writing situation. A group of squatters taking over a building on London's Picadilly some years ago wrote this now famous graffiti: "We are the writing on your wall." Graffiti is, literally, writing on a wall and this statement was their communication to the police, to the government trying to evict them, and to society at large, who, they assumed, might be watching smugly and feeling superior. The squatters created a whole social context with these simple words. They told their audience that they were the mythical writing on the wall, a warning of an unhappy future that could befall anyone in an uncertain world. Also, with great irony, they reminded their readers that they were little more than words splashed in paint. They had been reduced to paint to make their point.

What power there is in that short statement! What power in all graffiti that are witty, paradoxical, and to the point: an *international* form of public expression:

1. "'God is dead'—Nietzsche.
   'Nietzsche is dead'—God" (New York subway).

2. "Is there intelligent life on earth? Yes, but I'm only visiting" (Cambridge, England).

3. "Russian circus in town. Do not feed the animals" (Czechoslovakia).

4. "If Superman is so clever then why does he wear his underpants on the outside of his trousers?" (England).

Where does the power of such graffiti come from? From writing concisely and from summarizing a situation—even one that is hard to understand or tolerate—with an ironic twist, a clever change of meaning. In the ambiguous summary comes understanding and defiance. We can invert statements, as in #1 above, or pun, as in #3, or use a word in two different senses, as in #2. We can talk about the silliness of the obvious (#4). These are common word tricks with graffiti. But we can actually learn a lot about the human spirit from the writing on walls which aims to be funny and not merely smutty. We can also learn a lot about writing.

In fact, in the statement "we are the writing on your wall," we have an accurate summary of what happens when we write. The power lies not just with the writer but with the reader who possesses the text. We are part of everything we write. But our power is transferred to the reader who is clever enough to get the joke, catch the irony, make the meaning. And the reader then admires the writing, giving it back to the writer. That is the dialogue of writing.

Exercises

1. Here are three graffiti:

    "Love is a many-gendered thing."
    "A woman who strives to be like a man lacks ambition."
    "If men got pregnant, abortion would be a sacrament."

    (a) Describe the problems or situations you think the writers are referring to.
    (b) Explain how each of the graffiti gains its effects on you, and whether you think the graffiti are effective. Give reasons for your reactions.
    (c) What is the combined effect of these three graffiti on you and how do they relate to any specific social conditions you know of?

2. Take the following sayings and develop them, responding to each to form a whole graffito. For example, "'God is dead'—Nietzsche" is countered by "'Nietzsche is dead'—God" and from that *inversion* God would appear to have the last word when the two are placed together. In writing your graffiti, you want to *develop a point wittily* in the original statement or to have the last word in some way.

Life is like a rainbow: _____

Love is a four-letter word: _____

Blow your mind: _____

Might is right: _____

Writing for a Reader   We have been discussing the fact that all writing is not simply an effort to communicate with a reader, but an effort to make meaning with a reader in mind. In fact, writing involves a special three-part relationship with reading which must be developed anew for every piece of writing we do. These three aspects of the reading–writing connection can take place in any order:

- *Imagining the reader of the text you want to write:* To whom am I talking and why? How does my knowledge of reading help me talk to other readers?

- *Talking to the reader in the text:* How can I shorten the distance between the reader and me? How can I interest and persuade the reader?

- *Becoming the reader of the text you are writing:* As I write, I must read what I have written, so how would I as a reader respond to my writing? How can I revise and improve my text in the light of my reading?

We have discussed the first two points, and throughout this text you will rehearse them many times. But let us concentrate on the last aspect of the relationship between writing and reading for a moment. When we write, we not only speak our minds, we also discover *what is in our minds and what we really want to say.* We read our thoughts, our intentions, our audience. It is an old saying, but nonetheless true: We do not know what we want to say in writing until we have written it. We literally have to read our own feelings and ideas as we write. That is, *in writing we have to become our own readers.*

This is one of the most exciting, unpredictable, and rewarding aspects of writing. We are not merely expressing ideas we already have or communicating with a premeditated aim. Writing is a way of discovering and developing our responses to an event, text, or situation. It is a process of revision and rereading, of coming into consciousness of our ideas and feelings. It can tell us what we actually believe. Writing actually *writes us* the more we get involved with it, the more we read it.

We are the words we write. We become the words we read. No matter how mysterious, introverted, frustrating, or complex the act of writing may seem, the pleasures of writing have much to do with self-creation and self-discovery.

Exercise

Using *one or more* of the following quotations as a starting point, try some *freewriting*. When you do so, turn off your mental censors and simply write down what comes into your mind, regardless of what it is and without paying attention to grammar and punctuation. Try writing complete sentences, but if that fails, don't worry. Just write non-stop until you're tired of each quotation.

"Whenever a friend succeeds, a little something in me dies." (Gore Vidal)
"To be clever enough to get all that money, one must be stupid enough to want it." (G. K. Chesterton)
"There can be no fifty–fifty Americanism in this country. There is room here for only one hundred per cent Americanism." (Theodore Roosevelt)
"It starts when you sink in his (her) arms and ends with your arms in his (her) sink." (Graffito)

Rereading our own writing is a process not simply of checking for grammatical errors, but of *rethinking* our texts. It is impossible to think clearly without being aware of the *problems* of thinking clearly. Thinking is a process of probing, experimenting, associating, inferring, and going through numerous other reasonable and unreasonable acts of understanding and misunderstanding as we contemplate ideas in the theater of our imagination.

Insofar as writing is a form of thinking, so too is reading our writing a form of rethinking, of *entering into a critical dialogue with our work*. The central experience of writing, in fact, is *rewriting*, and that does not mean simply correcting grammar mistakes. It means developing our ideas and maybe even changing them.

So writing is one of the most self-conscious of human activities. It shapes our thoughts; it opens up new ideas; it can switch a thought and reroute it on another track. It quickly shows us what we do not know as well as what we do. It can take us places where we have not been before because ideas automatically associate as we write. When we write, we cannot sustain coherently connected thoughts sentence after sentence, page after page. Sometimes we have trouble keeping a clear direction from one line to the next. But we can stop, reread, reflect on our words, and rewrite. Writing is a cumulative act: We write by rewriting.

Exercises

1. Read what you wrote in your freewriting exercise above, *underlining* words, phrases, and sentences that you think are important.

    (a)   Keeping in mind the most important of these words and phrases, write a paragraph about each quotation, developing as clearly as you can your key insights in the freewriting exercise.
    (b)   Reread your paragraphs, and consider what you found out about *yourself*, your beliefs and personality. Write a page describing yourself honestly for an audience of your peers.

2. Write a letter to your English instructor describing what you think is the *ideal* working relationship you can have with a teacher of writing and, specifically, with the instructor. Explain how a relationship can be forged by your efforts as a responsible writer and by your teacher's efforts as a responsible reader. Discuss what you think the writer–reader relationship is and how it affects revision. When your instructor has read all your letters, he or she will write one back to the class on the very same subject, and the class will discuss his or her response.

Here is an essay, "Cramming," written by a student. Read it carefully *out loud* to yourself and do the exercises that follow it.

Cramming

As a beginning freshman at ———, I found my first few weeks of school to be a total disaster. The social life at ——— wasn't as good as I had anticipated; I got two parking tickets; and I wasn't prepared to spend the amount of time I needed to study for my classes. I knew it would take a while to adjust to these problems, but I couldn't seem to adjust to spending more of my free time studying. Not knowing how valuable it was to study during my free time, the night before my first history test, I started cramming the material at 11:00. Studying all night at the kitchen table, with the brewing of the coffee pot echoing in the background, I tried to remember as many historians and events as I could. When I got to class the next day, I thought I knew the material well enough to get a passing grade. After glancing over the test, my mind went blank. I couldn't remember one thing I had just studied; therefore when I got the test results back and I had an F staring me in the face, my first history grade reflected that I had put my social life before studying for my test. More worried about having a good social life and making new friends, new freshmen in college might have to spend all night cramming for their first couple of tests.

To avoid cramming for a test all night, a change in study habits may require studying and preparing earlier instead of the night before the test. This last minute studying, or better known as cramming, the night before the test in order to receive a good passing grade was almost the only study habit I knew in high school; however, if I didn't receive a passing grade, I knew I could make a poster for extra credit, or the homework I turned in would help. I tried this cramming for my first test at ————, and the grade received wasn't a passing one. There also wasn't any extra credit poster to do or any homework to help raise my grade; therefore, I had to teach myself the self-discipline to study my notes daily, do the daily readings in my textbooks, and do the assigned homework to avoid cramming for a test. Studying two hours for each individual class and reviewing with someone else in my class was the best way I found to prepare for a test and to avoid cramming.

A lot of beginning freshmen procrastinate their homework until the last minute and don't want to put in the hours they need to study effectively for a test. I fit in as one of these who wasn't ready to put in all the time I needed. My first two test scores reflected that I hadn't spent the adequate amount of time preparing. If my friends called me up and asked me to do something with them, I would go no matter how much homework I had to do. I would much rather have watched T.V., cleaned my room, or worked out at the fitness center just so I could postpone doing my homework. After pulling an all-nighter a couple of times, I knew I would have to quit procrastinating until midnight, because physically I couldn't function the next day. I would walk around the campus like a zombie with my eyes bloodshot and half shut, my hair not curled, barely wearing any makeup, and wearing anything that felt the most comfortable, usually a sweat suit. To avoid appearing like this at school, I knew I would have to give up my social life a little bit and quit procrastinating my homework until late at night.

If homework is put off until late at night, studying for a test all night takes different techniques to stay awake. Not every technique used works the same for everybody. I found that if I study in a sitting position at the kitchen table or at a desk, I am more awake and can study better with my body sitting up instead of lying down. Some people like to lie in bed while they are studying, but I find myself more apt to fall asleep and to become fatigued faster. To keep from falling asleep, I take a break for about ten minutes every hour; this helps free my mind from becoming disarrayed. Along with taking breaks, drinking coffee can make some people more alert. When I drink coffee to stay awake while studying, though, I spend more than half the night in the bathroom on the toilet when I could have been studying. Although taking a shower in the middle of the night may seem different, it may really help wake you up. I find taking a shower helps pep me up more than anything else. I feel fresher and more alert to what I am studying. Even though some of these things may seem out of the ordinary to be doing late at night, if someone has to prepare for a test the next day, they will resort to anything to help stay awake. All of these techniques to keep me awake could have been avoided if I would have studied differently at first.

People learn by their mistakes, and I learned the hard way by flunking my first two tests, which hurt my grades for the classes. I had to decide either to strive for better grades or to strive for a good social life and the fun college can offer. After pulling a couple of all-nighters, I decided my grades were more important, because my education and good grades would pay off in the end for a good job or a diploma to look back at and be proud of. Whereas, cramming all night because I put my homework off and flunking tests will get me nothing. ☐

Exercises

1. Write a paragraph or two that describes the *effect* of the essay on you, the reader. You are interested not so much in what the essay "means"

as in what the essay *does* to you. Did you find it easy reading? What did you like best about the writing? Least? Which parts of the text intrigued you most? Which parts slipped right by, or had to be reread for any effect to take place? Does the writer set up a dialogue with you?

2. Write a paragraph or two describing the writer and her intentions. What do you think she is like? What do you think she wants to say?

3. Write a paragraph or two in which you *develop* some of the ideas in this essay, adding your opinions and thoughts, and drawing on your own experience.

4. Now cross out sentences in the original essay that you think might be cut because they are not essential to the writer's account. As you read and annotate, consider the following *aims of your revision:*

    (a) You are looking for one or more statements that provide the main thrust of the text: sentences that had the strongest impact on you and where you think the writer's voice is strongest. Underline these statements and identify them as "main statements" ("MS") in the margin.

    (b) You are trying to shorten the text and make it as *concise* as possible. You want to remove repetitions or sentences that add nothing to the strong statements.

    (c) You are looking for parts of the text where the focus becomes fuzzy, or long-winded, or simply disappears, and you need to decide whether these sentences, phrases, and so on, should be rewritten or removed altogether. These are the moments when the writer's dialogue with his or her topic and audience seems to be breaking down, and you found yourself rereading more than once, or your attention wavered. Underline these passages and indicate with a question mark or a comment that you have a problem with them.

    (d) You are looking for the development of a strong and justified opinion or argument, based on clear evidence and rational comments. Passages that seem to you to be especially honest and articulate deserve underlining and commenting on, as do passages that reveal contradictory thoughts, or changes of opinion that need to be resolved.

CHAPTER 2

Writing from Reading

Why write about a text? For these reasons at least. First, because writing about a text leads us to read it attentively, to see things about it we might overlook on a more casual reading. Second, because writing stimulates thinking. Putting words on paper provokes thought, gets our minds into gear. Third, we may want to react strongly to what a text says, either to endorse its views or to disagree with them. And finally, writing about a text gives us power over it, allowing us to absorb it into our knowledge and experience.

In this chapter we explore different reasons for writing about texts and different ways to go about it. To that end the chapter is divided into three parts. Each concentrates on a different purpose for writing about a text; each describes different techniques and procedures for doing so; and each offers a different way to write about the writing you read. Here are the three parts:

Writing to understand a text
Writing to explain a text
Writing to evaluate a text

In writing to understand texts we are concerned primarily with how to read and make sense of them. Our emphasis is on making observations and connections largely for ourselves. The kind of writing associated with these goals is personal and exploratory. It assumes the forms of freewriting, annotating, listing, and journalizing.

In writing to explain texts, we are concerned largely with interpretation, with making inferences based on our observations about texts. (An inference is a statement about the unknown that we derive from the known—in short, an interpretation.) The writing in this section is more formal than informal, more public than private, more explanatory than exploratory.

In writing to evaluate texts we are concerned primarily with judging them, with measuring them against aesthetic criteria and against moral and cultural values. Our emphasis is on arriving at conclusions about how we value them and why.

WRITING TO UNDERSTAND A TEXT

When we understand a text we are able to make sense of it, to explain it to ourselves. In doing so, we follow its argument and consider its implications. In writing to understand a text we attempt to open ourselves to it, allowing the text to stimulate both our feelings and our thoughts. Consider, for example, the implications of the following words, which serve as the title of a text: "symptoms of love." Even before reading the text itself, seeing its title evokes our feelings and thoughts about the experience of being in love. It may suggest something about the nature of love as a disease, for which there are recognizable symptoms. Moreover, the words may trigger memories of our own experience; they may remind us of things we have seen, heard, read, or imagined.

Exercises

1. Write about what the title "Symptoms of Love" suggests to you. Don't worry about a "correct" response.

2. If you found yourself either unable or unwilling to perform this exercise before reading the poem, then return to the exercise after you read it. Even if you have done the exercise, you may wish to return and expand your writing based on feelings, thoughts, and memories the poem's details may evoke.

3. Describe the situation the poem depicts and the feelings it describes. Consider its portrayal of the lover.

Symptoms of Love
Robert Graves

Love is a universal migraine,
A bright stain on the vision
Blotting out reason.

Symptoms of true love
Are leanness, jealousy,
Laggard dawns;

Are omens and nightmares—
Listening for a knock.
Waiting for a sign:

For a touch of her fingers
In a darkened room,
For a searching look.

Take courage, lover!
Could you endure such pain
At any hand but hers?

In following through on the previous exercises you have been doing freewriting, a kind of writing in which you think about a subject or a text as you write. You did some freewriting in Chapter 1. Here, in responding to the text about love, your freewriting may be more focused—on the text itself or on its subject, love. As in the more open kind of freewriting, in the focused freewriting we invite you to do in this chapter, you needn't confine yourself to a single aspect of the subject. And you needn't organize your writing into a clearly discernible pattern of organization. Write to explore your feelings and thoughts about the text and its subject. In the process you may wander from the main concerns of the text. You may also discover thoughts and feelings you didn't know you had. The important thing is to respond naturally and honestly, to allow your responses full and free play.

Here is another text for you to respond to, this time an essay. Like Graves's poem, the title of Richard Selzer's essay, "Love Sick," offers a clue to its subject. It should also provide a stimulus to your own response. As you read, consider how you feel as well as what you think.

Love Sick

Richard Selzer

Love is an illness, and has its own set of obsessive thoughts. Behold the poor wretch afflicted with love: one moment strewn upon a sofa, scarcely breathing save for an occasional sigh upsucked from the deep well of his despair; the next, pacing *agitato*, his cheek alternately pale and flushed. Is he pricked? What barb, what gnat stings him thus?

At noon he waves away his plate of food. Unloved, he loathes his own body, and refuses it the smallest nourishment. At half-past twelve, he receives a letter. She loves him! And soon he is snout-deep in his dish, voracious as any wolf at entrails. Greeted by a friend, a brother, he makes no discernible reply, but gazes to and fro, unable to recall who it is that salutes him. Distraught, he picks up a magazine, only to stand wondering what it is he is holding. Was he once clever at the guitar? He can no longer play at all. And so it goes.

Ah, Cupid, thou wanton boy. How cruel thy sport!

See how the man of sorrows leans against a wall, one hand shielding his eyes from vertigo, the other gripping his chest to muffle the palpitations there. Let some stray image of his beloved flit across his mind, her toe perhaps, or scarf, and all at once, his chin and brow gleam with idiotic rapture. But wait! Now some trivial slight is recalled, and once again, his face is a mask of anguish, empurpled and carved with deep lines.

Such, such are the joys of love. May Heaven protect us, one and all, from this happiness. One marvels at the single-celled paramecium, who, without the least utterance of distemper, procreates by splitting in two. One can but envy the paramecium his solitary fission.

Love is an illness and, not unlike its sister maladies, hysteria, hypochondriasis, and melancholia, has its own set of obsessive thoughts. In love, the *idée fixe* that harries the patient every waking hour is not remorse, nor the fear of cancer, nor the dread of death, but that single other *person*. Every disease has its domain, its *locus operandi*. If, in madness, it is the brain, in cirrhosis, the liver, and lumbago, the spine, in love it is that web of knobs and filaments known as the autonomic nervous system. How ironic that here, in this all but invisible network, should lie hidden the ultimate carnal mystery. Mischievous Nature, having arranged to incite copulation by assigning opposite hormones to half the human race, and sculpted the curves of the flesh to accommodate the process, now throws over the primitive rite a magic veil, a web of difficulty that is the autonomic nervous system. It is the malfunction, the deficiency of this system that produces the disease of love. Here it fulminates, driving its luckless victims to madness or suicide. How many the lovers that have taken that final tragic step, and were found swinging from the limb of some lonely tree, airing their pathetic rags? The autonomic nervous system! Why not the massive liver? The solid spleen? Or the skin, from which the poison might be drawn with knife or poultice?

Lying upon the front of each of the vertebrae, from the base of the skull to the tip of the coccyx, is a paired chain of tiny nodes, each of which is connected to the spinal cord and to each other. From these nodes, bundles of nerves extend to meet at relay stations scattered in profusion throughout the body. These ganglia are in anatomical touch with their fellows by a system of circuitry complex and various enough to confound into self-destruction a whole race of computers. Here all is chemical rush and wave-to-wave ripple. Here is fear translated for the flesh, and pride and jealousy. Here dwell zeal and ardor. And love is contracted. By microscopic nervelets, the impulses are carried to all the capillaries, hair follicles and sweat glands of the body. The smooth muscle of the intestine, the lachrymal glands, the bladder, and the genitalia are all subject to the bombardment that issues from this vibrating harp of knobs and strings. Innumerable are the orders delivered: Constrict! Dilate! Secrete! Stand erect! It is all very busy, effervescent.

In defense of the autonomic nervous system, it must be said that it is uncrippled by the intellect or the force of the will. Intuition governs here. Here is one's flesh wholly trustworthy, for it speaks with honesty all the attractions and repulsions of our lives. Consciousness here would be an intruder, justly driven away from the realm of the transcendent. One *feels*; therefore one *is*. No opinion but spontaneous feeling prevails. Is tomorrow's love expected? Yesterday's recalled? Instantly, the thought is captured by the autonomic nervous system. (And alchemy turns wish and dream to ruddy reality.) The billion capillaries of the face dilate and fill with blood. You blush. You are prettier. Is love spurned? Again the rippling, the dance of energy, and the bed of capillaries constricts, squeezing the blood from the surface to some more central pool. Now you blanch. The pallor of death is upon you. Icy are your own fingertips. It is the flesh responding to the death of love with its own facsimile.

Imagine that you are in the painful state of unrequited love. You are seated at a restaurant table with your beloved. You reach for the salt; at the same moment, she for the pepper goes. Your fingers accidentally touch cellar-side. There is a sudden instantaneous discharge of the autonomic nervous system, and your hand recoils. It is singed by fire. Now, the capillaries of your cheeks are commanded to dilate. They fill with blood. Its color is visible in your skin. You go from salmon pink to fiery red. "Why, you are blushing," she says, and smiles cruelly. Even as she speaks, your sweat glands have opened their gates, and you are coated with wetness. You sop. She sees, and raises one eyebrow. Now the sounds of your intestine, those gurgles and gaseous pops called borborygmi, comes distinctly to your ears. You press your abdomen to still them. But, she hears! The people at the neighboring tables do, too. All at once, she turns her face to the door. She rises. Suddenly, it is time for her to go. Unhappy lover, you are in the grip of your autonomic nervous system, and by its betrayal you are thus undone.

Despite that love is an incurable disease, yet is there reason for hope. Should the victim survive the acute stages, he may then expect that love will lose much of its virulence, that it will burn itself out, like other self-limiting maladies. In fact, this is becoming more and more the natural history of love, and a good thing at that. Lucky is he in whom love dies, and lust lives on. For he who is tormented by the protracted fevers of chronic undying love awaits but a premature and exhausted death. While lust, which engages not the spirit, serves but to restore the vigor and stimulate the circulation.

Still, one dreams of bringing about a cure. For the discoverer of such, a thousand Nobels would be too paltry a reward. Thus I have engaged the initial hypothesis (call it a hunch) that there is somewhere in the body, under the kneecap perhaps, or between the fourth and fifth toes . . . somewhere . . . a single, as yet unnoticed master gland, the removal of which would render the person so

[handwritten: "Who would you want to be annoyed to love."]

operated upon immune to love. Daily, in my surgery, I hunt this
glans amoris, turning over membranes, reaching into dim tunnels,
straining all the warm extrusions of the body for some residue that
will point the way.

Perhaps I shall not find it in my lifetime. But never, I vow it,
shall I cease from these labors, and shall charge those who come
after me to carry on the search. Until then, I would agree with my
Uncle Frank, who recommends a cold shower and three laps around
the block for the immediate relief of the discomforts of love. □

[handwritten: Why not let love take a chance?]

Exercises

1. Write a response to Selzer's description of love. Your writing might
    take the form of a diary or journal entry in which you talk to yourself
    about Selzer's essay, perhaps relating it to your experience. Or it
    might be a series of notes and questions you would like to ask the
    author.

2. Compare your responses to Selzer's essay with your responses to
    Graves's poem. Are they similar? Different? Why?

3. Write a few paragraphs about "being in love" or about "falling in
    love." Consider what you know, feel, or think about either idea.

Thus far we have invited you to write both before and after
you read a text. We will have more to say, later, about writing *after*
you read a text. For now we concentrate on writing *as* you read.

ANNOTATING

Annotation is one way to increase your involvement in reading a text by writing about it while you read. When you annotate or
make notes about a text you respond actively to it. Usually annotations are made in the margins around a text, but they can also be
made within it, taking the form of underlined words, circled phrases,
bracketed sentences or paragraphs, arrows, question marks, and various other abbreviations.

Annotating a text offers a convenient and relatively painless
way to begin writing about it. Your annotations can get you started
in zeroing in on what you see as important. They can also signal
textual details that may puzzle or disconcert you. Annotations generally assume one or another of the following forms:

- Labels or shorthand abbreviations of your reactions. You might write, for example, "good" or "nonsense" or "yes." You might also use labels to highlight important textual features with annotations such as "main point" or "evidence" or "irony."

- Summaries of important ideas or attitudes you discover in the text. These marginal notes are more extensive than the labels just described, but they are still brief, condensed statements or questions. Here are a few examples:

  These characters are struggling to control each other.
  Selzer limits his discussion of love to love as a disease. He seems
  to ignore other possibilities.
  Graves's last stanza turns the poem upside down: love seems
  worth it after all.

- Questions and uncertainties that develop as you read. Your questions may be as brief as "Why this?" or "Significant?" Or they may be more extensive, as the following examples suggest:

  Is this scene related to the first two?
  Where does love as a feeling or as a state of mind come in?
  Does Bacon believe that love is inevitable? Is Bacon serious after
  all?

In annotating a text you begin to clarify your understanding of it. The act of writing such notes, however brief, encourages you to focus both on the writer's point and on what you think of it. Annotation stimulates your thinking, with the pen becoming an extension of your brain. A further advantage of annotation is that if you write no more, you have at least marked up the text for rereading and subsequent study. And if you write about the text in a more formal way later, your annotations have at least signaled key passages, noted significant details, and raised important questions for you to consider later.

Exercises

1. Return to one of the selections you wrote about earlier and annotate it.

2. Annotate the following texts. Underline; circle; draw arrows. Raise questions. Comment and react.

NW Ayer Incorporated

Let Me Not to the Marriage of True Minds
William Shakespeare

Let me not to the marriage of true minds
Admit impediments. Love is not love
Which alters when it alteration finds,
Or bends with the remover to remove:

Oh, no! it is an ever-fixéd mark,
That looks on tempests and is never shaken;
It is the star to every wandering bark,
Whose worth's unknown, although his height be taken.
Love's not Time's fool, though rosy lips and cheeks
Within his bending sickle's compass come;
Love alters not with his brief hours and weeks,
But bears it out even to the edge of doom.
If this be error and upon me proved,
I never writ, nor no man ever loved.

If a text engages you strongly—or if you are required to write about it at length—you might consider both annotating it and freewriting on it as well. In fact, if you performed both of the previous exercises, you have already done that. If you haven't (if, for example, you've annotated one of the texts in the previous exercise), consider freewriting about it, taking off from your annotations. Together annotation and freewriting will prompt your thinking and release your feelings so you'll have something to say to others in a more formal paper.

After reading the following annotated essay, write a paragraph or two discussing your sense of what it says.

Of Love
Francis Bacon

Bacon asserts, then qualifies. Exceptions as proofs, as qualifications?

Love is dangerous, destructive.

The stage is more beholding to Love than the life of man. For as to the stage, love is ever matter of comedies, and now and then of tragedies, but in life it doth much mischief, sometimes like a syren, sometimes like a fury. You may observe that amongst all the great and worthy persons (whereof the memory remaineth, either ancient or recent) there is not one that hath been transported to the mad degree of love, which shows that

Love as excess.

Love involves flattery.

Central idea?

Wisdom and love as contradictory.

great spirits and great business do keep out this weak passion. You must except nevertheless Marcus Antonius, the half partner of the empire of Rome, and Appius Claudius, the decemvir and lawgiver; whereof the former was indeed a voluptuous man, and inordinate, but the latter was an austere and wise man; and therefore it seems (though rarely) that love can find entrance not only into an open heart, but also into a heart well fortified, if watch be not well kept. It is a poor saying of Epicurus, *Satis magnum alter alteri theatrum sumus*, as if man, made for the contemplation of heaven and all noble objects, should do nothing but kneel before a little idol, and make himself a subject, though not of the mouth (as beasts are), yet of the eye, which was given him for higher purposes. It is a strange thing to note the excess of this passion, and how it braves the nature and value of things, but this: that the speaking in a perpetual hyperbole is comely in nothing but in love. Neither is it merely in the phrase, for whereas it hath been well said that the arch-flatterer, with whom all the pretty flatterers have intelligence, is a man's self, certainly the lover is more. For there was never proud man thought so absurdly well of himself as the lover doth of the person loved; and therefore it was well said, *That it is impossible to love and to be wise.* Neither doth this weakness appear to others only, and not to the party loved, but to the loved most of all, except the love be reciproque. For it is a true rule that love is ever rewarded either with the reciproque or with an inward and secret contempt. By how much the more men ought to beware of this passion, which loseth not only other things but itself. As for the other losses, the poet's relation doth well figure them: that he that preferred Helena quit-

Love = loss of riches and wisdom.

Love as child of folly.

Love and wine both as "rewards"—for dangers encountered by men in war.

Is the love of mankind good?

An ironic criticism of friars?

Bacon uses one word, "love," for different states of being and feeling.

ted the gifts of Juno and Pallas. For whosoever esteemeth too much of amorous affection quitteth both riches and wisdom. This passion hath his floods in the very times of weakness, which are great prosperity and great adversity, though this latter hath been less observed, both which times kindle love, and make it more fervent, and therefore show it to be the child of folly. They do best who, if they cannot but admit love, yet make it keep quarter and sever it wholly from their serious affairs and actions of life, for if it check once with business, it troubleth men's fortunes, and maketh men that they can no ways be true to their own ends. I know not how, but martial men are given to love; I think it is but as they are given to wine, for perils commonly ask to be paid in pleasures. There is in man's nature a secret inclination and motion towards love of others, which if it be not spent upon some one or a few, doth naturally spread itself towards many, and maketh men become humane and charitable, as it is seen sometime in friars. Nuptial love maketh mankind; friendly love perfecteth it; but wanton love corrupteth and embaseth it.

Exercises

1. Write two or three sentences that illustrate each of the following metaphorical descriptions and definitions of love.

   (a) Love is a disease.
   (b) Love is madness.
   (c) Love is war.
   (d) Love is magic.
   (e) Love is an adventure.
   (f) Love is a physical force.

2. Annotate (and/or freewrite about) the passage below. It is taken from the Bible, the First Letter to the Corinthians, Chapter 13.

If I speak in the tongues of men and of angels, but have not love, I am a noisy gong or a clanging cymbal. And if I have prophetic powers, and understand all mysteries and all knowledge, and if I have all faith, so as to remove mountains, but have not love, I am nothing. If I give away all I have, and if I deliver my body to be burned, but have not love, I gain nothing.

Love is patient and kind; love is not jealous or boastful; it is not arrogant or rude. Love does not insist on its own way; it is not irritable or resentful; it does not rejoice at wrong, but rejoices in the right. Love bears all things, believes all things, hopes all things, endures all things.

Love never ends; as for prophecies, they will pass away; as for tongues, they will cease; as for knowledge, it will pass away. For our knowledge is imperfect and our prophecy is imperfect; but when the perfect comes, the imperfect will pass away. When I was a child, I spoke like a child, I thought like a child, I reasoned like a child; when I became a man, I gave up childish ways. For now we see in a mirror dimly, but then face to face. Now I know in part; then I shall understand fully, even as I have been fully understood. So faith, hope, love abide, these three; but the greatest of these is love. □

LISTING

Thus far we have recommended two ways to engage texts actively while you read them and after. Both focused freewriting and annotating are informal methods for writing in response to texts. Both respect the subjectivity for your response, allowing you to record how you feel about texts as well as what you think about them. To these strategies we add a third—listing.

Although an informal strategy, which allows you to begin writing about a text with a minimum of preparation, listing will move you beyond personal response and subjective reactions. To explain a text to others, one way to get started is to make a list of your observations about it. Particularly worthy of listing are any recurrent features of a text. In Bacon's "Of Love," for example, you may notice the recurrence of words and phrases suggesting a shift of perspective. In Selzer's "Love Sick" you find many details suggesting a physiological description of love. In Graves's poem "Symptoms of Love" you saw a change of direction and tone in the final stanza.

These and other observations we can make *as* we read a text. We may or may not record them in annotations or freewriting. By collecting such observations and listing them together individually, we are in a better position to see them clearly and to discern connections among them: to discover related features and patterns. At one time or another, most of us have used lists to help us remember what to buy, whom to thank, what we have to do. Just as a list aids your memory at the grocery store, a writer's list provides details to create or re-create an experience.

In the following poem, Langston Hughes recounts his life to his freshman English teacher in college. In doing so, he provides us with a list of things about himself. As you read through the poem, list some facts about Hughes's life.

Theme for English B
Langston Hughes

The instructor said,

> *Go home and write*
> *a page tonight.*
> *And let that page come out of you—*
> *Then, it will be true.*

I wonder if it's that simple?

I am twenty-two, colored, born in Winston-Salem.
I went to school there, then Durham, then here
to this college on the hill above Harlem.
I am the only colored student in my class.
The steps from the hill lead down into Harlem,
through a park, then I cross St. Nicholas,
Eighth Avenue, Seventh, and I come to the Y.
the Harlem Branch Y, where I take the elevator
up to my room, sit down, and write this page:

It's not easy to know what is true for you or me
at twenty-two, my age. But I guess I'm what
I feel and see and hear. Harlem, I hear you:
hear you, hear me—we two—you, me, talk on this page.
(I hear New York, too.) Me—who?

Well, I like to eat, sleep, drink, and be in love.
I like to work, read, learn, and understand life.
I like a pipe for a Christmas present,
or records—Bessie, bop, or Bach.
I guess being colored doesn't make me *not* like
the same things other folks like who are other races.

So will my page be colored that I write?
Being me, it will not be white.
But it will be
a part of you, instructor.
You are white—
yet a part of me, as I am a part of you.
That's American.
Sometimes perhaps you don't want to be a part of me.
Nor do I often want to be a part of you.
But we are, that's true!
As I learn from you,
I guess you learn from me—
although you're older—and white—
and somewhat more free.

This is my page for English B.

In the act of telling his teacher who he was, of listing facts about his life, Hughes came to understand himself better. He gained an awareness of how his identity fits within a complex personal and social network. But just what kind of facts has Hughes included? How revealing are they? And how are they related?

Exercises

1. Write a brief prose autobiography to appear in your local newspaper shortly after your graduation from college. Use specific details so your readers can acquire a sense of who you are and what you've done.
     After you finish, reflect on how you went about recording the information you included. Did you list events from your life on a sheet in a particular order? Did you let your mind wander and then jot down details as they came to you? Or did you do something else? Compare your writing method and the product (your autobiography) with those of your classmates.

2. Make a list of things you notice about the following advertisement:

1984 Revlon, Inc.

JOURNALIZING: KEEPING A DOUBLE-ENTRY NOTEBOOK

Keeping a journal is still another way you can write to understand texts. In this journal you can record your thoughts about texts and your emotional responses to them. You can include brief summaries of the texts you encounter. The journal can function, in addition, as a common place for you to collect and copy sentences, phrases, ideas you would like to preserve. In it you can record your growing understanding of the significance and value of what you read. It can also serve as an arena to develop your thinking about issues that emerge from your reading.

An especially useful kind of journal is one that has been called a "double-entry" notebook or a "dialectical" notebook.* To make your notes dialectical you must allow for a divided or two-part organization of your journal pages. On one side you "take notes," recording more or less what you think a given text says. You summarize and paraphrase and quote the text. On the other side of the notebook pages you react by noting your own responses and questions. Here you record what you think and how you feel. You question and criticize the text, relating it to what you have experienced and what you have learned. This part makes the notebook or journal "dialectical." Here you *make* notes rather than *take* them. You react to the text, and you react to your notes on the text. The result is a dialogue in which you first talk with the texts you read and then talk with yourself about them. Here is an example:

St. Augustine and the Bullfight
Katherine Anne Porter

W. B. Yeats remarked—I cannot find the passage now, so must say it in other words—that the unhappy man (unfortunate?) was one whose adventures outran his capacity for experience, capacity for experience being, I should say, roughly equal to the faculty for understanding what has happened to one. The difference then between mere adventure and a real experience might be this? That adventure is something you seek for pleasure, or even for profit, like

---

*On the double-entry notebook, I am indebted to Ann E. Berthoff, who describes it in her books *Forming, Thinking, Writing* and *The Making of Meaning* (Upper Montclair, N.J.: Boynton/Cook Publishers, 1978; 1981).

a gold rush or invading a country; for the illusion of being more alive than ordinarily, the thing you will to occur; but experience is what really happens to you in the long run; the truth that finally overtakes you.

Adventure is sometimes fun, but not too often. Not if you can remember what really happened; all of it. It passes, seems to lead nowhere much, is something to tell friends to amuse them, maybe. "Once upon a time," I can hear myself saying, for I once said it, "I scaled a cliff in Boulder, Colorado, with my bare hands, and in Indian moccasins, bare-legged. And at nearly the top, after six hours of feeling for toe- and fingerholds, and the gayest feeling in the world that when I got to the top I should see something wonderful, something that sounded awfully like a bear growled out of a cave, and I scuttled down out of there in a hurry." This is a fact. I had never climbed a mountain in my life, never had the least wish to climb one. But there I was, for perfectly good reasons, in a hut on a mountainside in heavenly sunny though sometimes stormy weather, so I went out one morning and scaled a very minor cliff; alone, unsuitably clad, in the season when rattlesnakes are casting their skins; and if it was not a bear in that cave, it was some kind of unfriendly animal who growls at people; and this ridiculous escapade, which was nearly six hours of the hardest work I ever did in my life, toeholds and fingerholds on a cliff, put me to bed for just nine days with a complaint the local people called "muscle poisoning." I don't know exactly what they meant, but I do remember clearly that I could not turn over in bed without help and in great agony. And did it teach me anything? I think not, for three years later I was climbing a volcano in Mexico, that celebrated unpronounceably named volcano, Popocatepetl, which everybody who comes near it climbs sooner or later; but was that any reason for me to climb it? No. And I was knocked out for weeks, and that finally did teach me: I am not supposed to go climbing things. Why did I not know in the first place? For me, this sort of thing must come under the head of Adventure.

I think it is pastime of rather an inferior sort; yet I have heard men tell yarns like this only a very little better: their mountains were higher, or their sea was wider, or their bear was bigger and noisier, or their cliff was steeper and taller, yet there was no point whatever to any of it except that it had happened. This is not enough. May it not be, perhaps, that experience, that is, the thing that happens to a person living from day to day, is anything at all that sinks in? is, without making any claims, a part of your growing and changing life? what it is that happens in your mind, your heart? □

Now, here's the journal entry:

Summarizing and taking notes *(the writer's thoughts)*	**Reacting and making notes** *(our thoughts)*
Porter begins by paraphrasing Yeats's observation that men whose adventure or experience outruns their capacity for understanding it are indeed either unhappy or unfortunate. (Porter can't seem to remember which.)	Does she mention Yeats as an authority? Porter devalues adventures and values "experience." Experience is "real," she says; adventures are "mere" adventures. She also further judges them by calling adventure "illusion" and experience "truth."
Her second paragraph continues the indictment of adventure. She says it isn't fun—not much of it, most of the time. This paragraph contains an anecdotal description of Porter's mountain-climbing adventures. She knocks the experience by saying she didn't learn anything from it, and by noting how she suffered from it physically.	Does she mean that adventure provides only the "illusion" of fun? An illusion created or re-created *via* our faulty selective remembering of our adventures? This would suggest that the adventures were not "fun" in our experience of them; only that we delude ourselves into thinking they were in retrospect. We remember them as happy, exciting, successful, because we must—we need to, since we invested our time, money, energy, self-image.
Her third and final paragraph adds a twist: that many people's adventures are not really different from hers—the differences are of *degree* rather than *kind*.	Her tone further condemns adventure, which she reduces (unfairly?) to "climbing things." For her, perhaps this was true; but for me? for others?
Her final evaluation is that such experience—"adventures"—are not enough; adventure is only *what* happens, not what the happening means.	For Porter, experience is far more valuable.

Adventure is external experience only; *real experience* is what happens to us after the adventure is over. This real experience is intellectual and emotional, not merely external and physical.

A rhetorical observation: she uses questions and raises her ideas somewhat tentatively. A ploy? There seems no question about what she thinks. Then why this hesitant, questioning tone? Perhaps to make herself sound more persuasive, more reasonable, as if she is thinking things out rather than insisting on them.

Experience, in short, changes the mind and the heart, adventure changes nothing.

Porter's distinction can be allied with others: adventurous experience vs. real experience—the real experience going on quietly within.

And isn't her distinction here related to the idea that wisdom, growth, maturity, etc., come from considered, deliberative reflection on what happens to us?

A question: Hasn't Porter made *experience*, in her sense of the word, out of her adventures? Hasn't she redeemed something from it by reflecting on it as she does?

Exercises

1. Enter the dialogue by adding your comments and questions to the sample double-entry notebook selection. Comment on Porter's text, then react to our observations and responses as well.

2. Select a short work or a passage from a longer text and write a double-entry notebook response to it. The passage can come from one of your textbooks; from a book, magazine, or newspaper you're reading for pleasure; or from less formalized writing such as graffiti.

WRITING TO EXPLAIN A TEXT

When we write to explain a text our concern is largely one of making our understanding of it clear to others. Such writing will be based not only on our impressions of the text, but on our interpretation or considered understanding of it. In this section we explore ways to write about texts that are less personal, less informal, and less subjective than those described in the previous section. We emphasize ways to develop your reading into an interpretive essay. And we suggest forms of explanation your writing about texts may assume.

We began this movement from reading to interpretation in the previous section when we asked you to make lists of your observations and to begin relating the items on your lists. That act of discovering relationships, of seeing patterns, of making connections among details is crucial for interpretation. It is a necessary step but not a sufficient one, since to arrive at an interpretation you must come up with an *idea about the text* based on the connections you discern.

When we write an interpretation or explanation of the meaning of a text, our goal is clarity. This clarity is twofold. First it involves a clarity of understanding. (We need to know, in short, what we think.) And second, it requires a clarity of explanation. (We need to convey our thinking effectively to others.) One way to begin clarifying our understanding of a text for others is to summarize it or to paraphrase a crucial part of it.

Summarizing a Text   A summary is a succinct account of a work. As a condensation or compression, a summary is shorter than the work it summarizes. Here is a brief summary of Katherine Anne Porter's "Saint Augustine and the Bullfight":

> Porter's essay is both a meditation on and a definition of what she means by *experience*. She begins by paraphrasing Yeats's idea that experiences must be understood and not merely undergone. For Porter, having "adventures" or "experiences" without reflecting on them and arriving at their meaning is fruitless. Some experiences or adventures, she suggests, may be valueless not only because no meaning can be gleaned from them, but also because they are dangerous or unpleasant. Real experience, Porter contends, is something radically different. It is what happens to us intellectually and emotionally; it makes an indelible impression on the mind and the heart.

This summary recounts the gist of Porter's essay. It does not attempt to make a judgment about it. Typically, although a summary of a text requires some thought about its meaning, it usually does not include an evaluation of its validity. A summary, however, does more than catalogue the contents of a text or describe what happens in it. It must also explain the point of the text. In summarizing Bacon's essay "Of Love," for example, we must explain what Bacon says or what we think he says. We can do this in a single sentence or we can do it more extensively in a few paragraphs. Here is a one-sentence version:

> In "Of Love" Francis Bacon warns against the dangers of taking love too seriously.

If we push on for an additional sentence or two we might note this:

> In fact, Bacon lists the shortcomings of love, suggesting that it is akin to madness, idolatry, blindness, flattery, and folly. His point seems to be that love produces more problems than pleasures.

Any fuller summary would go on to specify some of the virtues Bacon claims for love, along with its positive consequences for the one who loves and for those loved. It would comment on the multiple meanings of love included in the essay's final sentence. And it would attempt to explain his qualifications and exceptions.

Exercises

1. Write one-sentence summaries of any two texts you've read so far.
2. For one or both of these, expand your summary to a paragraph of seven to ten sentences.

Paraphrasing a Text A paraphrase differs from a summary in the following ways. First, it is more extensive than a summary. Unlike a summary, which compresses the essence of a text into a brief compass, a paraphrase will generally equal the length of the text paraphrased. Second, a paraphrase follows the structure or the order of details of the text. The major differences between summary and paraphrase thus involve scale and organization. The paraphrase is inclusive, the summary selective; the paraphrase depends on the structure of the text; the summary does not. An additional distinction must also be made. Whereas you summarize whole works (or large sections of them), you generally paraphrase much briefer segments—a bit of dialogue from a play, a stanza or two from a poem, a paragraph or so from a story or essay. The summary telescopes much into little; the paraphrase puts a small slide of text under the microscope of our attention.

Let's consider a few examples of paraphrase. Here, first, is a paraphrase of the first two paragraphs of Richard Selzer's essay "Love Sick."

> According to Selzer, love is an "illness" that obsesses its victim. In the opening paragraphs Selzer depicts a physically debilitated lover suffering from the affliction of being in love. He mopes and swoons, uninterested in food until, receiving an acknowledgment that "she" loves him, he can again return to a brief period of normalcy— long enough, at least, to eat. But he is so distracted by his thoughts of her that he ignores those who would converse with him. Nor can he muster sufficient attention to read a magazine or play his guitar.

Notice how the paraphrase does not attempt to analyze or evaluate Selzer's picture of the lover. Instead it represents it, casting it in the reader's words while respecting Selzer's idea and observing the order in which he develops it.

In paraphrasing any text we move toward interpretation, specifically toward explication and analysis. Interpretation is a way of seeing a text, offering one perspective, one way of considering it, among many. An interpretation, moreover, presents a claim about what the text says or implies, then supports that claim with evidence. The evidential support comes primarily from the text itself. But it also emerges in the way writers reason about the textual details they marshal in support of their interpretations. And, on occasion, writers go beyond the text to include "extratextual" evidence to support their interpretive claims. An interpreter of a literary work, for example, may support his or her way of seeing the text with references to other works by the author, to the author's letters or biography, or even to interpretations published by other readers. But regardless of the type of extratextual evidence brought to bear on an interpretation of a given text, the writer's essential task is to present a way of seeing that text and to support that interpretation as clearly and richly as possible. We will have more to say about certain types of extratextual evidence later in this chapter. For now, we simply acknowledge that you may bring such knowledge to bear on your interpretation of any given text, although it often is not necessary. The important thing is to read the text, interpret it, and explain your way of seeing in writing.

An additional point must be made: Interpretations of texts often differ. Your view of the central concerns of a text and your understanding of its implications are not necessarily shared by other readers. Nor are their interpretations necessarily congruent with each other. This does not mean that interpretation is merely the voicing of opinions. It suggests, rather, that texts are rich sources of meaning and feeling that have various results when brought to life by readers. Because readers bring different kinds of knowledge, types of experience, and degrees of perception to their reading of texts, they see those texts in different ways. In fact readers often come to see the same text in different ways after they see what others say about it, as they come to know the text better, and as they grow and mature as individuals and as readers themselves.

Finally, we should remember that in developing our explanation of texts for other readers, in laying out our thinking for others to read, we first make use of the strategies of thinking and writing described in Chapters 1 to 5 and at the beginning of this chapter. As a way of summarizing and consolidating our advice about writing an interpretation or explanation of a text for other readers, we illustrate the process from start to finish with a single thorough reading.

Exercise

Read the following text and annotate it.

How It Feels to Be Colored Me
Zora Neale Hurston

I

I am colored but I offer nothing in the way of extenuating circumstances except the fact that I am the only Negro in the United

States whose grandfather on the mother's side was *not* an Indian chief.

I remember the very day that I became colored. Up to my thirteenth year I lived in the little Negro town of Eatonville, Florida. It is exclusively a colored town. The only white people I knew passed through the town going to or coming from Orlando. The native whites rode dusty horses, the Northern tourists chugged down the sandy village road in automobiles. The town knew the Southerners and never stopped cane chewing when they passed. But the Northerners were something else again. They were peered at cautiously from behind curtains by the timid. The more venturesome would come out on the porch to watch them go past and got just as much pleasure out of the tourists as the tourists got out of the village.

The front porch might seem a daring place for the rest of the town, but it was a gallery seat for me. My favorite place was atop the gate-post. Proscenium box for a born first-nighter. Not only did I enjoy the show, but I didn't mind the actors knowing that I liked it. I usually spoke to them in passing. I'd wave at them and when they returned my salute, I would say something like this: "Howdy-do-well-I-thank-you-where-you-goin'?" Usually automobile or the horse paused at this, and after a queer exchange of compliments, I would probably "go a piece of the way" with them, as we say in farthest Florida. If one of my family happened to come to the front in time to see me, of course negotiations would be rudely broken off. But even so, it is clear that I was the first "welcome-to-our-state" Floridian, and I hope the Miami Chamber of Commerce will please take notice.

During this period, white people differed from colored to me only in that they rode through town and never lived there. They liked to hear me "speak pieces" and sing and wanted to see me dance the parse-me-la, and gave me generously of their small silver for doing these things, which seemed strange to me for I wanted to do them so much that I needed bribing to stop. Only they didn't know it. The colored people gave no dimes. They deplored any joyful tendencies in me, but I was their Zora nevertheless. I belonged to them, to the nearby hotels, to the county—everybody's Zora.

But changes came in the family when I was thirteen, and I was sent to school in Jacksonville. I left Eatonville, the town of the oleanders, as Zora. When I disembarked from the river-boat at Jacksonville, she was no more. It seemed that I had suffered a sea change. I was not Zora of Orange County any more. I was now a little col-

ored girl. I found it out in certain ways. In my heart as well as in the
mirror. I became a fast brown—warranted not to rub nor run.

II

But I am not tragically colored. There is no great sorrow
dammed up in my soul, nor lurking behind my eyes. I do not mind
at all. I do not belong to the sobbing school of Negrohood who hold
that nature somehow has given them a lowdown dirty deal and
whose feelings are all hurt about it. Even in the helter-skelter skir-
mish that is my life, I have seen that the world is to the strong
regardless of a little pigmentation more or less. No, I do not weep
at the world—I am too busy sharpening my oyster knife.

Someone is always at my elbow reminding me that I am the
granddaughter of slaves. It fails to register depression with me. Slavery is sixty years in the past. The operation was successful and the
patient is doing well, thank you. The terrible struggle that made me
an American out of a potential slave said "On the line!" The Recon-
struction said "Get set!": and the generation before said "Go!" I am
off to a flying start and I must not halt in the stretch to look behind
and weep. Slavery is the price I paid for civilization, and the choice
was not with me. It is a bully adventure and worth all that I have
paid through any ancestors for it. No one on earth ever had a greater
chance for glory. The world to be won and nothing to be lost. It is
thrilling to think—to know that for any act of mine, I shall get twice
as much praise or twice as much blame. It is quite exciting to hold
the center of the national stage, with the spectators not knowing
whether to laugh or to weep.

The position of my white neighbors is much more difficult. No
brown specter pulls up a chair beside me when I am down to eat.
No dark ghost thrusts its leg against mine in bed. The game of keeping what one has is never so exciting as the game of getting.

III

Sometimes it is the other way around. A white person is set
down in our midst, but the contrast is just as sharp for me. For
instance, when I sit in the drafty basement that is The New World
Cabaret with a white person, my color comes. We enter chatting

about any little nothing that we have in common and are seated by the jazz waiters. In the abrupt way that jazz orchestras have, this one plunges into a number. It loses no time in circumlocutions, but gets right down to business. It constricts the thorax and splits the heart with its tempo and narcotic harmonies. This orchestra grows rambunctious, rears on its hind legs and attacks the tonal veil with primitive fury, rending it, clawing it until it breaks through to the jungle beyond. I follow those heathen—follow them exultingly. I dance wildly inside myself; I yell within, I whoop; I shake my asse-gai above my head. I hurl it true to the mark *yeeeeooww!* I am in the jungle and living in the jungle way. My face is painted red and yellow and my body is painted blue. My pulse is throbbing like a war drum. I want to slaughter something—give pain, give death to what, I do not know. But the piece ends. The men of the orchestra wipe their lips and rest their fingers. I creep back slowly to the veneer we call civilization with the last tone and find the white friend sitting motionless in his seat, smoking calmly.

"Good music they have here," he remarks, drumming the table with his fingertips.

Music. The great blobs of purple and red emotions have not touched him. He has only heard what I felt. He is far away and I see him but dimly across the ocean and the continent that have fallen between us. He is so pale with his whiteness then and I am *so* colored.

I do not always feel colored. Even now I often achieve the unconscious Zora of Eatonville before the Hegira. I feel most colored when I am thrown against a sharp white background.

For instance at Barnard. "Beside the waters of the Hudson" I feel my race. Among the thousand white persons, I am a dark rock surged upon, and overswept, but through it all, I remain myself. When covered by the waters, I am; and the ebb but reveals me again.

IV

At certain times I have no race, I am *me.* When I set my hat at a certain angle and saunter down Seventh Avenue, Harlem City, feeling as snooty as the lions in front of the Forty-Second Street Library, for instance. So far as my feelings are concerned, Peggy

Hopkins Joyce on the Boule Mich with her gorgeous raiment, stately carriage, knees knocking together in a most aristocratic manner, has nothing on me. The cosmic Zora emerges. I belong to no race nor time. I am the eternal feminine with its string of beads.

I have no separate feeling about being an American citizen and colored. I am merely a fragment of the Great Soul that surges within the boundaries. My country, right or wrong.

Sometimes, I feel discriminated against, but it does not make me angry. It merely astonishes me. How *can* any deny themselves the pleasure of my company? It's beyond me.

But in the main, I feel like a brown bag of miscellany propped against a wall. Against a wall in company with other bags, white, red and yellow. Pour out the contents, and there is discovered a jumble of small things priceless and worthless. A first-water diamond, an empty spool, bits of broken glass, lengths of string, a key to a door long since crumbled away, a rusty knife-blade, old shoes saved for a road that never was and never will be, a nail bent under the weight of things too heavy for any nail, a dried flower or two still a little fragrant. In your hand is the brown bag. On the ground before you is the jumble it held—so much like the jumble in the bags, could they be emptied, that all might be dumped in a single heap and the bags refilled without altering the content of any greatly. A bit of colored glass more or less would not matter. Perhaps that is how the Great Stuffer of Bags filled them in the first place—who knows? □

Focusing   After you have made your first reading of this text, you may or may not be in a position to say that you have a strong opinion about it. You may even be perplexed over Hurston's role as a black woman. This is not surprising because although you have been reacting and annotating, you'll probably find that your tendency to cluster ideas together is being countered by facts, ideas, and reactions that as yet do not make sense to you. Perhaps one of the following occurred to you:

- You developed a strong reaction to the text. Did you feel, for example, that Hurston is witty and open-minded about her blackness, that she is or is not complaining about being black? Or did you feel that she does not have a liberated black consciousness?

- You found a few statements at least which stand out, some incidents that are memorable and worth *paraphrasing*. It's a good idea after you've read an essay to make sure you have *annotated* what you remember most strongly. (Perhaps the scene in Zora's hometown as the whites drive or ride by; perhaps her delight in being on center stage; perhaps the scene in the jazz club?) *Concentrate on the most concrete and memorable incidents and ideas.*

- You found statements that bother you. These might be things, such as the tone of voice the writer is using or the significance of one or more incidents. What does Zora mean by "colored me"? Why does she say she is "the only Negro in the United States whose grandfather on the mother's side was not an Indian chief"? What does she really feel about whites and about blacks?

Listing   You have already begun to accumulate information through labeling and paraphrasing when you annotated things such as Zora sitting on the fence calling out to the white passers-by, or Zora getting inside the music at the jazz club and "going primitive," or Zora saying that she is not "tragically colored." Or you have made a paraphrase of an event such as "Zora only feels colored once she gets to a mixed-color town." By paraphrasing you reduce an event to one or more memorable qualities. You focus on the event.

A good interpretation depends on an adequate accumulation of information. You know the information you have is adequate when you have sufficient labels or paraphrases for each section of the text. Make a list of the important points. Here are a few.

- Hurston won't apologize for being colored.

- Hurston sees herself as a performer with an audience of whites.

- Hurston finds herself irrevocably colored in mixed society.

- There's no tragedy in being colored.

- The world is Hurston's oyster.

- Slavery is the price paid for civilization.

- Being black means getting twice as much praise or blame.

- Blackness is a white problem.

The points listed may strike you as containing the main theme or thesis in Hurston's essay. This central idea or feeling should be used to form the basis of a short summary statement in your own words, one that contains your interpretation of the essay's most important ideas. Check your marginal notes and use them to make your summary as well as the list of main points. Keep the summary short and, at this point in your interpretation, assume that it is tentative. You might say, for example, working from the paraphrases above, that the essay is about a black woman's discovery of her own color and how she develops a strong self-image. Or you might say that the essay reveals a lack of consciousness of what it really means to be black in America.

If you have trouble writing a summary from your annotations, a good idea is to *select one or two main ideas from your list of main points and cluster the other points around them.* This will let you make connections between the statements and give you a better chance of selecting important details.

Clustering   Clustering is the act of associating your reading responses around a nucleus idea or emotion. The writing process allows you to do this by free association. Your annotated text and your list of main points already offer a set of events and possible connections. Don't be disturbed by contradictions or paradoxes in your list. They are signs that you must reread the text to decide whether they can remain, whether they are important. You may have trouble deciding, for example, whether Hurston is sufficiently aware of her blackness in a politically informed, mid-twentieth-century way. And you may have trouble deciding where and to what extent she is being ironic.

Let's assume that you've decided that your main point concerns *color.* Simply list under the heading the most relevant of the main points.

Color

no apologies from Hurston
Hurston wants a white audience
no tragedy in being black
slavery has led to civilization
being black leads to extreme praise or blame
a white man's problem
color is skin deep, though a jumble within

Or perhaps you think Zora's self-image is the dominant idea:

Self-image

confident performer
world's her oyster
powerful emotional roots in being black
eternal feminine
a jumble within

As you can see, it's possible to accumulate the same information around more than one dominant idea. Whichever one you
choose, write a brief summary statement once your list is made. A
summary from the color issue could be that it is basically a white
problem, for example, and Hurston tries to handle color consciousness without guilt or defensiveness. On the other hand, Hurston's
self-image, her confident performance, lies in developing her role as
a black female artist. Your summary need not be made out of two
related statements like "color" and "self-image," for you may find
only one main point among your paraphrases, or you may find two
or three. The effort you make to link all the main points into one
summary statement is an important step toward understanding and
explaining the text.

From a simple summary of a sentence or two you can develop
a paragraph explaining your interpretation. Here's one possibility:

> In "How It Feels to Be Colored Me" Zora Neale Hurston
> reveals a black woman's confidence in her color, her talent, and her
> femininity. She sees the issue of color as intrinsically skin deep and
> primarily a white problem which need not result in tragic conse-
> quences for blacks. In the first part of the essay Hurston indicates the
> significant change that took place in her self-perception when she
> moved from Eatonville to Jacksonville. She learned there what it
> meant to be "a little colored girl." In the second part she makes clear
> that although she felt the sting of discrimination, she doesn't wallow
> in self-pity but instead looks hopefully to her opportunities as a
> human being and as an artist, seeing the world as her oyster. Part
> three reveals the differences she feels between herself and her white
> friend. It also includes the important revelation that she feels most
> black when she is with white people. In the fourth and final section
> Hurston describes her paradoxical sense of being a small part of a
> complex and multifaceted cosmic whole while retaining a distinctive
> and significant sense of selfhood.

In writing a still more elaborate interpretation of Hurston's essay, you would provide evidence in the form of textual detail to support your thinking. You would return, that is, to your detailed notes of specific observations and questions that led you to your conclusion about the piece. An alternative would be to consider still additional questions about the *values* that emerge in your reading and of *your evaluation* of the essay. You might ask yourself, for example, whether Hurston's description is accurate, whether it reflects the views of contemporary blacks generally. And you might consider whether she convinces you that her experience illustrates any truths about racial prejudice or about the resilience and resources of human character. You need to decide, in short, first whether you believe Hurston, and then whether you agree with her—and why.

Exercises

Read the following text, then follow the instructions for writing.

Beer Can
John Updike

This seems to be an era of gratuitous inventions and negative improvements. Consider the beer can. It was beautiful—as beautiful as the clothespin, as inevitable as the wine bottle, as dignified and reassuring as the fire hydrant. A tranquil cylinder of delightfully resonant metal, it could be opened in an instant, requiring only the application of a handy gadget freely dispensed by every grocer. Who can forget the small, symmetrical thrill of those two triangular punctures, the dainty *pfff*, the little crest of suds that formed eagerly in the exultation of release? Now we are given, instead, a top beetling with an ugly, shmoo-shaped "tab," which, after fiercely resisting the tugging, bleeding fingers of the thirsty man, threatens his lips with a dangerous and hideous hole. However, we have discovered a way to thwart Progress, usually so unthwartable. *Turn the beer can upside down and open the bottom.* The bottom is still the way the top used to be. True, this operation gives the beer an unsettling jolt, and the sight of a consistently inverted beer can might make people edgy, not to say queasy. But the latter difficulty could be eliminated if manufacturers would design cans that looked the same whichever end was up, like playing cards. What we need is Progress with an escape hatch. □

1. Select an everyday object like Updike's beer can and write a paragraph about it. Do more than simply describe the object. Instead, interpret its significance.

2. Take the object you wrote about in Exercise 1 or select another, and write an extended paragraph explaining its function and significance 100 years from now.

3. Study the paintings by Degas, Peale, Tooker, and Ghirlandaio (Color Plates 1–4, following p. 174) and write an interpretation of one of them.

4. Here are two selections with accompanying interpretations. Comment on the persuasiveness of each interpretation. Support or refute either in a brief interpretive paper of your own. Remember that in interpreting any text you are not looking for the single correct way to understand it. Instead you are offering your way of seeing the text and attempting to convince other readers to accept what you say.

Crumbling is not an instant's Act
Emily Dickinson

Crumbling is not an instant's Act,
A fundamental pause
Dilapidation's processes
Are organized Decays.

'Tis first a Cobweb on the Soul,
A Cuticle of Dust,
A Borer in the Axis,
An Elemental Rust—

Ruin is formal—Devil's work,
Consecutive and slow—
Fail in an instant, no man did.
Slipping—is Crash's Law.

The central idea of the poem is expressed in its opening line. We might paraphrase it this way: crumbling does not happen instantaneously; it is a gradual process, occurring slowly, cumulatively over time. The remainder of the first stanza further establishes this idea by accenting how "crumbling" is a consequence of dilapidation, which is a result of "decay." The deterioration that results is progressive; it is an organized, systematic process: one stage of decay leads to the next until destruction inevitably follows.

The gradual nature of decay is further emphasized with the statement that no one ever failed in an "instant," that the catastrophe occurs after, and as a consequence of, a series of failures. We can thus read the poem as a statement about the process of ruin (personal, emotional, financial) as well as a description of the process of decay. And we can summarize its theme thus: failure and destruction can be traced to small-scale elements that precede and cause them.

This theme is further extended in the second stanza, which contains four images of decay: cobweb, rust, dust, and the borer in the axis. These images are all accompanied by bits of specifying detail. The dust is a "cuticle," an image with suggestions of something at the "edges," of something on the outside and also of something human; the "cobweb on the soul" suggests spiritual deterioration ("cobwebs" suggest neglect); the "elemental" rust puts decay at the heart of things, at the center and vital core where the "borer" is operating. We can consider each of these images of decay as applying to a person, particularly to his or her soul: the dust encircling it, the cobweb netting it, the borer eating into it, and the rust corroding it. Such an emphasis on spiritual decay seems further warranted by the first line of the third stanza: "Ruin is formal—Devil's work." Ruin is perhaps the word most strongly suggestive of human and spiritual collapse; "Devil's work" speaks for itself. Thus, a statement of the poem's theme must accomodate the idea of spiritual decay.

Humpty Dumpty

Humpty Dumpty sat on a wall.
Humpty Dumpty had a great fall.
All the king's horses and all the king's men
Couldn't put Humpty Dumpty together again.

Although this poem is familiar as a nursery rhyme, we should not ignore its important theme. For "Humpty Dumpty" is, finally, not a children's verse at all. It is, rather, a warning about the danger of *hubris* or pride, the sin of the first man, Adam, which, to quote Milton's *Paradise Lost,* "brought death into the world and all our woe."

Why is Humpty Dumpty a symbol of pride? Primarily because as an egg sitting on a wall, he is in a very dangerous situation, a situation in which he should never have placed himself. By sitting on the wall, Humpty Dumpty tries to go beyond his limits as an egg, for an egg doesn't belong on a wall. In sitting there Humpty Dumpty tries to reach beyond himself, to be like a man, something he decidedly is not. This is very much like Adam, who as a man, wanted to be like God. And like Adam, too, Humpty Dumpty deserves his "fall," the loss of what he had. In fact "fall" is the most important word in the poem. Literally, it describes Humpty Dumpty's precipitous decline and his consequent destruction. Symbolically, it represents the *fall* of man from grace into sin. Like Adam, who was cast out of Paradise and who suffered physical hardship as a result of his excessive pride, so Humpty Dumpty, the nursery rhyme Adam, is broken by his fall, never to be made whole again.

WRITING TO EVALUATE A TEXT

Our emphasis in this section is on criticism, or the evaluation of texts. Critical evaluation involves making judgments about the value of texts. To evaluate a text, however, you first have to understand it. You need to have a clear sense of what it says and what it implies. Evaluation thus is grounded in interpretation; our conclusions about what texts mean affect how we value them.

Our first problem in evaluating a text is deciding on suitable and appropriate criteria for evaluation. Such criteria form the basis of our critical judgments of any text. Consequently, it is a good idea to make these criteria explicit rather then allowing them to remain implicit. We can consider what this means by examining a particular case.

Following are three brief texts, all headlines for the same news event, the murder of a woman:

1. Queens Woman Stabbed to Death in Front of Home

2. Help Cry Ignored, Girl Dies of Knifing

3. Queens Barmaid Stabbed, Dies

To evaluate these we need to establish our criteria of judgment. What are our standards of judgment for headlines? Factual accuracy? Reliability? Interest? Efficiency?

The criteria we establish will influence our judgment about the relative merit of these headlines. If, for example, factual accuracy and objectivity assume priority, the first headline is best. (Why? Aside from its objective tone, this headline gets the facts right: the victim, Kitty Genovese, was twenty-eight years old, and hence not a "girl"; nor was she a "barmaid," though she was employed at an establishment where she served alcoholic beverages.) If, however, human interest and reader involvement are more important than objectivity or accuracy, the second headline is better. Besides inviting our sympathy for the victim and igniting our anger at those who ignore her cry for help, this headline encapsulates in miniature the dramatic nature of the experience: a girl cries out—"Help! Help!"; people ignore her cries; a man knifes her to death.

Does the third headline have anything to commend it? Efficiency, perhaps. And a matter-of-fact tone that implies that this sort of thing happens frequently and shouldn't much concern us. Note in particular how the victim is *judged* by the word "barmaid." Note also how in the second headline, by identifying her as a "girl," the writer engages our sympathy for her. The method, ironically, is the same—using words heavy with connotation to evoke our emotional responses. The effect, however, is dramatically different, affecting our judgment of Kitty Genovese in opposite ways. By identifying the victim simply as a *woman*, the first headline deliberately avoids the kinds of responses invited by the other headlines.

We can continue this discussion a bit further by considering the opening sentences of the news accounts that followed these headlines.

1.   A 28-year-old Queens woman was stabbed to death early this morning outside her apartment house in Kew Gardens.

2.   The neighbors had grandstand seats for the slaying of Kitty Genovese. And yet, when the pretty, diminutive brunette cried for help, she cried in vain.

3.   An attractive 28-year-old brunette, who had given up a more prosaic life for a career as a barmaid and residence in a tiny Bohemian section of Queens, was stabbed to death early this morning.

In evaluating the three news stories we would again set up criteria of judgment against which to measure them. The opening of the second story does more than provide information in the manner of the first. Our sense of the legitimacy of introducing emotion and judgment into news accounts will determine how we value the second and third of these story leads. We may decide, of course, that the first headline and its accompanying story are exemplary in accomplishing what they set out to do: to present the facts as objectively as possible. At the same time, however, we may respond to the human drama and the plight of the victim as revealed in the headline and opening sentence of the second example. The important thing is that we know what our criteria are when we make such judgments, that we know why we value what we do.

Exercises

1. Compare two texts of a similar nature with the purpose of evaluating them. Be sure to make your criteria explicit. Suggestions: two newspaper editorials on the same subject; two political speeches on a similar subject, perhaps given before the same audience; two recipes for the same dish; two sets of directions; two birthday or get-well cards; two sonnets, two short stories, two essays, perhaps by the same writer, perhaps on a the same subject; two newspaper or magazine accounts of the same subject or event.

2. Examine the advertisements on pages 93 and 94. Develop a set of criteria for evaluating them. Consider their implied audience and purpose; their language and pictures; their style.

Thus far we have been encouraging you to consider evaluation as a way of measuring a text's success at being what it is, at fulfilling its textual role. In doing so you have been measuring one text against standards of excellence achieved by other texts of that kind. Very likely, however, other criteria emerged in your evaluation as well, criteria that derive less from generic considerations than from moral, ethical, and cultural values. It is important to recognize how strongly our moral values and cultural attitudes shape our responses to and judgment of texts. Since such value-based judgments are largely inescapable, we should not avoid them. Rather we should be aware of why and how we make the judgments we do.

The revolution is over.

While Nike is singing the praises of their revolution, let us introduce you to something that really deserves the term.

Introducing the Reebok Energy Return System.™

The Energy Return System™ from Reebok. E.R.S.™

This system actually saves a significant amount of the energy you put into running... and then returns it to you just when you need it most.

No other shoe has ever been designed to do this. That's why the Reebok World Trainer™ with E.R.S. actually returns up to 30% more energy per mil-

limeter of compression than either the Nike Air Max or the Tiger Gel 100.

What's more, this energy return is accomplished with no loss in either cushioning or stability. In fact, the World Trainer surpasses most shoes on *both* counts.

Oddly enough, energy return is nothing new. Lots of everyday objects have natural energy return systems. Springs. Pogo sticks. Diving boards. But no running shoes did. Until now.

Our Energy Return System is surprisingly simple. Basically, it's a series of four tubes carefully positioned in the midsole under your heel.

These tubes are made of one of the most resilient materials on earth. DuPont Hytrel.™ It's the same stuff they make car bumpers out of.

When your foot strikes the ground, the Hytrel tubes store up the energy. As your foot rolls forward, the tubes return to their original shape and release the energy.

Kind of like a spring being sprung.

It makes the Reebok World Trainer the first running shoe that actually propels the

runner on his way.

You see, we're not so foolish as to think we could create a revolution out of thin Air. Revolutions require bigger ideas. Like giving power back to the people. Or in this case, energy back to the runner.

Reebok ⊞
Running Shoes.

1988 Reebok International Ltd.

Cosmair, Inc.

We can clarify this point with reference to the following texts, each of which displays strongly felt cultural dispositions and moral values. The first is a brief interchapter from Ernest Hemingway's fictional work *In Our Time.**

> While the bombardment was knocking the trench to pieces at Fossalta, he lay very flat and sweated and prayed oh jesus christ get me out of here. Dear jesus please get me out. Christ please please please christ. If you'll only keep me from getting killed I'll do anything you say. I believe in you and I'll tell every one in the world that you are the only one that matters. Please please dear jesus. The shelling moved further up the line. We went to work on the trench and in the morning the sun came up and the day was hot and muggy, and cheerful and quiet. The next night back at Mestre he did not tell the girl he went upstairs with at the Villa Rossa about Jesus. And he never told anybody.

This text, though brief, is rich in cultural and moral implications. It assumes a modest knowledge of war as it was fought in the early twentieth century. It assumes, for example, that we know what trenches are, what shelling is, and also that we can make sense of the soldier's behavior. It also assumes some familiarity with a soldier going "upstairs" with a "girl" at a place like the "Villa Rossa."

The text, however, is reticent about these and other matters. It says little directly. It's close-mouthed and tight-lipped, in addition, about what it expects from us as readers—somewhat like the soldier who "never told anybody" about his experience. But it makes a strong statement by implication, nonetheless, about its three central subjects: love, war, and religion. And it does this largely by playing off conventional expectations about these subjects. The soldier, for example, does not acquit himself heroically. Instead he cringes in the trenches to avoid being hit by enemy shells (though we may wonder what else he could do). And he prays to a God he probably ignores under normal circumstances. Moreover, his approach to prayer is to bargain with God: If you'll do this for me, I'll do something else for you. But it's a bargain he doesn't keep. Our response to this soldier's language and behavior is influenced by the cultural values we share and the moral dispositions we bring to both our reading and our living.

---

*For the Hemingway and Le Guin examples we are indebted to Robert Scholes's discussion in *Textual Power* (New Haven: Yale University Press, 1985).

Our evaluation of him turns on considerations such as whether he really believes in Jesus, and what such a belief may mean. It turns on whether you think the soldier's prayer is "answered" by God in a providential intervention to move the shelling "farther up the line," or whether you see that as a coincidence, attributable purely to luck. It turns also on whether his going to a house of prostitution is something you can understand, sympathize with, and approve of—or not; and whether his not telling the girl or anybody else about Jesus is a serious violation of a solemn vow, or an excusable, perfectly understandable response.

Besides evaluating the behavior of the soldier, we also make a judgment about the values we think the text espouses. Does the author seem to display sympathy for the soldier? Does he judge him harshly? The narrative voice is noncommittal, concerned more with portraying a situation than with commenting on it. This stance of objectivity is itself a "value," an attitude or disposition we must eventually assess, as we must also respond to the fact that the world depicted is a man's world, a world of war and violence, in which women (or *girls* as the text stipulates them) figure only marginally, and then only as they can be used by men. (We know, for example, what the man feels and fears, but we are told nothing about the girl's thoughts and emotions.) Our sexual identity along with our religious disposition and our general cultural awareness and values will strongly influence what we make of and take from this text.

So too will these factors affect our response on the very different text that follows. If Hemingway's text can be described generally as "realistic," then the next one must be characterized as "fantastic," or nonrealistic. It is excerpted from a science fiction novel about an alien society whose most striking feature concerns the sexual identity of its inhabitants: They possess the possibility of becoming men or women interchangeably many times. As the text has it: "The mother of several children may be the father of several more."

We are made aware of their condition in a report on these "Gethenians" (inhabitants of Gethen) by a man from Earth who has traveled to their wintry world. His report reveals that, strange as their sexuality is, it shares features with our human sexuality and provokes us to realize how influential and affecting it is. Here is an excerpt from this report:

The sexual cycle averages 26 to 28 days (they tend to speak of it as 26 days, approximating it to the lunar cycle). For 21 or 22 days the individual is *somer*, sexually inactive, latent. On about the 18th day hormonal changes are initiated by the pituitary control and on the 22nd or 23rd day the individual enters *kemmer*, estrus. In this first phase of kemmer (Karh. *secher*) he remains completely androgynous. Gender, and potency, are not attained in isolation. A Gethenian in first-phase kemmer, if kept alone or with others not in kemmer, remains incapable of coitus. Yet the sexual impulse is tremendously strong in this phase, controlling the entire personality, subjecting all other drives to its imperative. When the individual first finds a partner in kemmer, hormonal secretion is further stimulated (most importantly by touch—secretion? scent?) until in one partner either a male or female hormonal dominance is established. The genitals engorge or shrink accordingly, foreplay intensifies, and the partner, triggered by the change, takes on the other sexual role (?without exception? If there are exceptions, resulting in kemmer-partners of the same sex, they are so rare as to be ignored). This second phase of kemmer (Karh. *thorharmen*), the mutual process of establishing sexuality and potency, apparently occurs within a time-span of two to twenty hours. If one of the partners is already in full kemmer, the phase for the new partner is liable to be quite short; if the two are entering kemmer together, it is likely to take longer. Normal individuals have no predisposition to either sexual role in kemmer; they do not know whether they will be the male or the female, and have no choice in the matter.

The man who makes this report also presents these additional reflections on sexual difference both as we know it in our lives as men and women, and as he sees it in the lives of the androgynous Gethenians:

> When you meet a Gethenian you cannot and must not do what a bisexual naturally does, which is to cast him in the role of Man or Woman, while adopting towards him a corresponding role dependent on your expectations of the patterned or possible interactions between persons of the same or the opposite sex. Our entire pattern of socio-sexual interaction is nonexistent here. They cannot play the game. They do not see one another as men or women. This is almost impossible for our imagination to accept. What is the first question we ask about a newborn baby? . . . A man wants his virility regarded, a woman wants her femininity appreciated, however indirect and subtle the indications of regard and appreciation. On Winter (Gethen) they will not exist. One is respected and judged only as a human being. It is an appalling experience.

Such a conception is staggering, for it lies outside the realm of possibility for us, while striking at the heart of our tendency to establish polarized categories that include but also extend beyond man–woman and male–female. These categories also include (and we probably and inevitably judge the Gethenians according to them): normal–abnormal, right–wrong, familiar–strange, us–them. Throughout her novel, Ursula Le Guin repeatedly invites us to consider the pernicious consequences of making judgments according to values grounded in such polar oppositions. Her book, *The Left Hand of Darkness*, while requiring us to respond according to the cultural dispositions and values we have inherited, simultaneously directs us to transcend them.

Exercises

1. In his book *The ABC of Reading* Ezra Pound suggests that the best way to develop aesthetic discrimination is to compare texts rather than evaluate them in isolation. Pound puts it this way:

    The proper METHOD for studying poetry and good letters is the method of contemporary biologists, that is, careful firsthand examination of the matter, and continued COMPARISON of one "slide" or specimen with another.

    Select two texts, one whose moral or cultural values you share and another that represents values you find disagreeable. Identify the values each text reflects. Explain your evaluation, and argue for the value of one text over the other. (You may use, if you like, the Hemingway and Le Guin texts.)

2. Evaluate the following paired texts. Also evaluate the paired paintings by Eakins and Rubens (Color Plates 5 and 6).

(1) *Aunt Jennifer's Tigers*
Adrienne Rich

Aunt Jennifer's tigers prance across a screen,
Bright topaz denizens of a world of green.
They do not fear the men beneath the tree;
They pace in sleek chivalric certainty.

Aunt Jennifer's fingers fluttering through her wool
Find even the ivory needle hard to pull.
The massive weight of Uncle's wedding band
Sits heavily upon Aunt Jennifer's hand.

When Aunt is dead, her terrified hands will lie
Still ringed with ordeals she was mastered by.
The tigers in the panel that she made
Will go on prancing, proud and unafraid.

(2) *Women*
May Swenson

```
Woman             Or they
  should be         should be
  pedestals         little horses
  moving            those wooden
  pedestals         sweet
  moving            oldfashioned
  to the            painted
  motions           rocking
  of men            horses

      the gladdest things in the toyroom.

    the               feelingly
    pegs              and then
    of their          unfeelingly
    ears              To be
    so familiar       joyfully
    and dear          ridden
    to the trusting   rockingly
    fists             ridden until
  To be chafed        the restored

egos dismount and the legs stride away

Immobile      willing
  sweetlipped     to be set
  sturdy          into motion
  and smiling     Women
  women           should be
  should always   pedestals
  be waiting        to men
```

(1) This Is Just to Say
William Carlos Williams

I have eaten
the plums
that were in
the icebox

and which
you were probably
saving
for breakfast

Forgive me
they were delicious
so sweet
and so cold.

(2) *Variations on a Theme by William Carlos Williams*
Kenneth Koch

1
I chopped down the house that you had been saving to live in next
     summer.
I am sorry, but it was morning, and I had nothing to do
     and its wooden beams were so inviting.

2
We laughed at the hollyhocks together
and then I sprayed them with lye.
Forgive me. I simply do not know what I am doing.

3
I gave away the money that you had been saving to live on for the
     next ten years.
The man who asked for it was shabby
and the firm March wind on the porch was so juicy and cold.

4

Last evening we went dancing and I broke your leg.
Forgive me. I was clumsy, and
I wanted you here in the wards, where I am the doctor!

CHAPTER 3

Writing and Thinking

Each of us discovers ideas in individual ways, sometimes in rather personal ways that reflect our views of life, our backgrounds, and our role models. In this chapter we explore some strategies writers use to get themselves started, to discover how they feel about a topic, what they think about it, and why. As you read through this chapter, do not forget that each occasion for writing requires particular purposes, characteristics, and demands. Whatever helps you get started writing one day might not help you another day. And whatever your friends or colleagues use to get themselves started might not always help you. However, you can experiment and practice with warm-up techniques many writers use, providing you use each of these strategies for what it is—a creative tool designed to stimulate your thinking. Of course, we do not expect you to use all of these strategies each time you write. In fact, we suggest that you not use any technique that becomes an obstacle or impediment to writing. We do hope, however, that whenever you have difficulty writing, you will use the discovery technique that feels right for you.

Exercises

1. Think about your own writing strategies. Recollect on a sheet of paper the steps you went through in your last writing assignment. Record

every step you took, including avoidance techniques such as procrastination. What do you think your writing process reveals about you?

2. Compare your approach to writing with two fellow writers. How and why are your approaches similar to theirs? Different from theirs?

PREPARING TO WRITE

Our writing habits—how often we write, where, when, and why—contribute greatly to our attitude toward writing. How we feel about writing partly determines how effective our writing will be.

Pause for a moment and consider your feelings, habits, and predispositions about writing.

- How often and how much do you write? Daily? Weekly? As little or as much as possible?

- What kinds of writing do you do? Personal experiences? Private thoughts? Letters? Class notes? Business notes? Memos? Lists? Reports? Fiction? Poetry? Annotations on readings?

- What is your favorite kind of writing?

- What do you usually write with? Pen? Pencil? Typewriter? Word processor?

- What is your favorite writing instrument? Why?

- Do you have a special place for writing?

- Where do you feel most comfortable writing? Why?

- What kind of writing do you enjoy reading? Who is your favorite writer?

- What do you like best about your writing?

- What do you think "effective" writing is?

By analyzing our writing habits, we can discover the elements that create a good writing environment for us, and we can reduce some of the distractions that prevent us from thinking and writing. A pleasant—or at least a predictable—writing environment often puts us in a receptive frame of mind and encourages us to focus our attention on the task before us.

Exercises

1. Describe your *actual* writing environment and your *ideal* one. How much does your writing "space" contribute to your attitude toward writing and detract from your ability to meet deadlines?

2. Describe your best piece of writing. Discuss the circumstances— assignment, deadline, personal strategies, and processes—that evoked your work.

PERCEPTUAL BLOCKS TO WRITING

As writers, we must establish an attitude conducive to writing, a state where our minds can freely receive new stimuli, a context that encourages us to experiment and do our best. And we must teach ourselves to accept without judgment some of the thoughts that pour from our minds during a creative, thoughtful period.

Georgi Lozanov, a Bulgarian psychiatrist and educational researcher, thinks we create self-protective barriers that prevent us from being bombarded by too many stimuli. We restrict our beliefs and admit only stimuli and ideas that seem logical and compatible with our values, perceptions, and self-confidence. In effect, our self-imposed barriers often prevent us from seeing the world differently, from learning, from accommodating new ideas into our existing beliefs.

In the following excerpt from *Time, Space, and Medicine,* Larry Dossey explains how another barrier, the cultural "mind set," prevented the Patagonian Indians from perceiving Darwin's ship, the *Beagle.* Notice the interplay among mind set, observations, and interpretations.

Scientists and Patagonians
Larry Dossey

> . . . *since we have come to the understanding that science is*
> *not a description of "reality" but a metaphorical ordering of*
> *experience, the new science does not impugn the old. It is not*

a question of which view is "true" in some ultimate sense.
Rather, it is a matter of which picture is more useful in
guiding human affairs.

WILLIS HARMAN

SCIENCE: WHAT DO WE MEAN?

How exactly, does science work? How do scientists go about "doing" science?

Ordinarily, we think science proceeds in a straight forward way. Ideally scientists make observations, formulate hypotheses, and test those hypotheses by making further observations. When there is discrepancy between what is observed and what is predicted by the hypothesis, the hypothesis is revised. Science proceeds in this way, which is a gradual method of finding the best fit between observation and prediction.

But this idealized version of how one "does" science is naive. Although science demands proof that observations made by one observer be observable by other observers using the same methods, it is by no means clear that, even when confronted with identical phenomena, different observers will report identical observations. And it is most certain that, even if the same observations are made, the conclusions as to the meaning of the observations frequently differ. These variations in observation and in formulating ideas about what is observed are crucial to the studies dealing with human consciousness that follow.

The fact is that all of us, scientists included, see differently. Variations in human perception are well known and have been studied extensively. Distortions in perception are frequently seen among observers, even though they may be in identical settings viewing identical phenomena.

A documented misperception from history can be found in the experience of Darwin. His ship, *Beagle*, after anchoring off the Patagonian coast, dispatched a landing party in small rowboats. Amazingly, the Patagonian natives watching from shore were blind to the *Beagle*, but could easily see the tiny rowboats! They had no prior experience of monstrous sailing ships, but canoes—small rowing vessels—were an everyday part of their life. Rowboats fit their model of the world and brigantines did not. Their model determined their perceptions.

The Patagonians' previous perceptions formed a conceptual framework that shaped their interpretations of reality, even of events they had never before experienced. Like them, we fit experiences, observations, and ideas into conceptual molds and view reality from a preconceived perspective. When we become familiar with something we often take it for granted and accept it unquestioningly, allowing our familiarity with it to control the number and kinds of responses we have about it. By shifting perspectives or frames of references, we remove some of our mental barriers, alter our views of reality, and give ourselves new topics to write about. □

Exercises

1. Recall a "Patagonian" experience in which your knowledge or expectation of an event prevented you from "seeing the obvious" surrounding that event. Describe the steps you underwent to reach a fuller understanding of the event.

2. Discuss the underlying wisdom in each of the following statements:

    (a) "You can't see the forest for the trees."
    (b) "You don't need a weatherman to know which way the wind blows." (Bob Dylan)

3. List as many perceptual barriers that blur thinking processes as you can think of.

PREWRITING STRATEGIES

For most of us, getting started is often the hardest part of writing. A blank page, begging to be filled with ink, can be intimidating, especially when our words come slowly or when our minds go blank. Usually we do not know what we want to say until we see our words lying before us on the page. As we mentioned in Chapter 1, writing is a recursive act, a process of reading, rereading, and revising our words and ideas. Consequently, our words generate other words and ideas, much like the give-and-take exchanges that occur in a dialogue.

Prewriting is the complex network of initial mental sequences we undergo when we write a paper. Sometimes we generate words from scratch; other times we reread words we have written to see if they jog our memories of past, often forgotten knowledge or create new ideas we have not yet formulated in our own minds. Regardless of where we are in our writing, we must allow our thoughts free rein until we have a "working" draft we can revise and respond to.

Although many prewriting strategies exist, the following techniques can remove some of the perceptual barriers that prevent us from thinking. They encourage us to accept all of our ideas as potentially good ones. Some of these techniques help us generate random ideas that will later become a "working" text, whereas others require us to revise previously accumulated ideas, shaping them into the actual "working" text.

GENERATING STRATEGIES

Listing   Although listing appears to be a prewriting strategy, it is really a method of transcribing information generated by numerous prewriting strategies. Listing frees writers from the structures of sentences, paragraphs, and even the spelling of words, enabling them to keep pace with their thoughts. By recording thoughts in lists, often through the use of abbreviations, scribbling, and drawings, you create a skeletal framework of your thinking—a kind of impressionistic outline—you can flesh out later.

Since listing is such a familiar activity, it is easy to overlook its effectiveness and rely on traditional vertical and horizontal columns of information. As you work on the prewriting strategies in this chapter, experiment with listing, particularly in innovative patterns such as circles, diagonals, clusters, or tree diagrams, which encourage fresh perspectives on your topics.

Exercises

1.   The famous coat of arms on the next page is a symbolic representation of one family's character and history. Each symbol has significance for the family and its role in society. Make a list of the symbols you see and jot down under each symbol a list of its possible meanings.

2. Review your lists of symbols and meanings. Compare your lists with those of a peer. Did you both use similar formats—vertical, horizontal, diagonal, circular—to record your information? What effect, if any, does the format of ideas have on interpretation of those ideas?

3. Write a one-page descriptive interpretation of the family's coat of arms.

Brainstorming   A form of free association similar to freewriting, brainstorming is a problem-solving strategy commonly used by groups of people. In many instances, a group of people forms a think-tank and explores ideas together in pursuit of a common goal. Brainstorming works particularly well when you really do not know what to do or think, or when you cannot make a decision.

For example, you might have sat with a group of friends in a steamy café early one winter's evening trying to decide what to do for the weekend. As you talked, you explored some available options—a basketball game, a movie, a concert, a study session. If you kept your mind open, you listened to each person who offered a suggestion before settling on a diversion. And if you were lucky, you learned there were more things available than you first imagined.

Brainstorming is a powerful public strategy for generating information and ideas because it taps a group's potential and brings numerous viewpoints and backgrounds to a problem. For it to work effectively, however, you must create a receptive atmosphere, an environment that accepts all ideas as possible solutions for the problems or steps toward the goal.

In brainstorming we become nonjudgmental recorders of thoughts, regardless of how humorous or how crazy they seem at first. We ignore spelling, punctuation, grammar, even logic, because we just want to record the flood of information, attitudes, ideas, or feelings we hear voiced around us. At a later time, when we have a collection of data and when we have discovered what is really on our minds, we will arrange this information to suit our purposes, shaping and editing it for our readers.

Exercises

1. Form a group of four people and use the brainstorming strategy to generate a series of captions for the following pictures. Write for four minutes on each topic, jotting down all ideas mentioned by your group. Do not take time to write in sentences or edit your notes; simply record the information as it occurs.

Charles Bell. *Gumball #15.* (1983). 89 × 61 inches. Oil on canvas. Private collection, courtesy Louis K. Meisel Gallery.

2.   With the same group members, review the information generated in Exercise 1 and select from your notes the most appropriate caption for each work. Write a paragraph explaining why your group's choice for each work is an effective one.

Freewriting   Although freewriting is a form of free association similar to brainstorming, it is a private, personal information-gathering strategy. As we discovered in earlier chapters, freewriting "turns off our mental censors" and lets us gather information, unencumbered by the barrier of correctness.

Freewriting is an effective method of generating ideas that form an initial, working text. As in all free association techniques, freewriting asks us to suspend our judgments and preferences and record all ideas as potentially significant, a determination made later during revision. By giving our minds free rein, we often record words and ideas that lie buried beneath our current concerns. Or perhaps we set off a series of personal associations that form a complex network of interrelated ideas. A familiar parallel to freewriting occurs often in spirited conversation when we retrace the topics of our discussion to see how we arrived where we are.

Exercise

Freewrite for four minutes on each of the following topics. Jot down as many thoughts as you can; use whichever technique you feel comfortable with—listing, abbreviating, scribbling—to record your ideas. Be sure to record information as quickly as you can without stopping or correcting your work.

1. "Television—the plug-in drug."

2. The popularity of violence in movies.

3. The impact of computers on daily life.

4. The business of sports.

5. The public's fascination with Elizabeth Taylor.

As you glance over the notes you took, are you surprised by anything you jotted down? Which topic triggered the most information? Did any specific word snowball into an avalanche of associations? If so, why?

Journal Keeping   We study the past to measure change and growth and to gain insights about the present. As time passes, however, our recollections often are dulled, leaving us fuzzy images, shapeless forms, and vague remembrances. Many writers keep a notebook—really a verbal scrapbook—of their thoughts, experiences, and ideas to help them later when they need a reference or an impression of some past event.

Unlike diaries, which record details of daily life, journals record significant personal impressions and reactions to events. The diarist preserves the factual details of an event in the form of a finished text; the journal writer preserves collected materials—experiences, overheard conversations, anecdotes, and impressions—as a source for future texts.

In the following excerpt Joan Didion, a contemporary American writer, discusses her journal and its relationship to her life as a writer. As you read her discussion, try to see how a journal can become important for your writing.

On Keeping a Notebook
Joan Didion

"'That woman Estelle,'" the note reads, "'is partly the reason why George Sharp and I are separated today.' *Dirty crepe-de-Chine wrapper, hotel bar, Wilmington RR, 9:45 a.m. August Monday morning.*"

Since the note is in my notebook, it presumably has some meaning to me. I study it for a long while. At first I have only the most general notion of what I was doing on an August Monday morning in the bar of the hotel across from the Pennsylvania Railroad station in Wilmington, Delaware (waiting for a train? missing one? 1960? 1961? why Wilmington?), but I do remember being there. The woman in the dirty crepe-de-Chine wrapper had come down from her room for a beer, and the bartender had heard before the reason why George Sharp and she were separated today. "Sure," he said, and went on mopping the floor. "You told me." At the other end of the bar is a girl. She is talking, pointedly, not to the man beside her but to a cat lying in the triangle of sunlight cast through the open door. She is wearing a plaid silk dress from Peck & Peck, and the hem is coming down.

Here is what it is: the girl has been on the Eastern Shore, and now she is going back to the city, leaving the man beside her, and all she can see ahead are the viscous summer sidewalks and the 3 a.m. long-distance calls that will make her lie awake and then sleep drugged through all the steaming mornings left in August (1960? 1961?). Because she must go directly from the train to lunch in New York, she wishes that she had a safety pin for the hem of the plaid silk dress, and she also wishes that she could forget about the hem and the lunch and stay in the cool bar that smells of disinfectant and malt and make friends with the woman in the crepe-de-Chine wrapper. She is afflicted by a little self-pity, and she wants to compare Estelles. That is what that was all about.

Why did I write it down? In order to remember, of course, but exactly what was it I wanted to remember? How much of it actually happened? Did any of it? Why do I keep a notebook at all? It is easy to deceive oneself on all those scores. The impulse to write things down is a peculiarly compulsive one, inexplicable to those who do not share it, useful only accidentally, only secondarily, in the way that any compulsion tries to justify itself. I suppose that it begins or does not begin in the cradle. Although I have felt compelled to write things down since I was five years old, I doubt that my daughter ever will, for she is a singularly blessed and accepting child, delighted with life exactly as life presents itself to her, unafraid to go to sleep and unafraid to wake up. Keepers of private notebooks are a different breed altogether, lonely and resistant rearrangers of things, anxious malcontents, children afflicted apparently at birth with some presentiment of loss.

My first notebook was a Big Five tablet, given to me by my mother with the sensible suggestion that I stop whining and learn to amuse myself by writing down my thoughts. She returned the tablet to me a few years ago; the first entry is an account of a woman who believed herself to be freezing to death in the Arctic night, only to find, when day broke, that she had stumbled onto the Sahara Desert, where she would die of the heat before lunch. I have no idea what turn of a five-year-old's mind could have prompted so insistently "ironic" and exotic a story, but it does reveal a certain predilection for the extreme which has dogged me into adult life; perhaps if I were analytically inclined I would find it a truer story than any I might have told about Donald Johnson's birthday party or the day my cousin Brenda put Kitty Litter in the aquarium.

So the point of my keeping a notebook has never been, nor is it now, to have an accurate factual record of what I have been doing or thinking. That would be a different impulse entirely, an instinct for reality which I sometimes envy but do not possess. At no point have I ever been able successfully to keep a diary; my approach to daily life ranges from the grossly negligent to the merely absent, and on those few occasions when I have tried dutifully to record a day's events, boredom has so overcome me that the results are mysterious at best. What is this business about "shopping, typing piece, dinner with E, depressed"? Shopping for what? Typing what piece? Who is E? Was this "E" depressed, or was I depressed? Who cares?

In fact I have abandoned altogether that kind of pointless entry; instead I tell what some would call lies. "That's simply not true," the members of my family frequently tell me when they come up against my memory of a shared event. "The party was *not* for you, the spider was *not* a black widow, *it wasn't that way at all.*" Very likely, they are right, for not only have I always had trouble distinguishing between what happened and what merely might have happened, but I remain unconvinced that the distinction, for my purposes, matters. The cracked crab that I recall having for lunch the day my father came home from Detroit in 1945 must certainly be embroidery, worked into the day's pattern to lend verisimilitude; I was ten years old and would not now remember the cracked crab. The day's events did not turn on cracked crab. And yet it is precisely that fictitious crab that makes me see the afternoon all over again, a home movie run all too often, the father bearing gifts, the child weeping, an exercise in family love and guilt. Or that is what it was to me. Similarly, perhaps it never did snow that August in Vermont; perhaps there never were flurries in the night wind, and maybe no one else felt the ground hardening and summer already dead even as we pretended to bask in it, but that was how it felt to me, and it might as well have snowed, could have snowed, did snow.

How it felt to me: that is getting closer to the truth about a notebook. I sometimes delude myself about why I keep a notebook, imagine that some thrifty virtue derives from preserving everything observed. See enough and write it down, I tell myself, and then some morning when the world seems drained of wonder, some day when I am only going through the motions of doing what I am supposed to do, which is write—on that bankrupt morning I will simply open my notebook and there it will all be, a forgotten account with accumulated interest, paid passage back to the world out there: dialogue overheard in hotels and elevators and at the hat-check counter in Pavillon (one middle-aged man shows his hat check to another and says, "That's my old football number"); impressions of Bettina Aptheker and Benjamin Sonnenberg and Teddy ("Mr. Acapulco") Stauffer; careful *aperçus* about tennis bums and failed fashion models and Greek shipping heiresses, one of whom taught me a significant lesson (a lesson I could have learned from F. Scott Fitzgerald, but perhaps we all must meet the very rich for ourselves) by asking, when I arrived to interview her in her orchid-filled sitting room on the second day of a paralyzing New York blizzard, whether it was snowing outside.

I imagine, in other words, that the notebook is about other people. But of course it is not. I have no real business with what one stranger said to another at the hat-check counter in Pavillon; in fact I suspect that the line "That's my old football number" touched not my own imagination at all, but merely some memory of something once read, probably "The Eighty-Yard Run." Nor is my concern with a woman in a dirty crepe-de-Chine wrapper in a Wilmington bar. My stake is always, of course, in the unmentioned girl in the plaid silk dress. Remember what it was to be me: that is always the point.

It is a difficult point to admit. We are brought up in the ethic that others, any others, all others, are by definition more interesting than ourselves; taught to be diffident, just this side of self-effacing. ("You're the least important person in the room and don't forget it," Jessica Mitford's governess would hiss in her ear on the advent of any social occasion; I copied that into my notebook because it is only recently that I have been able to enter a room without hearing some such phrase in my inner ear.) Only the very young and the very old may recount their dreams at breakfast, dwell upon self, interrupt with memories of beach picnics and favorite Liberty lawn dresses and the rainbow trout in a creek near Colorado Springs. The rest of us are expected, rightly, to affect absorption in other people's favorite dresses, other people's trout.

And so we do. But our notebooks give us away, for however dutifully we record what we see around us, the common denominator of all we see is always, transparently, shamelessly, the implacable "I." We are not talking here about the kind of notebook that is patently for public consumption, a structural conceit for binding together a series of graceful *pensées*; we are talking about something private, about bits of the mind's string too short to use, an indiscriminate and erratic assemblage with meaning only for its maker.

And sometimes even the maker has difficulty with the meaning. There does not seem to be, for example, any point in my knowing for the rest of my life that, during 1964, 720 tons of soot fell on every square mile of New York City, yet there it is in my notebook, labeled "FACT." Nor do I really need to remember that Ambrose Bierce like to spell Leland Stanford's name "£eland $tanford" or that "smart women almost always wear black in Cuba," a fashion hint without much potential for practical application. And does not the relevance of these notes seem marginal at best?:

> In the basement museum of the Inyo County Courthouse in Independence, California, sign pinned to a mandarin coat: "This MANDARIN COAT was often worn by Mrs. Minnie S. Brooks when giving lectures on her TEAPOT COLLECTION."
> Redhead getting out of car in front of Beverly Wilshire Hotel, chinchilla stole, Vuitton bags with tags reading:
>
> MRS LOU FOX
>
> HOTEL SAHARA
>
> VEGAS

Well, perhaps not entirely marginal. As a matter of fact, Mrs. Minnie S. Brooks and her MANDARIN COAT pull me back into my own childhood, for although I never knew Mrs. Brooks and did not visit Inyo County until I was thirty, I grew up in just such a world, in houses cluttered with Indian relics and bits of gold ore and ambergris and the souvenirs my Aunt Mercy Farnsworth brought back from the Orient. It is a long way from that world to Mrs. Lou Fox's world, where we all live now, and is it not just as well to remember what I am? Might not Mrs. Lou Fox help me to remember what I am not?

But sometimes the point is harder to discern. What exactly did I have in mind when I noted down that it cost the father of someone I know $650 a month to light the place on the Hudson in which he lived before the Crash? What use was I planning to make of this line by Jimmy Hoffa: "I may have my faults, but being wrong ain't one of them"? And although I think it interesting to know where the girls who travel with the Syndicate have their hair done when they find themselves on the West Coast, will I ever make suitable use of it? Might I not be better off just passing it on to John O'Hara? What is a recipe for sauerkraut doing in my notebook? What kind of magpie keeps this notebook? *"He was born the night the Titanic went down."* That seems a nice enough line, and I even recall who said it, but is it not really a better line in life than it could ever be in fiction?

But of course that is exactly it: not that I should ever use the line, but that I should remember the woman who said it and the afternoon I heard it. We were on her terrace by the sea, and we were finishing the wine left from lunch, trying to get what sun there was, a California sun. The woman whose husband was born the night the *Titanic* went down wanted to rent her house, wanted to go back to her children in Paris. I remember wishing that I could afford the house, which cost $1,000 a month. "Someday you will," she said lazily. "Someday it all comes." There in the sun on her terrace it seemed easy to believe in someday, but later I had a low-grade afternoon hangover and ran over a black snake on the way to the supermarket and was flooded with inexplicable fear when I heard the checkout clerk explaining to the man ahead of me why she was finally divorcing her husband. "He left me no choice," she said over and over as she punched the register. "He has a little seven-month-old baby by her, he left me no choice." I would like to believe that my dread then was for the human condition, but of course it was for me, because I wanted a baby and did not then have one and because I wanted to own the house that cost $1,000 a month to rent and because I had a hangover.

It all comes back. Perhaps it is difficult to see the value in having one's self back in that kind of mood, but I do see it; I think we are well advised to keep on nodding terms with the people we used to be, whether we find them attractive company or not. Otherwise they turn up unannounced and surprise us, come hammering on the mind's door at 4 a.m. of a bad night and demand to know who deserted them, who betrayed them, who is going to make amends. We forget all too soon the things we thought we could never forget. We forget the loves and the betrayals alike, forget what we whispered and what we screamed, forget who we were. I have already lost touch with a couple of people I used to be; one of them, a seventeen-year-old, presents little threat, although it would be of some interest to me to know again what it feels like to sit on a river levee drinking vodka-and-orange-juice and listening to Les Paul and Mary Ford and their echoes sing "How High the Moon" on the car radio. (You see I still have the scenes, but I no longer perceive myself among those present, no longer could even improvise the dialogue.) The other one, a twenty-three-year-old, bothers me more. She was always a good deal of trouble, and I suspect she will reappear when I least want to see her, skirts too long, shy to the point of aggravation, always the injured party, full of recriminations and little hurts and stories I do not want to hear again, at once saddening me and angering me with her vulnerability and ignorance, an apparition all the more insistent for being so long banished.

It is a good idea, then, to keep in touch, and I suppose that keeping in touch is what notebooks are all about. And we are all on our own when it comes to keeping those lines open to ourselves: your notebook will never help me, nor mine you. *"So what's new in the whiskey business?"* What could that possibly mean to you? To me it means a blonde in a Pucci bathing suit sitting with a couple of fat men by the pool at the Beverly Hills Hotel. Another man approaches, and they all regard one another in silence for a while. "So what's new in the whiskey business?" one of the fat men finally says by way of welcome, and the blonde stands up, arches one foot and dips it in the pool, looking all the while at the cabaña where Baby Pignatari is talking on the telephone. This is all there is to that, except that several years later I saw the blonde coming out of Saks Fifth Avenue in New York with her California complexion and a voluminous mink coat. In the harsh wind that day she looked old and irrevocably tired to me, and even the skins in the mink coat were not worked the way they were doing them that year, not the way she would have wanted them done, and there is the point of the story. For a while after that I did not like to look in the mirror, and my eyes would skim the newspapers and pick out only the deaths, the cancer victims, the premature coronaries, the suicides, and I stopped riding the Lexington Avenue IRT because I noticed for the first time that all the strangers I had seen for years—the man with the seeing eye dog, the spinster who read the classified pages every day, the fat girl who always got off with me at Grand Central—looked older than they once had.

It all comes back. Even that recipe for sauerkraut: even that brings it back. I was on Fire Island when I first made that sauerkraut, and it was raining, and we drank a lot of bourbon and ate the sauerkraut and went to bed at ten, and I listened to the rain and the Atlantic and felt safe. I made the sauerkraut again last night and it did not make me feel any safer, but that is, as they say, another story. □

For Didion and many others, the journal recaptures quintessential experiences and evokes the mood associated with a particular event. A journal entry creates a series of recollections similar to those spawned by an old record played on the radio.

Exercises

1. Keep a journal for five days, jotting down information about a topic, event, or person that intrigues you each day. You may record notes from your reading, conversations, or personal experiences. Jot down enough details so you can recall the significance or impact of the experience at a later date.

2. Rewrite any one of Didion's journal entries as if it were a daily diary entry. How does your information change as you switch from journal writer to diarist?

3. Write a one-page definition of an effective journal entry. How does the information in a journal differ from the information gathered by brainstorming, freewriting, or listing?

QUESTIONS AND ANSWERS

Prewriting is a process of overcoming mental inertia, generating thoughts, and eliminating stereotypical or superficial thinking about a topic. By asking yourself questions about a topic, you can accumulate a wealth of information. A series of well-planned questions, applied methodically to a topic, can deepen your understanding of it and offer you interesting insights to write about.

Questioning moves us from observing simple physical details to discovering complexities inherent in a topic and its environment. Ultimately, questions encourage us to reevaluate our understanding of a topic and see it differently than we have ever seen it before. However, to expand our ideas and prevent Patagonian-like "conditioned responses" to our questions, we must ask as many questions as we can about a topic. As a rule of thumb, the more questions you ask, the better your insights.

The following prewriting strategies use questions to generate fresh responses for various writing tasks. As you work on each of these strategies, be sure to generate information in each category defined by the technique.

The Reporter's Questions   Some journalism textbooks recommend that their students provide the answer to six questions—who, what, when, where, why, and how—in the introductions of their news stories. Such questions create important contexts for newspaper readers; they can also be powerful prewriting resources for writers.

Questions often generate more questions, thereby opening the mind to more possibilities than it originally imagined. Whether the technique generates factual information or new lines of inquiry, questioning can be an effective strategy. Below is an exploratory questioning of Picasso's *Three Musicians* (Color Plate 7). As you read over the questions and responses, look for possible paper topics or topics for further exploration.

Notes on Picasso's *Three Musicians*—Reporter's Questions

WHO   Who are they? a flutist, a guitarist, a singer?

WHAT   What are they doing? What are they playing? What do they represent?

WHEN   When did he paint it?

WHY   Why did he paint it?
       Why did he paint musicians?
       Why did he paint this way?
       Why is there a dog in it?
       Why am I confused?
       Why is the background dark?

WHERE Where did he learn to paint this way?

HOW   How am I supposed to react?
       How does his style affect me?
       How does this painting relate to music?

Since our questions generate more questions, they emphasize an area of interest for us. The WHY question produced the greatest response, an indication perhaps that the writer should continue exploring this productive area. As writers think about answers to questions like these, they might discover certain aspects of the artist or the painting that broaden their perspectives, give them insight, or send them to the library to explore in depth new angles of vision for a paper. By jotting down our responses to our questions, we formulate the raw material for our writing, the bits and pieces we will connect later into a revised text.

Cubing   Cubing offers us a more systematic method of asking questions and generating ideas than do reporters' questions.

Cubing provides six perspectives from which to ask questions or to observe a topic: describe, compare, associate, analyze, apply, and argue for or against. By referring to the different written perspectives on each side of a real or imaginary cube, you can shift your views on a topic and avoid stereotypical thinking about a subject.

If we apply the cubing strategy to Picasso's painting, we will accumulate different kinds of questions. Note how cubing expands the range of responses from factual observations of the painting to abstract explorations concerning its significance and complexity.

Notes on Picasso's *Three Musicians*—Cubing Strategy

DESCRIBE   *Side 1:* A trio of musicians—a flutist(?), a guitarist, and singer are playing in a room. A dog lies under a table or behind them. It seems content and at ease with the musicians. Arms, hands, and faces don't seem clearly attached to their bodies. The painting has many straight lines and right angles.

COMPARE   *Side 2:* Reminds me vaguely of a studio portrait; but can it be a portrait if we can't see the subjects? Did Picasso do portraits? If so, when? How would a photographer have rendered this scene? Since Picasso calls this *Three Musicians* maybe he wants me to compare it with music. The colors create a harmony; they are quite pleasant. Is melody equivalent to color? I have heard people say a piece of music is colorful.

ASSOCIATE   *Side 3:* The piece is abstracted and might represent something, but what? Is this like Picasso's other work? Is it like a poem with symbols and metaphors that I just can't see yet? Somehow it reminds me of a good MTV production. It also reminds me of Southwest Indian figurines and Cycladic figurines.

ANALYZE   *Side 4:* Why would a person paint a portrait of abstracted people? Through hints, such as shapes of hands, feet, legs, instruments, and faces, Picasso lets me see forms. Maybe shapes and forms are more important than distinct features; perhaps Picasso sees more similarities than differences among people and objects. By drawing our attention to broad impressions, he forces us to see a unity in life. Are universals more important than particulars?

APPLY   *Side 5:* How can I apply this? Maybe I can transfer these insights to his other work, to other artists, to other art forms. Sculpture has always eluded me. Maybe if I learn to understand or like Picasso, I'll understand modern sculpture. Abstract forms really do stress essences. I know that. I learned it when I lost my glasses. My blurred vision made many people look alike; I mistakenly waved at strangers all day.

ARGUE   *Side 6:* I think I can make a case for abstract art as a way of seeing life differently. Picasso lets me see the essence of a trio and their dog. I don't think I want to argue against this painting because I like it now. Maybe I could show why I changed my mind, how I felt at first and now.

Exercise

Glance over the cubing notes above and find five topics that might be developed into an essay or research paper. Briefly discuss the processes you would go through to generate more ideas for your new topic.

Particle-Wave-Field Like cubing, the particle-wave-field (PWF) strategy systematizes our freewriting responses and encourages new insights through a series of specific perspectives. Rather than relying on superficial responses from familiar viewpoints, PWF forces us to see subjects as they exist in isolation and in contexts.

As particles, objects exist by themselves, composed of the particular characteristics that make them unique. When we view something as a particle, we see its physical details, motionless like the subject of a photograph. We describe *The Three Musicians* as a painting filled with color, strokes, and subject matter. Our notes resemble the descriptions of an object much like the blurbs under an item in a mail order catalogue. By describing the details of something, we learn to see it as it exists, the verifiable entity that others see, touch, hear, or smell.

If we view Picasso's painting as a wave, we see different aspects of it. The painting becomes a point in the artist's life, a culmination of techniques and interpretations that will develop into something else later. Perhaps this painting was a turning point in Picasso's career. Perhaps the shape of a musician represents a single step in Picasso's journey to an even more abstracted form for the human body. If so, where did his art take him next? The dynamics of the wave can reflect growth, a form of motion, as well as movement. In essence, the wave perspective asks us to consider something as it functions and changes over time.

By viewing an object in its field, we study it in a large context—its place in the environment, history, or discipline of study. From this perspective we view *The Three Musicians* as representative of cubism, a symbol of twentieth-century art, or a philosophical statement on human displacement in a technological world.

Overall, the PWF strategy shifts our attention from the concrete to the abstract. It offers us a multidimensional view of something in a more comprehensive manner than cubing did. The PWF strategy focuses us on the interrelatedness of things, encouraging us to see meaning where we might have thought none existed.

Exercise

Study the painting *The Cradle*, by Berthe Morisot (Color Plate 8), for a few minutes. Then use the reporter's questions, cubing or PWF to record as many thoughts and observations as you can in five minutes. Compare your notes and your strategy with those of two peers. Who used the most effective strategy to accumulate information? Why did one strategy work better than another?

Clustering Clustering is the act of associating your prewriting responses around a nucleus or dominant idea. In Chapter 2 we clustered our annotations on Zora Neale Hurston's "How It Feels to Be Colored Me" around the dominant ideas "color" and "self-image." In clustering as a prewriting strategy, you return to previously generated material, sift through it, look for a pattern to emerge, or impose one on it.

Study the following notes for a history essay on the Nez Perce and arrange them into some kind of order, perhaps around dominant ideas. As you think about them, realize you may scrap ideas that lead nowhere and eliminate ideas that no longer appeal to you or fit within the clusters of meaning you are creating.

American Indian tribe from the Wallowa Valley in northeastern Oregon

Valued the Appaloosa horse for its markings

Extremely generous

Lived in lodges, sheltering 30 or more people

Believed the earth was their mother

Only punishment was derisive laughter

Ironic name because they didn't believe in mutilation of face or body

To the Nez Perce farming meant disfiguring the mother earth by cutting her skin

Acquired horses by 1700

Cutting wheat or corn was the same as cutting their mother's hair

Early Nez Perce hunted on foot for game and fished for survival

If a Nez Perce misbehaves, he or she must walk through the village as others laugh at him or her

After acquiring horses, they ranged far in search of buffalo

By 1811 fur trappers had reached the Nez Perce

By 1835 Christian missionaries had reached the area

During the tribe's flight, the most devastating battle occurred at Big Hole, Montana, where U.S. soldiers annihilated most of the sleeping women and children before warriors could arm themselves

Lewis and Clark in 1806 reached the tribe, commented on their peacefulness, and felt they had discovered "a lost Eden"

Nez Perce is French for "pierced nose"

General Howard of the U.S. Army was sent to quell the war

Fur trappers introduced materialism and competition to the tribe

Chief Joseph epitomized their peace-loving spirit

White man's law reached the Wallowa Valley in 1842, beginning a series of quarrels, disagreements, and finally warfare

The Lewis and Clark expedition would have starved to death during the winter had the Nez Perce not shared their meager supplies with them

An 1855 treaty divided lands between them and the white settlers

Mining to the Nez Perce violates the earth mother by cutting into her heart

They believed each person has a *Weyakin,* an inner spirit symbolized by something in nature

The Battle of Big Hole was as devastating to the Nez Perce as the Little Big Horn was to the whites

Farmers, prospectors, and ranchers violated the treaty so much that war broke out in 1877

Trappers introduced to the Nez Perce alcoholism and venereal disease

After several indecisive battles, Joseph led his tribe in flight across
thousands of miles of rough terrain

They surrendered to the white army at Bear Paws, Montana

They fled across the Lolo Trail in Idaho, down the Bitterroot Valley,
through Yellowstone, and up the Bear Paws Valley near the Cana-
dian border

When Joseph and his tribe reached the Bear Paw Mountains, they
were too tired to fight any longer

Joseph's famous surrender speech displays the peaceful spirit of the
Nez Perce:

> I am tired of fighting . . . the old men are all dead. It is cold and
> we have no blankets. . . . I want to have time to look for my
> children and see how many I can find. Maybe I shall find them
> among the dead. Hear me, my chiefs. I am tired: my heart is
> sick and sad. From where the sun now stands, I will fight no
> more forever.

In reading through the Nez Perce notes, you probably sorted
the information into clusters or groups of information and began
forming impressions about the tribe. Although you might have
known nothing about the Nez Perce, these bits of information
allowed you to act, react, see families of details, and bring other
experiences to bear on the new information before you.

Clustering information is important to forming an opinion, an
impression, or an interpretation of the details you have generated in
prewriting. By listening to yourself and returning to your notes, you
can find something to write about, an idea or impression that
occurred to you long after the fervor of your prewriting session.

Exercises

1. Write a paragraph based on one of the clusters of information you
   created on the Nez Perce fact sheet. If you remembered any additional
   information during the clustering process, incorporate it into your
   writing.

2. Study each of the following groups of topics for a few minutes. Then
   use any prewriting strategy or combination of strategies you wish—
   listing, brainstorming, freewriting, questions, cubing, PWF, or

clustering—to generate as much specific information as you can about one topic from each of the groups.

Group 1:

A description of your favorite dining place
A scene from your favorite movie or play
The process of performing a simple high-tech job such as "booting up" a computer program or withdrawing money from a computerized teller

Group 2:

The importance of space exploration
The impact of television on your life
The convenience or inconvenience of air travel

Group 3:

Discrimination against AIDS victims
Prayer in the public schools
A national lottery

Study the information these topics generated. Which group of topics elicited the most information and why? Did you find some prewriting strategies more effective than others? Why? Under which circumstances do you think each of the prewriting strategies works best?

3.   Make a chart of prewriting strategies, listing their advantages and disadvantages.

MAKING CONNECTIONS

All of the strategies discussed in this chapter and in previous chapters help you break down perceptual blocks and gain fresh insights into many topics. Each strategy is a tool, designed for particular situations; few are universally effective. In some instances, a specific strategy will yield less information than another technique. If a strategy leads nowhere after several minutes, select another one and begin again.

Each of the prewriting strategies we have discussed allows us to probe our minds and lay bits of information in front of us so we can later interpret them, see patterns among ideas and facts, and discover what we think about a topic. And each strategy creates raw material for a text, but stops short of producing that text. The information we generate has little meaning until we sift through and connect it to our lives in some significant way and then, clearly and logically, share it with our readers.

Exercises

The following readings present different perceptual problems and show how two people handled them. Read each selection carefully, collecting information by means of your favorite prewriting technique. Write a one- or two-page paper for each reading, identifying the main characters' perceptual problems and analyzing the effectiveness of the problem-solving process he or she used.

1. This excerpt from Robert Pirsig's *Zen and the Art of Motorcycle Maintenance* describes a student's difficulty in finding something to write about.

One of them, a girl with strong-lensed glasses, wanted to write a five-hundred-word essay about the United States. He was used to the sinking feeling that comes from statements like this, and suggested without disparagement that she narrow it down to just Bozeman.

When the paper came due she didn't have it and was quite upset. She had tried and tried but she just couldn't think of anything to say.

He had already discussed her with her previous instructors and they'd confirmed his impressions of her. She was very serious, disciplined and hardworking, but extremely dull. Not a spark of creativity in her anywhere. Her eyes, behind the thick-lensed glasses, were the eyes of a drudge. She wasn't bluffing him, she really couldn't think of anything to say, and was upset by her inability to do as she was told.

It just stumped him. Now *he* couldn't think of anything to say. A silence occurred, and then a peculiar answer: "Narrow it down to the *main street* of Bozeman." It was a stroke of insight.

She nodded dutifully and went out. But just before her next class she came back in *real* distress, tears this time, distress that had obviously been there for a long time. She still couldn't think of anything to say, and couldn't understand why, if she couldn't think of anything about *all* of Bozeman, she should be able to think of something about just one street.

He was furious. "You're not *looking!*" he said. A memory came back of his own dismissal from the University for having *too much* to say. For every fact there is an *infinity* of hypotheses. The more you *look* the more you *see*. She really wasn't looking and yet somehow didn't understand this.

He told her angrily, "Narrow it down to the *front* of *one* building on the main street of Bozeman. The Opera House. Start with the upper left-hand brick."

Her eyes, behind the thick-lensed glasses, opened wide.

She came in the next class with a puzzled look and handed him a five-thousand-word essay on the front of the Opera House on the main street of Bozeman, Montana. "I sat in the hamburger stand across the street," she said, "and started writing about the first brick, and the second brick, and then by the third brick it all started to come and I couldn't stop. They thought I was crazy, and they kept kidding me, but here it all is. I don't understand it."

Neither did he, but on long walks through the streets of town he thought about it and concluded she was evidently stopped with the same kind of blockage that had paralyzed him on his first day of teaching. She was blocked because she was trying to repeat, in her writing, things she had already heard, just as on the first day he had tried to repeat things he had already decided to say. She couldn't think of anything to write about Bozeman because she couldn't recall anything she had heard worth repeating. She was strangely unaware that she could look and see freshly for herself, as she wrote, without primary regard for what had been said before. The narrowing down to one brick destroyed the blockage because it was so obvious she had to do some original and direct seeing. □

2.   This fictional piece, "Zen in the Art of Tennis," by Calvin Tomkins, demonstrates a person's ability to interpret reality from one perspective, regardless of the facts involved.

Three years ago this spring, I began to have serious trouble with my tennis game. At first it seemed nothing more than the customary early-season awkwardness and bad timing, but when my double faults and netted backhands carried over into mid-July, causing me public humiliation and private anguish, I knew that some drastic therapy was needed. The three men I usually played with were patient and understanding. They gave various advice, but none of it helped until that hot Saturday morning in August when Wally Michaels took me aside between sets and asked, casually enough, "Have you ever thought of trying Zen?"

Coming from Wally, a steady, somewhat plodding backcourt player, the question startled me. This was long before Zen Buddhism had become a commonplace in suburbia, and hard as it is to believe now, the books of Daisetz T. Suzuki, pioneer of Zen in America, were then known to very few tennis players. Cocktail-party guests had not yet begun to ask each other Zen *koans*, the riddle questions designed to coerce the mind into a state of nonrational awareness. It was even possible to spend a whole evening talking to an old friend without having to hear about his *satori* (enlightenment) or having to argue the relative merits of beatnik Zen, square Zen, and ladies' Zen. I usually find myself a little ahead of contemporary trends, however, and I had recently read five or six of Dr. Suzuki's early books on Zen, and was then in the midst of a lovely small volume, by a German Zen addict named Eugen Herrigel, called *Zen in the Art of Archery*. Wally's question therefore dropped like a stone into deep water. I knew, suddenly and inexplicably, that Zen could well be the answer to my tennis problem.

The question was, where could I find a teacher? Wally Michaels surprised me again by saying he would ask his *roshi*, or Zen Master, whom he had been going to for about two years in hopes of increasing his annual sales record (*Zen in the Art of Salesmanship*). He did so that same afternoon, but the *roshi* was unable to suggest anyone. "Try the Yellow Pages," said Wally. "You never know." Without much enthusiasm, I dug out the Classified and leafed through it until I came to "Tennis Instruction." About halfway down the page, my eye was arrested by an unmistakably Japanese, Zen-sounding name, I. Ashikawa, which was followed by a cryptic message "Fish & Birds" and an address on upper Broadway, in the Bronx. I sprang to my feet with a cry of triumph. What a perfect Zen analogy—tennis balls darting like fish, flying like birds! My wife suggested, in her literal way, that it sounded like a pet shop that had slipped into the tennis listings by mistake, but I knew better. Without a doubt, Ashikawa was my man.

The next afternoon, I took the car and drove to the upper-Broadway address, which turned out to be a small shop sandwiched between two early-Bronx-baroque apartment houses. The dusty windows of the shop were full of bird cages and tropical-fish tanks—a nice bit of deception. In my eagerness, I rang the bell repeatedly for ten minutes or so, forgetting that novices often wait outside a Zen monastery for days or even weeks before being considered worthy to be admitted. Finally, the door opened and a feathery wisp of a man, with white hair and a yellow sleeveless shirt, put his head out and said brusquely, "Closed. Go away."

"I've come to see about tennis lessons," I said breathlessly. "Are you a *roshi?* Do you teach the *dharma?*" Instead of replying, he flung a handful of birdseed in my face, slammed the door, and disappeared.

Imagine my delight! Here was proof that I had stumbled on a true Zen Master, who would break down my slavish habits of rational, logical thought, and in so doing perhaps cure my wrongheaded backhand. I drove home with a high heart, certain that I was well begun on my quest for enlightenment.

The next day, I was back. When Ashikawa threw the birdseed at me this time, I managed to bow politely before he slammed the door. Two days later, I was able to pick up a pinch of seed and hand it back to him. The following Monday, he let me come in.

The place did give somewhat the appearance of a pet shop. Bird cages lined one side wall and tropical-fish tanks the other. Mr. Ashikawa led me to a small, cluttered office in the back, where a tethered myna bird glared at me with bloodshot eyes and said, enigmatically, "Porry want a clacker?" Ashikawa asked me if I wanted to buy the bird, and when I declined he demanded to know just what it was I did want.

"Whatever you can teach me," I said, as humbly as possible. He stared at me for a long time, obviously trying to make out whether I was a restless dilettante or a serious Zen seeker. At length, he gave a little grunt and nodded his white head. At such a moment, words would have been superfluous.

From then on, I came every morning for an hour, before going to my office downtown. Ashikawa showed me how to clean the bird cages and the fish tanks, and I was content to do so. I remembered reading the story of the young samurai who went to a famous Zen Master to learn swordsmanship and was put to work building fires and cooking the Master's meals. When he unwisely asked how long it would be before they could begin lessons in swordsmanship, the Master struck him smartly on the head with a heavy stick, and from that time forward the Master would sneak up behind him every time his back was turned and give him a thrashing. After several years of this, the samurai became adept at dodging blows from any angle. One day, he saw the Master himself bending over a cooking fire, and, unable to resist the temptation, raised his own stick to strike him. Without even looking up, the Master caught the blow on the lid of a pot. This opened the samurai's eyes to the real secrets of swordsmanship, and he was forever grateful to the Master, although his wits became so confused by the repeated blows on the head that he never amounted to much as a swordsman himself. Determined to avoid the samurai's mistake, I said not a word about tennis lessons for a full six weeks.

Finally my impatience overcame me. In a foolish attempt to force the issue, I appeared one morning with my tennis racket and some balls. The Master had the grace to look puzzled rather than angry. It was at this point that he asked me the first *koan*. "What have you got there?" he said. There was no doubt in my mind that this was a *koan*. Obviously, Ashikawa knew a tennis racket when he saw one, so his question must have been intended to jolt my mind into the kind of nonrational awareness I was so anxious to achieve. I was a good deal deeper into Zen by this time. I had read nine or ten more books by Daisetz T. Suzuki and had become increasingly certain that all my tennis problems could be traced back to that old troublemaker the rational mind. I had also been wondering when Ashikawa would let me sink my teeth into a *koan*, so when he repeated the question now, saying sharply, "What have you got there?" I bowed low and emitted a wild Zen laugh. At last we were getting somewhere.

After that, I brought the racket every day. This seemed to please the Master, who used to remove the press and let the myna bird sit on the strings, where it hopped up and down, croaking "Porry want a clacker?" It was typical of a Zen tennis sage to treat the racket itself—centerpiece of his art—with such merry irreverence.

Autumn drifted into winter. There were times, I confess, when the prospects looked discouraging. Ashikawa seemed far more interested in his fish and birds than in the teaching of Zen tennis. At home, I suffered stoically through such indignities as hearing my wife tell our friends that she had become a Zen Mother, while my two children clamored for ice-cream *koans*. But I was determined to stick it out.

On January 19th, I solved the first *koan*. When the Master

pointed to my tennis racket and asked me, as he did nearly every morning, "What have you got there?" I felt a sudden wave of anger and I answered, *without thinking*, "A bird stand, for God's sake!" He doubled over with laughter. Suddenly I knew that I had penetrated to the heart of the *koan*, because Ashikawa stopped laughing and asked me another one, far more difficult than the first. "Are you crazy?" he said.

Instead of answering straight off and making a fool of myself, I decided to seize this propitious moment to begin our Zen tennis lessons. Motioning to Ashikawa to follow me, I strode out the door and around the corner to a vacant lot I had been eying for several months. It was bounded on two sides by tumble-down fences, and at the rear by the smooth windowless wall of a garage. "How about it?" I said. "I'm ready if you are."

"Are you crazy?" Ashikawa repeated, pretending to be uneasy.

Without more ado, I addressed myself to the back wall, tossed up a ball, and served. It was a good first serve, hard and flat. The ball hit about four feet up the wall and came back at an angle, bouncing off pieces of brick and tin cans and eventually disappearing under a parked Pontiac. I stole a glance at the Master who looked dubious. "I know," I said quickly, eager to impress him. "I was trying to *aim* it. I should just let it *fall* from the racket naturally—is that right?" This falling bit was right out of Herrigel's book on archery, and it must have distressed Ashikawa no end to have me thus parade my pitiful learning. He said nothing, but motioned for me to serve again. This time the ball didn't reach the wall. The third serve slid off the handle and went bouncing erratically down the street. A tatterdemalion youth fielded it and made off with it around the corner. I retrieved the remaining two balls and continued serving. The Master watched me closely, muttering in Japanese from time to time but never offering the least particle of advice. I had hoped he would make a few suggestions, although I was well aware that Zen cannot be taught—that, in fact, "One knows it by not knowing it." By the time we stopped, I could hardly hit the ball.

Our lessons followed this pattern for several months. After cleaning the fish tanks and bird cages, we would go back to the vacant lot, where I would serve for half an hour or so, often in snow or rain. My serve grew steadily worse, to the intense delight of the hordes of neighborhood toughs who came out to watch and jeer. The Master was incredibly patient. When I offered him the racket, hoping he would demonstrate, he merely backed away, giggling. He obviously meant for me to learn by direct experience. Remembering my readings in Suzuki, I tried to keep my mind locked up in the lower part of my abdomen, "just below the navel" (so that I might adjust myself "with the shifting situation from moment to moment"), but it was no use. This only gave me cramps.

Then one day in late spring, totally without warning, I served a perfect ball. It seemed to float effortlessly from my racket, without conscious guidance, in a pure and beautifully anti-intellectual arc, to the exact center of the back wall. I turned eagerly to see the Master's reaction. To my amazement, he was nowhere in sight. Where he had been standing a moment ago, there was now a large blue policeman, watching me coldly. I started to tell him about the shot, but something in his manner suggested that he might have trouble understanding, so I merely started walking away. The policeman followed me to my car, and I thought it best to drive away without bothering Ashikawa again that day.

So great was my joy at having approached for the first time, through that perfect serve, the inner spirit of Zen tennis that I was not even particularly surprised to be denied entrance to Ashikawa's shop the next morning. The door was locked. When I rang, the Master came to the window shaking his head and waving angrily. He refused to let me in. It was, in its way, an exquisite gesture. He took this means of telling me he had no more to teach, that I must now find another Master or proceed on my own.

In the years since that day, I have often sought a new tennis Master to carry on Ashikawa's work, and I am still looking. But the way of Zen has not been closed to me—not by any means. My tennis is rather strange now, by our club standards, and it has become increasingly difficult for me to get up a game. I seldom put the ball in court on my serve, and my ground strokes have a way of soaring over the backstop and off into space, like swallows. But the great thing is, *this no longer concerns me.* I rarely think now in terms of winning. As I penetrate ever closer into the real spirit of tennis, I become increasingly aware that the server and the receiver are really one person, and the goal of both is not points but *satori.* The transformation of my entire life is at hand. I can even derive pleasure from mixed doubles.

Yesterday I solved the second *koan.* As I missed an overhead smash, it suddenly swept over me that the answer to the question, "Are you crazy?" was simply, to paraphrase Descartes, "I think, therefore I *must* be crazy." My sudden peal of pure Zen laughter startled the three ladies I was playing with, I'm afraid, but I felt no embarrassment; someday soon, I knew, I would be able to stop thinking altogether and attain *satori*. I only wish old Master Ashikawa had been around to see my next double fault, which was perfect. □

CHAPTER **4**

Writing and Form

There is no single best way to organize an essay. The forms your essays assume will vary, depending on your audience, your purpose, and the occasion or circumstances that motivate the writing. In this chapter we explore different approaches to forming and shaping an essay. We consider both the standard organizational patterns such as the five-paragraph essay, and some other more open, less prescriptive structures. Our purpose is to suggest a variety of approaches to developing ideas and structuring them in ways readers can understand. We believe strongly that a rich and varied consciousness of form is essential in learning to read well and write effectively.

THREE-PART FORMS

Form can be either mechanical or organic. Mechanical forms are those built on the model of the machine. They are efficient and practical with each part serving a function in the whole. Organic forms are modeled on nature. Their principle of organization is that of growth and development. An example of mechanical form in writing is the five-paragraph essay. This form requires an introductory paragraph that identifies your subject and introduces your thesis, or main idea. It requires three supporting paragraphs in which you extend and explain your idea. And it requires a concluding paragraph in which you sum up your argument or identify its implications. Such an organizational form can be efficient and useful for expository writing, but it limits possibilities for more creative and interesting structural arrangements of thought. Mechanical forms tend to be predictable. They tend also to limit thought to what can be contained within their very strict boundaries. In the five-paragraph essay, for example, you are required to use three supporting examples or arguments—no more, no less. Why? Because the form demands it.

We should point out, however, that the constraints of the five-paragraph form simultaneously compel you to think. To complete the form, you need to fill five slots: introduction, conclusion, and three body points. You have to think of something to say for each of them.

For some of the essays you write in college this form of organization will suit your subject, audience, and thought. On other occasions, however, it will not. In writing autobiographical essays based on personal experience, in narrative and descriptive writing, in writing reports and critical interpretations, and in various kinds of creative writing, you will turn to other organizational forms, other ways of shaping content.

One of the best ways to begin developing a sense of form in writing is to read with an eye to seeing how writers organize their thinking. Here is a short essay that illustrates with near-mathematical precision the formal characteristics of the classic five-paragraph essay. As you read it, make marginal notes to identify the function and point of each paragraph.

What I Have Lived For
Bertrand Russell

Three passions, simple but overwhelmingly strong, have governed my life: the longing for love, the search for knowledge, and unbearable pity for the suffering of mankind. These passions, like great winds, have blown me hither and thither, in a wayward course, over a deep ocean of anguish, reaching to the very verge of despair.

I have sought love, first, because it brings ecstasy—ecstasy so great that I would often have sacrificed all the rest of life for a few hours of this joy. I have sought it, next, because it relieves loneliness—that terrible loneliness in which one shivering consciousness looks over the rim of the world into the cold unfathomable lifeless abyss. I have sought it, finally, because in the union of love I have seen, in a mystic miniature, the prefiguring vision of the heaven that saints and poets have imagined. This is what I sought, and though it might seem too good for human life, this is what—at last—I have found.

With equal passion I have sought knowledge. I have wished to understand the hearts of men. I have wished to know why the stars shine. And I have tried to apprehend the Pythagorean power by which number holds sway above the flux. A little of this, but not much, I have achieved.

Love and knowledge, so far as they were possible, led upward toward the heavens. But always pity brought me back to earth. Echoes of cries of pain reverberate in my heart. Children in famine, victims tortured by oppressors, helpless old people a hated burden to their sons, and the whole world of loneliness, poverty, and pain make a mockery of what human life should be. I long to alleviate the evil, but I cannot, and I too suffer.

This has been my life. I have found it worth living, and would gladly live it again if the chance were offered me. □

Notice how Russell's explanation begins with a clear statement of his thesis or central idea (that three passions have governed his life); how it continues by explaining them one by one; and how it concludes with an affirmation of his point. Even though Russell divides his essay into five paragraphs, we can see it essentially as a three-part form: introduction (paragraph 1), body (paragraphs 2 to 4) and conclusion (paragraph 5). This three-part structure offers a traditionally efficient way to construct an essay or to construe one. When you read an essay, decide where the introduction ends and the body of the text begins. Identify also the end of this body or support section and the start of the conclusion. Sometimes (often, in fact) essays employ a three-part form but not strictly in the five-paragraph format.

Consider the following example. Again, as you read, make marginal notes about the essay's structure. Identify its introduction, body, and conclusion. Comment on what the writer does in each part, and why. Comment also on the way the body paragraphs develop. Ask yourself how one paragraph relates to those that precede and follow it. In doing this you will be reading not merely for a sense of the essay's overall structure, but also for a sense of its developing argument, for the ordering of its thought.

Blame the Victim
Ellen Goodman

There is a sign I pass every day on the way to work which says in bold letters: Health Thyself. The sign is "A Friendly Message" from the Blue Cross/Blue Shield people, who have, I know, a vested interest in its meaning.

But the very tone of it, the sort of Eleventh Commandment, Thus Spake Blue Cross/Blue Shield attitude of it, sitting there above the highway, has slowly rubbed raw a small layer of my consciousness. I have begun to wonder whether the Self-Health movement—of which this sign is more symbol than substance—isn't another variation on our national theme song: Blame the Victim. How many measures, how many beats, how many half-notes is it from the order to Health Thyself to the attitude that blames the ill for their illness?

The titles on the bookshelf of my favorite store are a chorus stuck in this monotone: *Stay Out of the Hospital* instructs one; *The Anti-Cancer Diet* offers another; *You Can Stop* (smoking) cheerleads a third. They tell readers How To design their faces, control their migraines, lose weight, bear children without pain and psych themselves out of everything from back pain to heart disease.

Perhaps the most typical of them is one which touts *Preventing Cancer: What You Can Do to Cut Your Risks by Up to 50 Percent.* And another containing *Dr. Frank's No Aging Diet: Eat and Grow Younger.*

Now I am in favor—who is against it?—of proper diet and exercise. I am against—who is in favor of it?—smoking. I assume that a diet high in calories, cholesterol and cognac would eventually do me in. I think that self-consciousness about health, the desire to take responsibility for the shape of our lungs and calf muscles, is positive, and I agree that we are our own best screening system. But there is a risk. A risk that as we focus on the aspects of self-health we begin to look at all illness as self-inflicted and even regard death as a kind of personal folly.

There have been, among my acquaintances, the relatives of my relatives and friends of my friends, three heart attacks within the past year. One man, I was told, was, well, overweight. "He should have known better." Another woman was, her friends insist, a real "Type A." And the third man, I was assured by the most well-meaning of people, brought it on himself. "He was so out of shape."

Similarly, when people hear reports of cancer, how often do they inadvertently say that the victim should have stayed out of the sun, or off the pill, or away from nitrates?

Now maybe they are right and maybe they are wrong, but I fear that there are many who seek to know the cause of a disease not to cure it, but to judge its victims.

It is reassuring to hear that we can cut the risks of cancer by 50 percent. It is lovely to think that we can eat in special ways and grow younger. In a world of amorphous fears, where carcinogens are the new demons, it is very human to try to analyze illness in order to separate ourselves from it, to assure ourselves that we can be immune. There is a natural tendency to try to buy insurance packages—not of Blue Crosses and Blue Shields, but of diets and regimens and cautions.

But there is also something malignant about some of the extremists who make a public virtue of their health. It is the sort of self-righteousness that inspired a letter writer to suggest to me recently that we eliminate lung cancer research, because "smokers do it to themselves."

There is a judgmental attitude toward ill-health germinating in parts of the country and in parts of our minds that can be spread cruelly. It implies that those who do not "Health Thyself" are not only courting their own disasters, but are owed very little in the way of sympathy. It implies that illness is, at root, a punishment for foolishness.

This feeds into the hope, born of fear, that if we keep ourselves in shape and watch out, we can not only postpone death but prevent it. The notion that death is, in essence, suicide, and something we can avoid, is the most profound illusion of all. □

Exercises

1. Write an essay in which you imitate the overall form of Russell's "What I Have Lived For." You can write on the same topic if you like. Or you can modify it. Some suggestions: "What I Live By," "What I Love," "What I Fear," or "What I Have Learned."

2. Write an essay imitating the three-part form of "Blame the Victim." That is, arrange your essay as three identifiable parts: introduction, body, conclusion. You are not required to write either three or five paragraphs; you may write as few or as many paragraphs as you like (or as many as your instructor requires or your subject seems to call for). Label the three main parts of your essay.

   The essays you have been reading and writing exemplify what we have called three-part form. Grouping by three is a useful, natural, and familiar procedure. Think, for example, of how time is organized into past, present, and future; or how day is divided into morning, afternoon, and evening. Consider the film studio: lights, camera, action; the running track: on your marks, get set, go; the shooting range: ready, aim, fire. Or consider these other groups of three: man, woman, child; childhood, adolescence, adulthood; right field, center field, left field; thesis, antithesis, synthesis.

Exercises

1. Identify the three-part form of the following sentences and then write imitations of each.

   (a)   Crafty men condemn studies, simple men admire them, and wise men use them. (Francis Bacon)
   (b)   Some books are to be tasted, others to be swallowed, and some few to be chewed and digested. (Francis Bacon)
   (c)   Veni, vidi, vici. I came; I saw; I conquered. (Julius Caesar)

2. Find a photograph or painting organized as a three-part form. Identify the three parts and explain how they work together to form a harmonious whole.

3. Identify something from the natural world that exhibits three-part form. Explain how.

4. Identify a poem, a song, or other piece of music arranged as a three-part form. Comment on its organization.

TWO-PART FORMS

In the same way that we can learn to notice three-part forms in writing and in everyday life, so too can we notice and use two-part forms. Much of our experience, in fact, involves the use of two-part categories, usually related through opposition or complementarity: inside–outside; up–down; light–dark; youth–age; before–after; male–female. We can consider such forms either as contrasting opposites in conflict or as complementary completers of each other.

Aphorisms Two-part forms are pervasive in writing. We find and use small-scale two-part forms in sentences like the following:

> Buddies seek approval, but friends seek acceptance. (Ellen Goodman)
> What is now proved was once only imagined. (William Blake)
> It is not necessary to desire things in order to acquire them. (E. B. White)

These and other sentences that exhibit concisely formulated principles are called aphorisms. Identify a few aphorisms you are familiar with and explain how they exhibit two-part form.

Exercises

1. Write imitations of the two-part sentences quoted above.

2. Find examples of three two-part sentences from a newspaper, magazine, or book, and then write an imitation of each.

Dialogue A two-part form on a larger scale is exemplified by dialogue and conversation. In our everyday lives a good deal of our talk is with one other person at a time. We engage often in dialogue (to say nothing of the interior dialogue or talking to ourselves we engage in). Our dialogue or conversation with other people takes different forms and occurs for different purposes under varying circumstances. Our dialogues are spoken in differing tones of voice, with varying degrees of intimacy, and with diverse attitudes, feelings, and perspectives.

Consider the following dialogue from the opening of a one-act play. Listen carefully to the voices of the characters as you imagine how they might sound. Consider the nature of the two-part form this dialogue exhibits.

Suppressed Desires
Susan Glaspell

SCENE I

*A studio apartment in an upper story, Washington Square South. Through an immense north window in the back wall appear tree tops and the upper part of the Washington Arch. Beyond it you look up Fifth Avenue. Near the window is a big table, loaded at one end with serious-looking books and austere scientific periodicals. At the other end are architect's drawings, blueprints, dividing compasses, square, ruler, etc. At the left is a door leading to the rest of the apartment; at the right the outer door. A breakfast table is set for three, but only two are seated at it—*HENRIETTA *and* STEPHEN BREWSTER. *As the curtains withdraw* STEVE *pushes back his coffee cup and sits dejected.*

HENRIETTA: It isn't the coffee, Steve dear. There's nothing the matter with the coffee. There's something the matter with *you.*

STEVE *(doggedly):* There may be something the matter with my stomach.

HENRIETTA *(scornfully):* Your stomach! The trouble is not with your stomach but in your subconscious mind.

STEVE: Subconscious piffle! *(Takes morning paper and tries to read.)*

HENRIETTA: Steve, you never used to be so disagreeable. You certainly have got some sort of a complex. You're all inhibited. You're no longer open to new ideas. You won't listen to a word about psychoanalysis.

STEVE: A word! I've listened to volumes!

HENRIETTA: You've ceased to be creative in architecture—your work isn't going well. You're not sleeping well—

STEVE: How can I sleep, Henrietta, when you're always waking me up to find out what I'm dreaming?

HENRIETTA: But dreams are so important, Steve. If you'd tell yours to Dr. Russell he'd find out exactly what's wrong with you.

STEVE: There's nothing wrong with me.

HENRIETTA: You don't even talk as well as you used to.

STEVE: Talk? I can't say a thing without you looking at me in that dark fashion you have when you're on the trail of a complex.

HENRIETTA: This very irritability indicates that you're suffering from some suppressed desire.

STEVE: I'm suffering from a suppressed desire for a little peace.

HENRIETTA: Dr. Russell is doing simply wonderful things with nervous cases. Won't you go to him, Steve?

STEVE (*slamming down his newspaper*): No, Henrietta, I won't!

HENRIETTA: But Stephen—!

STEVE: Tst! I hear Mabel coming. Let's not be at each other's throats the first day of her visit.
(*He takes out cigarettes.* MABEL *comes in from door left, the side opposite* STEVE, *so that he is facing her. She is wearing a rather fussy negligee in contrast to* HENRIETTA, *who wears "radical" clothes.* MABEL *is what is called plump.*)

MABEL: Good morning.

HENRIETTA: Oh, here you are, little sister.

STEVE: Good morning, Mabel.
(MABEL *nods to him and turns, her face lighting up, to* HENRIETTA.)

HENRIETTA (*giving* MABEL *a hug as she leans against her*): It's so good to have you here. I was going to let you sleep, thinking you'd be tired after the long trip. Sit down. There'll be fresh toast in a minute and (*rising*) will you have—

MABEL: Oh, I ought to have told you, Henrietta. Don't get anything for me. I'm not eating breakfast.

HENRIETTA (*at first in mere surprise*): Not eating breakfast? (*She sits down, then leans toward* MABEL *who is seated now, and scrutinizes her.*)

STEVE (*half to himself*): The psychoanalytical look!

HENRIETTA: Mabel, why are you not eating breakfast?

MABEL (*a little startled*): Why, no particular reason. I just don't care much for breakfast, and they say it keeps down— (*A hand on her hip—the gesture of one who is "reducing"*) that is, it's a good thing to go without it.

HENRIETTA: Don't you sleep well? Did you sleep well last night?

MABEL: Oh, yes, I slept all right. Yes, I slept fine last night, only (*laughing*) I did have the funniest dream!

STEVE: S-h! S-t!

HENRIETTA (*moving closer*): And what did you dream, Mabel?

STEVE: Look-a-here, Mabel. I feel it's my duty to put you on. Don't tell Henrietta your dreams. If you do she'll find out that you have an underground desire to kill your father and marry your mother—

HENRIETTA: Don't be absurd, Stephen Brewster. (*Sweetly to* MABEL) What was your dream, dear?

MABEL (*laughing*): Well, I dreamed I was a hen.

HENRIETTA: A hen?

MABEL: Yes; and I was pushing along through a crowd as fast as I could, but being a hen I couldn't walk very fast—it was like having a tight skirt, you know; and there was some sort of creature in a blue cap—you know how mixed up dreams are—and it kept shouting after me, "Step, Hen! Step, Hen!" until I got all excited and just couldn't move at all.

HENRIETTA (*resting chin in palm and peering*): You say you became much excited?

MABEL (*laughing*): Oh, yes; I was in a terrible state.

HENRIETTA (*leaning back, murmurs*): This is significant.

STEVE: She dreams she's a hen. She is told to step lively. She becomes violently agitated. What can it mean?

HENRIETTA (*turning impatiently from him*): Mabel, do you know anything about psychoanalysis?

Exercises

1. Write the opening scene of a one-act play involving two characters in dialogue. (This might be done collaboratively with one or more other students.) Create a situation and set the characters talking. If you like, you can select one of the following contexts for your dialogue: two customers in line at a department store; manager and shopper at a supermarket; teacher and student discussing a paper or a literary text; baseball manager and umpire discussing a call.

2. Transcribe a conversation you overhear at work or school—in class, at lunch, in the library, on the playing field. Comment on the nature and form of the dialogue.

3. Transcribe a brief dialogue from a television show. Comment on the nature, form, and tone of the dialogue.

Before–After Sequence   Other two-part forms can serve as useful frameworks for organizing essays. You can use the dialogue framework discussed above as a way of thinking through your ideas about a subject. The voices in your mind would represent differing viewpoints or positions that you could work out in writing. A more common two-part organizational pattern you can use in writing is a before–after or once–now sequence. This framework is especially powerful in shaping your writing about personal experience. It is particularly effective for discussing patterns of change or turning points in your life, changes in belief, attitude, perspective, understanding. Some possible subjects are these:

> Once I was, now I am . . .
> Once I believed, now I believe . . .
> Once I thought, now I know . . .
> Once I dreamed (or hoped), now I . . .

To write an essay using this structure, you will most likely need to include both a *narrative*, a story of what happened to change you, and an *explanation*, an analysis of the significance of that change. The exciting thing about this form is its potential to release your feelings and thoughts about things you consider important. It encourages you to probe your past experience in relation to your present circumstances and to consider important differences between them.

Exercises

1. Write an essay based on the once–now or before–after pattern.
2. Read the following excerpt from *The Autobiography of Malcolm X*. Explain how it makes use of the pattern.

I kept close to the top of the class, though. The topmost scholastic standing, I remember, kept shifting between me, a girl named Audrey Slaugh, and a boy named Jimmy Cotton.

It went on that way, as I became increasingly restless and disturbed through the first semester. And then one day, just about when those of us who had passed were about to move up to 8-A, from which we would enter high school the next year, something happened which was to become the first major turning point of my life.

Somehow, I happened to be alone in the classroom with Mr. Ostrowski, my English teacher. He was a tall, rather reddish white man and he had a thick mustache. I had gotten some of my best marks under him, and he had always made me feel that he liked me. He was, as I have mentioned, a natural-born "advisor," about what you ought to read, to do, or think—about any and everything. We used to make unkind jokes about him: why was he teaching in Mason instead of somewhere else, getting for himself some of the "success in life" that he kept telling us how to get?

I know that he probably meant well in what he happened to advise me that day. I doubt that he meant any harm. It was just in his nature as an American white man. I was one of his top students, one of the school's top students—but all he could see for me was the kind of future "in your place" that almost all white people see for black people.

He told me, "Malcolm, you ought to be thinking about a career. Have you been giving it thought?"

The truth is, I hadn't. I never have figured out why I told him, "Well, yes, sir, I've been thinking I'd like to be a lawyer." Lansing certainly had no Negro lawyers—or doctors either—in those days, to hold up an image I might have aspired to. All I really knew for certain was that a lawyer didn't wash dishes, as I was doing.

Mr. Ostrowski looked surprised, I remember, and leaned back in his chair and clasped his hands behind his head. He kind of half-smiled and said, "Malcolm, one of life's first needs is for us to be realistic. Don't misunderstand me, now. We all here like you, you know that. But you've got to be realistic about being a nigger. A lawyer—that's no realistic goal for a nigger. You need to think about something you *can* be. You're good with your hands—making things. Everybody admires your carpentry shop work. Why don't you plan on carpentry? People like you as a person—you'd get all kinds of work."

The more I thought afterwards about what he said, the more uneasy it made me. It just kept treading around in my mind.

What made it really begin to disturb me was Mr. Ostrowski's advice to others in my class—all of them white. Most of them had told him they were planning to become farmers. But those who wanted to strike out on their own, to try something new, he had encouraged. Some, mostly girls, wanted to be teachers. A few wanted other professions, such as one boy who wanted to become a county agent; another, a veterinarian; and one girl wanted to be a nurse. They all reported that Mr. Ostrowski had encouraged what they had wanted. Yet nearly none of them had earned marks equal to mine.

It was a surprising thing that I had never thought of it that way before, but I realized that whatever I wasn't, I *was* smarter than nearly all of those white kids. But apparently I was still not intelligent enough, in their eyes, to become whatever *I* wanted to be.

It was then that I began to change—inside.

I drew away from white people. I came to class, and I answered when called upon. It became a physical strain simply to sit in Mr. Ostrowski's class.

Where "nigger" had slipped off my back before, wherever I heard it now, I stopped and looked at whoever said it. And they looked surprised that I did.

I quit hearing so much "nigger" and "What's wrong?"—which was the way I wanted it. Nobody, including the teachers, could decide what had come over me. □

Problem–Solution   Another convenient and useful two-part form for structuring a piece of persuasive writing is the problem–solution form. Although the basic pattern is simple enough, it can assume a variety of complicating elaborations. In its clearest and simplest form a problem–solution structure is just that. The first part of the piece identifies a problem; the second explains what to do about it—and perhaps also why and how it should be done. You can find examples of the form in the editorial pages of newspapers, including the editorials proper, the letters to the editor, and the "op-ed" page articles. Sometimes in these editorial articles and letters the writers include alternative solutions to the problem they identify. They include these alternatives only to reject them, to provide evidence of their inadequacy, and to set the stage for their own solution. In such cases, we find a three-part structure: identification of problem; discussion of unacceptable solutions; proposal of better solution.

The problem–solution organization is also frequently used in business writing, especially in reports and proposals. The form may appear in a brief memo as well as in an elaborate report. In a long report, the statement of the problem usually is divided into subsections, one of which generally is a history or narrative of how the problem developed. It might also include an analysis of the problem's various *causes*. The solution section can be similarly elaborated, perhaps taking the form of a series of alternatives—presented in the order of least to most promising, least to most costly, or some other commonsensical order.

Exercises

1. Select two newspaper or magazine editorial pieces and explain how they employ the problem–solution structure.

2. Write an editorial, letter to the editor, or op-ed column using a problem–solution organization.

3. Acquire a memorandum or report from your school or business and analyze its problem–solution framework.

4. Write a memorandum or report, setting it up as a problem–solution. If you write a report, decide how elaborate to make both the problem and solution sections and how much space to allot each. Decide also how to arrange each section—as a narrative, list, chart, or something else.

5. Read the following proposal and analyze its structure. Pinpoint its statement of a problem and its proposed solution.

In Defense of Literacy
Wendell Berry

In a country in which everybody goes to school, it may seem absurd to offer a defense of literacy, and yet I believe that such a defense is in order, and that the absurdity lies not in the defense, but in the necessity for it. The published illiteracies of the certified educated are on the increase. And the universities seem bent upon ratifying this state of things by declaring the acceptability, in their graduates, of adequate—that is to say, of mediocre—writing skills.

The schools, then, are following the general subservience to the "practical," as that term has been defined for us according to the benefit of corporations. By "practicality" most users of the term now mean whatever will most predictably and most quickly make a profit. Teachers of English and literature have either submitted, or are expected to submit, along with teachers of the more "practical" disciplines, to the doctrine that the purpose of education is the mass production of producers and consumers. This has forced our profession into a predicament that we will finally have to recognize as a perversion. As if awed by the ascendency of the "practical" in our society, many of us secretly fear, and some of us are apparently ready to say, that if a student is not going to become a teacher of his language, he has no need to master it.

In other words, to keep pace with the specialization—and the dignity accorded to specialization—in other disciplines, we have begun to look upon and to teach our language and literature as specialties. But whereas specialization is of the nature of the applied sciences, it is a perversion of the disciplines of language and literature. When we understand and teach these as specialties, we submit willy-nilly to the assumption of the "practical men" of business, and also apparently of education, that literacy is no more than an ornament: when one has become an efficient integer of the economy, *then* it is permissible, even desirable, to be able to talk about the latest novels. After all, the disciples of "practicality" may someday find themselves stuck in conversation with an English teacher.

I may have oversimplified that line of thinking, but not much. There are two flaws in it. One is that, among the self-styled "practical men," the practical is synonymous with the immediate. The long-term effects of their values and their acts lie outside the boundaries of their interest. For such people a strip mine ceases to exist as soon as the coal has been extracted. Short-term practicality is long-term idiocy.

The other flaw is that language and literature are always *about* something else, and we have no way to predict or control what they may be about. They are about the world. We will understand the world, and preserve ourselves and our values in it, only insofar as we have a language that is alert and responsive to it, and careful of it. I mean that literally. When we give our plows such brand names as "Sod Blaster," we are imposing on their use conceptual limits which raise the likelihood that they will be used destructively. When we speak of man's "war against nature," or of a "peace offensive," we are accepting the limitations of a metaphor that suggests, and even proposes, violent solutions. When students ask for the right of "participatory input" at the meetings of a faculty organization, they are thinking of democratic process, but they are *speaking* of a convocation of robots, and are thus devaluing the very traditions that they invoke.

Ignorance of books and the lack of a critical consciousness of language were safe enough in primitive societies with coherent oral traditions. In our society, which exists in an atmosphere of prepared, public language—language that is either written or being read— illiteracy is both a personal and a public danger. Think how constantly "the average American" is surrounded by premeditated language, in newspapers and magazines, on signs and billboards, on TV and radio. He is forever being asked to buy or believe somebody else's line of goods. The line of goods is being sold, moreover, by men who are trained to make him buy it or believe it, whether or not he needs it or understands it or knows its value or wants it. This sort of selling is an honored profession among us. Parents who grow hysterical at the thought that their son might not cut his hair are *glad* to have him taught, and later employed, to lie about the quality of an automobile or the ability of a candidate.

What is our defense against this sort of language—this language-as-weapon? There is only one. We must know a better language. We must speak, and teach our children to speak, a language precise and articulate and lively enough to tell the truth about the world as we know it. And to do this we must know something of the roots and resources of our language; we must know its literature. The only defense against the worst is a knowledge of the best. By their ignorance people enfranchise their exploiters.

But to appreciate fully the necessity for the best sort of literacy we must consider not just the environment of prepared language in which most of us now pass most of our lives, but also the utter transience of most of this language, which is meant to be merely glanced at, or heard only once, or read once and thrown away. Such language is by definition, and often calculation, not memorable; it is language meant to be replaced by what will immediately follow it, like that of shallow conversation between strangers. It cannot be pondered or effectively criticized. For those reasons an unmixed diet of it is destructive of the informed, resilient, critical intelligence that the best of our traditions have sought to create and to maintain—an intelligence that Jefferson held to be indispensable to the health and longevity of freedom. Such intelligence does not grow by bloating upon the ephemeral information and misinformation of the public media. It grows by returning again and again to the landmarks of its cultural birthright, the works that have proved worthy of devoted attention.

"Read not the Times. Read the Eternities," Thoreau said. Ezra Pound wrote that "literature is news that STAYS news." In his lovely poem, "The Island," Edwin Muir spoke of man's inescapable cultural boundaries and of his consequent responsibility for his own sources and renewals:

> Men are made of what is made,
> The meat, the drink, the life, the corn,
> Laid up by them, in them reborn.
> And self-begotten cycles close
> About our way; indigenous art
> And simple spells make unafraid
> The haunted labyrinths of the heart . . .

These men spoke of a truth that no society can afford to shirk for long: we are dependent, for understanding, and for consolation and hope, upon what we learn of ourselves from songs and stories. This has always been so, and it will not change.

I am saying, then, that literacy—the mastery of language and the knowledge of books—is not an ornament, but a necessity. It is impractical only by the standards of quick profit and easy power. Longer perspective will show that it alone can preserve in us the possibility of an accurate judgment of ourselves, and the possibilities of correction and renewal. Without it, we are adrift in the present, in the wreckage of yesterday, in the nightmare of tomorrow. □

PATTERNS OF EXPOSITION

We have been concerned with patterns of organization that conform to familiar two- and three-part forms. Much of the writing we read and produce can be viewed from such a perspective. But we also need to consider the traditional patterns of exposition.

Exposition is simply writing that explains; expository discourse is another name for explanatory prose. Exposition, theoretically, can be distinguished from argumentative discourse in that the purpose of expository writing, strictly speaking, is not to convince but to explain. Its goal is not persuasion, the goal of argumentative writing, but rather clarification and understanding. Expository writing, however, is combined as frequently with argumentation as it is with description and narration—the two other common modes of discourse. Yet even though expository writing rarely exists in isolation (as it usually is pressed into the service of persuasion or is accompanied by narrative anecdote or descriptive detail), we can identify some prevailing features of exposition and some common patterns in which it often occurs.

Causal Analysis   One of the most common patterns of exposition is causal analysis, which involves assessing why something happened or developed the way it did. It is a way of explaining how or why something is the way it is. If you were to consider, for example, your reasons for attending college, including why you chose the school and program you did, you would be engaged in causal analysis. Your analysis and ensuing explanation could be simple and brief or elaborate and complex. It might consider remote and subtle causal factors as well as immediate and readily apparent ones. However elaborate and complicated you were to make it, your focus on why you came to X college would illustrate only one part of a causal analysis sequence. Its flip side would involve an analysis of the effects of your choice.

This second aspect of causal analysis concerns the consequences of an action or the effects of a situation. These include both present consequences and future ones. In considering the consequences of your decision to attend a particular college and pursue a specific program, you would be looking forward rather than back. You would analyze the results of your action. Writing that employs causal analysis can be confined to analysis of either cause or effects or it can combine the two. The following examples illustrate the common possibilities.

Fear of Dearth
Carll Tucker

I hate jogging. Every dawn, as I thud around New York City's Central Park reservoir, I am reminded of how much I hate it. It's so tedious. Some claim jogging is thought conducive; others insist the scenery relieves the monotony. For me, the pace is wrong for contemplation of either ideas or vistas. While jogging, all I can think about is jogging—or nothing. One advantage of jogging around a reservoir is that there's no dry-shortcut home.

From the listless looks of some fellow trotters, I gather I am not alone in my unenthusiasm: Bill-paying, it seems, would be about as diverting. Nonetheless, we continue to jog; more, we continue to *choose* to jog. From a practically infinite array of opportunities, we select one that we don't enjoy and can't wait to have done with. Why?

For any trend, there are as many reasons as there are participants. This person runs to lower his blood pressure. That person runs to escape the telephone or a cranky spouse or a filthy household. Another person runs to avoid doing anything else, to dodge a decision about how to lead his life or a realization that his life is leading nowhere. Each of us has his carrot and stick. In my case, the stick is my slackening physical condition, which keeps me from beating opponents at tennis whom I overwhelmed two years ago. My carrot is to win.

Beyond these disparate reasons, however, lies a deeper cause. It is no accident that now, in the last third of the 20th century, personal fitness and health have suddenly become a popular obsession. True, modern man likes to feel good, but that hardly distinguishes him from his predecessors.

With zany myopia, economists like to claim that the deeper cause of everything is economic. Delightfully, there seems no marketplace explanation for jogging. True, jogging is cheap, but then not jogging is cheaper. And the scant and skimpy equipment which jogging demands must make it a marketer's least favored form of recreation.

Some scout-masterish philosophers argue that the appeal of jogging and other body-maintenance programs is the discipline they afford. We live in a world in which individuals have fewer and fewer obligations. The work week has shrunk. Weekend worship is less compulsory. Technology gives us more free time. Satisfactorily filling free time requires imagination and effort. Freedom is a wide and risky river; it can drown the person who does not know how to swim across it. The more obligations one takes on, the more time one occupies, the less threat freedom poses. Jogging can become an instant obligation. For a portion of his day, the jogger is not his own man; he is obedient to a regimen he has accepted.

Theologists may take the argument one step further. It is our modern irreligion, our lack of confidence in any hereafter, that makes us anxious to stretch our mortal stay as long as possible. We run, as the saying goes, for our lives, hounded by the suspicion that these are the only lives we are likely to enjoy.

All of these theorists seem to me more or less right. As the growth of cults and charismatic religions and the resurgence of enthusiasm for the military draft suggest, we do crave commitment. And who can doubt, watching so many middle-aged and older persons torturing themselves in the name of fitness, that we are unreconciled to death, more so perhaps than any generation in modern memory?

But I have a hunch there's a further explanation of our obsession with exercise. I suspect that what motivates us even more than a fear of death is a fear of dearth. Our era is the first to anticipate the eventual depletion of all natural resources. We see wilderness shrinking; rivers losing their capacity to sustain life; the air, even the stratosphere, being loaded with potentially deadly junk. We see the irreplaceable being squandered, and in the depths of our consciousness we are fearful that we are creating an uninhabitable world. We feel more or less helpless and yet, at the same time, desirous to protect what resources we can. We recycle soda bottles and restore old buildings and protect our nearest natural resource—our physical health—in the almost superstitious hope that such small gestures will help save an earth that we are blighting. Jogging becomes a sort of penance for our sins of gluttony, greed, and waste. Like a hairshirt or a bed of nails, the more one hates it, the more virtuous it makes one feel.

That is why *we* jog. Why *I* jog is to win at tennis. ☐

Notice how Tucker's essay offers a variety of reasons for why people jog. He begins and ends with a simple, personal reason. In between he considers a broad range of explanations, some more complex, less immediately apparent, and less directly related to everyday experience than others. And notice, too, how the first paragraphs introduce the essay's subject and how the introduction ends with an invitation to consider the question of what makes joggers run. Finally, consider Tucker's conclusion—really a triple conclusion. The first of his final three concluding paragraphs offers one explanation—fear of death. The second offers an alternative reason—fear of "dearth"—really penance out of guilt for our destruction of the planet. And, finally, in a bit of humor, Tucker returns to his first simple, personal reason—he jogs to win at tennis.

The following selection about the destructive effects of nuclear weapons exemplifies another form in which causal analysis appears as a pattern of exposition. Unlike Tucker's causal analysis, which considered the causes or reasons why something is done, Schell examines the probable effects or consequences of an event. Although his piece is cast as a single long paragraph, we can divide it into four paragraphs—where you see the ¶, or paragraph indicator. There are at least two reasons Schell arranged his list of consequences as a single paragraph. First, the selection is excerpted from a longer essay, which includes many long paragraphs. His long paragraph here is thus consistent with his paragraphing style in the essay overall. Second, accumulating all the consequences together without giving us readers a chance to breathe is more emotionally affecting and more persuasive than a series of short paragraphs.

As you read Schell's selection consider the order of the consequences.

The Destructive Power of a One-Megaton Bomb on New York City
Jonathan Schell

One way to begin to grasp the destructive power of present-day nuclear weapons is to describe the consequences of the detonation of a one-megaton bomb, which possesses eighty times the explosive power of the Hiroshima bomb, on a large city, such as New York. Burst some eighty-five hundred feet above the Empire State Building, a one-megaton bomb would gut or flatten almost every building between Battery Park and 125th Street, or within a radius of four and four-tenths miles, or in an area of sixty-one square miles, and would heavily damage buildings between the northern tip of Staten Island and the George Washington Bridge, or within a radius of about eight miles, or in an area of about two hundred square miles. A conventional explosive delivers a swift shock, like a slap, to whatever it hits, but the blast wave of a sizable nuclear weapon endures for several seconds and can surround and destroy whole buildings. People, of course, would be picked up and hurled away from the blast along with the rest of the debris. Within the sixty-one square miles, the walls, roofs, and floors of any buildings that had not been flattened would be collapsed, and the people and furniture inside would be swept down onto the street. (Technically, this zone would be hit by various overpressures of at least five pounds per square inch. Overpressure is defined as the pressure in excess of normal atmospheric pressure.) ¶ As far away as ten miles from ground zero, pieces of glass and other sharp objects would be hurled about by the blast wave at lethal velocities. In Hiroshima, where buildings were low and, outside the center of the city, were often constructed of light materials, injuries from falling buildings were often minor. But in New York, where the buildings are tall and are constructed of heavy materials, the physical collapse of the city would certainly kill millions of people. ¶ The streets of New York are narrow ravines running between the high walls of the city's buildings. In a nuclear attack, the walls would fall and the ravines would fill up. The people in the buildings would fall to the street with the debris of the buildings, and the people in the street would be crushed by this avalanche of people and buildings. ¶ At a distance of two miles or so from ground zero, winds would reach four hundred miles an hour, and another two miles away they would reach a hundred and eighty miles an hour. Meanwhile, the fireball would be growing, until it was more than a mile wide, and rocketing upward, to a height of over six miles. For ten seconds, it would broil the city below. Anyone caught in the open within nine miles of ground zero would receive third-degree burns and would probably be killed; closer to the explosion, people would be charred and killed instantly. From Greenwich Village up to Central Park, the heat would be great enough to melt metal and glass. Readily inflammable materials, such as newspaper and dry leaves, would ignite in all five boroughs (though in only a small part of Staten Island) and west to the Passaic River, in New Jersey, within a radius of about nine and a half miles from ground zero, thereby creating an area of more than two hundred and eighty square miles in which mass fires were likely to break out. □

Essays arranged as causal analyses can be organized chronologically if a narrative explanation fits the facts (as it would for explaining how you ended up where you are today). But they might also take the form of a list of reasons arranged according to their order of importance or their degree of complexity. In any case, you would begin with a description of the situation or problem—the success of the Boston Celtics, for example, or the increase in the divorce rate. You would then follow up with a series of explanations for the causes of that success or that increase. (Or you could analyze the consequences of either.) How widely you range in your analysis of causes and/or effects and how deeply you probe involve both matters of practicality (your available time; the constraints of the assignment) and of intentionality (how specific you decide to get; how hard you want to think about the subject). In writing about divorce, for example, you could restrict your focus to the consequences of divorce for the children of broken marriages. Or you could extend the range of your analysis to include its effects on the divorced partners themselves, the effects on their families and friends, and possibly even the consequences for society.

Your decision about how narrowly to focus your analysis will also affect how you organize it. Generally speaking, any causal analysis, whether of causes, effects, or both, and no matter how narrowly focused, can be organized as a simple list or a sequence.

Exercises

1. Write an essay analyzing the causes of some social problem or issue—alcoholism, drunk driving, overpopulation, divorce, teenage suicide, for example.

2. Analyze the effects of a social problem—an increase in violent crime, an increase in unemployment, the rise of AIDS—or one of those mentioned in Exercise 1.

3. Discuss the causes and probable effects of an important decision you've made or will make in the future.

Causal analysis is more than a pattern of exposition. It is essentially a mode of thinking, specifically a type of analytical thinking. It is important to realize this, for it is true of the other patterns of exposition as well. Each is indeed a way to organize and arrange your ideas about a subject. But each is also a way for you to think about that subject and to generate ideas that you can organize into one of the expository structures.

Process Analysis   Causal analysis (or the cause–effect pattern of thinking and writing) can be thought of as a dynamic or progressive pattern. Why? Because it ranges over time; it explains events by considering their relation to one another both sequentially and logically. Another progressive pattern for thinking and organizing is that of process analysis.

In organizing an essay that describes a process you generally do one of two things: either you explain step-by-step how to do something or you explain, again one stage at a time, how something is done (or how it has come about). In the first case, you give directions; in the second, you offer an explanation. Along the way you may employ a narrative structure: first this, then that, then something else. Or you may present a list of things to do or a set of considerations to bear in mind, without insisting on a strictly prescribed order. Much of this book follows such a how-to principle. So does the following selection about how to write the headline for an advertisement, excerpted from the chapter "How to Write Potent Copy," from David Ogilvy's lively book, *Confessions of an Advertising Man.*

The headline is the most important element in most advertisements. It is the telegram which decides the reader whether to read the copy.

On the average, five times as many people read the headline as read the body copy. When you have written your headline, you have spent eighty cents out of your dollar.

If you haven't done some selling in your headline, you have wasted 80 percent of your client's money. The wickedest of all sins is to run an advertisement *without* a headline. Such headless wonders are still to be found; I don't envy the copywriter who submits one to me.

A change of headline can make a difference of ten to one in sales. I never write fewer than sixteen headlines for a single advertisement, and I observe certain guides in writing them:

1. The headline is the "ticket on the meat." Use it to flag down the readers who are prospects for the kind of product you are advertising. If you are selling a remedy for bladder weakness, display the words *"Bladder Weakness"* in your headline; they catch the eye of everyone who suffers from this inconvenience. If you want *mothers*

to read your advertisement, display *"Mothers"* in your headline. And so on.

Conversely, do not say anything in your headline which is likely to *exclude* any readers who might be prospects for your product. Thus, if you are advertising a product which can be used equally well by men and women, don't slant your headline at women alone; it would frighten men away.

2. Every headline should appeal to the reader's *self-interest.* It should promise her a benefit, as in my headline for Helena Rubinstein's Hormone Cream: "How Women over 35 Can Look Younger."

3. Always try to inject *news* into your headlines, or new ways to use an old product, or new improvements in an old product.

The two most powerful words you can use in a headline are "Free" and "New." You can seldom use "Free," but you can almost always use "New"—if you try hard enough.

4. Other words and phrases which work wonders are "How To," "Suddenly," "Now," "Announcing," "Introducing," "It's Here," "Just Arrived," "Important Development," "Improvement," "Amazing," "Sensational," "Remarkable," "Revolutionary," "Startling," "Miracle," "Magic," "Offer," "Quick," "Easy," "Wanted," "Challenge," "Advice to," "The Truth About," "Compare," "Bargain," "Hurry," "Last Chance."

Don't turn up your nose at these clichés. They may be shopworn, but they work. That is why you see them turn up so often in the headlines of mail-order advertisers and others who can measure the results of their advertisements.

Headlines can be strengthened by the inclusion of *emotional* words, like "Darling," "Love," "Fear," "Proud," "Friend," and "Baby." One of the most provocative advertisements which has come out of our agency showed a girl in a bathtub, talking to her lover on the telephone. The headline: *Darling, I'm having the most extraordinary experience . . . I'm head over heels in DOVE.*

5. Five times as many people read the headline as read the body copy, so it is important that these glancers should at least be told what brand is being advertised. That is why you should always include the brand name in your headlines.

6. Include your selling promise in your headline. This requires long headlines. When the New York University School of Retailing ran headline tests with the cooperation of a big department store,

they found that headlines of ten words or longer, containing news and information, consistently sold more merchandise than short headlines.

Headlines containing six to twelve words pull more coupon returns than short headlines, and there is no significant difference between the readership of twelve-word headlines and the readership of three-word headlines. The best headline I ever wrote contained *eighteen* words: *At Sixty Miles an Hour the Loudest Noise in the New Rolls-Royce comes from the electric clock.*

7. People are more likely to read your body copy if your headline arouses their curiosity; so you should end your headline with a lure to read on.

8. Some copywriters write *tricky* headlines—puns, literary allusions, and other obscurities. This is a sin.

In the average newspaper your headline has to compete for attention with 350 others. Research has shown that readers travel so fast through this jungle that they don't stop to decipher the meaning of obscure headlines. Your headline must *telegraph* what you want to say, and it must telegraph it in plain language. Don't play games with the reader.

In 1960 the *Times Literary Supplement* attacked the whimsical tradition in British advertising, calling it "self-indulgent—a kind of middle-class private joke, apparently designed to amuse the advertiser and his client." Amen.

9. Research shows that it is dangerous to use *negatives* in headlines. If, for example, you write "Our Salt Contains No Arsenic," many readers will miss the negative and go away with the impression that you wrote "Our Salt Contains Arsenic."

10. Avoid *blind* headlines—the kind which mean nothing unless you read the body copy underneath them; most people *don't.* ☐

Exercises

1. Ogilvy organizes his discussion as a simple list. Reorganize it by consolidating his points into fewer paragraphs. Decide on a logical structure for your reordering.

2. Write an essay explaining how to perform some process you are familiar with. Examples: how to parallel ski, do a back flip, bake cookies, lose weight, get or break a date, study for an exam, do the breast stroke. Break the activity down into steps, stages, or parts. Put them in order. And explain how to get from one part or stage to another.

The following selection illustrates our alternative process analysis—the "how-it-is-done" approach.

How Dictionaries Are Made

S. I. Hayakawa

It is widely believed that every word has a correct meaning, that we learn these meanings principally from teachers and grammarians (except that most of the time we don't bother to, so that we ordinarily speak "sloppy English"), and that dictionaries and grammars are the supreme authority in matters of meaning and usage. Few people ask by what authority the writers of dictionaries and grammars say what they say. I once got into a dispute with an Englishwoman over the pronunciation of a word and offered to look it up in the dictionary. The Englishwoman said firmly, "What for? I am English. I was born and brought up in England. The way I speak *is* English." Such self-assurance about one's own language is not uncommon among the English. In the United States, however, anyone who is willing to quarrel with the dictionary is regarded as either eccentric or mad.

Let us see how dictionaries are made and how the editors arrive at definitions. What follows applies, incidentally, only to those dictionary offices where first-hand, original research goes on—not those in which editors simply copy existing dictionaries. The task of writing a dictionary begins with reading vast amounts of the literature of the period or subject that the dictionary is to cover. As the editors read, they copy on cards every interesting or rare word, every unusual or peculiar occurrence of a common word, a large number of common words in their ordinary uses, and also the sentences in which each of these words appear, thus:

pail
The dairy *pails* bring home increase of milk
Keats, *Endymion* I, 44–45

That is to say, the context of each word is collected, along with the word itself. For a really big job of dictionary-writing, such as the *Oxford English Dictionary* (usually bound in about twenty-five volumes), millions of such cards are collected, and the task of editing occupies decades. As the cards are collected, they are alphabetized and sorted. When the sorting is completed, there will be for each word anywhere from two or three to several hundred illustrative quotations, each on its card.

To define a word, then, the dictionary-editor places before him the stack of cards illustrating that word; each of the cards represents an actual use of the word by a writer of some literary or historical importance. He reads the cards carefully, discards some, rereads the rest, and divides up the stack according to what he thinks are the several senses of the word. Finally, he writes his definitions, following the hard-and-fast rule that each definition *must* be based on what the quotations in front of him reveal about the meaning of the word. The editor cannot be influenced by what *he* thinks a given word *ought* to mean. He must work according to the cards or not at all.

The writing of a dictionary, therefore, is not a task of setting up authoritative statements about the "true meanings" of words, but a task of *recording*, to the best of one's ability, what various words *have meant* to authors in the distant or immediate past. *The writer of a dictionary is a historian, not a lawgiver.* If, for example, we had been writing a dictionary in 1890, or even as late as 1919, we could have said that the word "broadcast" means "to scatter" (seed, for example), but we could not have decreed that from 1921 on, the most common meaning of the word should become "to disseminate audible messages, etc., by radio transmission." To regard the dictionary as an "authority," therefore, is to credit the dictionary-writer with gifts of prophecy which neither he nor anyone else possesses. In choosing our words when we speak or write, we can be *guided* by the historical record afforded us by the dictionary, but we cannot be *bound* by it, because new situations, new experiences, new inventions, new feelings are always compelling us to give new uses to old words. Looking under a "hood," we should ordinarily have found, five hundred years ago, a monk; today, we find a motorcar engine. □

Exercises

1. Explain how Hayakawa goes about correcting a popular misconception. Notice his use of contrast and example to clarify his point.

2. Outline the process of making a dictionary.

3. Write an essay explaining how something—beer, ice cream, wine, cola, pizza—is made. Or explain how something—a VCR, pinball machine, automobile engine, camera, telephone, sewing machine— works. Or explain how something is done: how birds build nests, how whales feed (or spiders or hummingbirds), how pictures are developed, how crabs mate, how movie sets are built, how the football draft (NFL) is conducted, how an orchestra or band rehearses for a performance.

Complementing the progressive expository patterns are the synchronic or static patterns of exposition—illustration, comparison and contrast, analogy, and classification. Unlike process and causal analysis, these patterns of thinking and writing are nonprogressive; they do not require establishing a time frame or sequence of actions, steps, or stages. They do, however, exhibit another characteristic— repetition—and hence can be described as repetitive patterns. The simplest and perhaps the most familiar of these is illustration or exemplification.

Illustration/Exemplification   To illustrate means to clarify by providing an example, a specific instance of a point or general idea. When you illustrate, you illuminate your point, shedding light on your subject. In the process you gain your readers' understanding. In organizing a piece of writing illustratively you will have to decide how many examples you will need to make your point and how extensively to develop each.

Consider the use of example in the following passage.

Animal Aid
Michel de Montaigne

As for the society and confederation that they form among themselves to league together and assist one another, it may be seen of oxen, hogs, and other animals that at the call of the one you injure, all the herd runs up to his aid and rallies in his defense. When the parrot fish has swallowed the fisherman's hook, his comrades gather in a swarm around him and gnaw through the line; and if by chance there is one that has got into the net, the others offer him their tail from outside, and he grips it as tight as he can with his teeth; thus they drag him out and take him away. Barbels, when one of their comrades is caught, set the line against their back, raising a spine they have which is toothed like a saw, and with which they saw it and cut it.

As for the particular aids we receive from one another in the service of life, many similar examples are seen among them. They maintain that the whale never moves unless it has ahead of it a little fish resembling the sea gudgeon, which for this reason is called the *guide*. The whale follows it, letting itself be led and turned as easily as the tiller turns the boat; and in recompense for this, whereas everything else, whether beast or vessel, that enters the horrible chaos of this monster's mouth, is straightway engulfed and lost, this little fish retires into it in all security and sleeps there, and during its sleep the whale does not budge. But as soon as it comes out, the whale starts in to follow it without stopping, and if by chance it loses the guide, it goes wandering here and there, and often bruising itself against the rocks, like a vessel that has no rudder. □

Montaigne's examples are more numerous and varied in the first of his two paragraphs. The opening sentence makes the point that animals help one another in time of trouble. Montaigne announces the idea while pointing in passing to the two examples of oxen and hogs. The second and third sentences of the first paragraph provide two more fully explained examples: parrot fish and barbels. The second paragraph continues support of the point with a still more elaborately developed example: the whale and its little guide. This last example makes the additional specific point that the relationship is mutually beneficial for the whale and its small companion.

In the same way that Montaigne organizes a paragraph through the framework of example we outlined above, you can organize an essay in a similar fashion. You could, for example, to suggest the most common pattern, structure your essay this way:

- *Opening paragraph*—Introduction to the subject and main idea.

- *Second paragraph*—First example or series of brief examples.

- *Third paragraph*—Second example or series of brief examples.

- *Fourth paragraph*—Third example or series of brief examples (through the final paragraph).

- *Final paragraph*—Final example—most important, extensive, or complex (final paragraph may be devoted to final example or may be a special "conclusion").

The following essay provides a clear example of this method.

Courtship Through the Ages
James Thurber

Surely nothing in the astonishing scheme of life can have non-plussed Nature so much as the fact that none of the females of any of the species she created really cared very much for the male, as such. For the past ten million years Nature has been busily inventing ways to make the male attractive to the female, but the whole business of courtship, from the marine annelids up to man, still lumbers heavily along, like a complicated musical comedy. I have been reading the sad and absorbing story in Volume 6 (Cole to Dama) of the *Encyclopaedia Britannica*. In this volume you can learn all about cricket, cotton, costume designing, crocodiles, crown jewels, and Coleridge, but none of these subjects is so interesting as the Courtship of Animals, which recounts the sorrowful lengths to which all males must go to arouse the interest of a lady.

We all know, I think, that Nature gave man whiskers and a mustache with the quaint idea in mind that these would prove attractive to the female. We all know that, far from attracting her, whiskers and mustaches only made her nervous and gloomy, so that man had to go in for somersaults, tilting with lances, and performing feats of parlor magic to win her attention; he also had to bring her candy, flowers, and the furs of animals. It is common knowledge that in spite of all these "love displays" the male is constantly being turned down, insulted, or thrown out of the house. It is rather comforting, then, to discover that the peacock, for all his gorgeous plumage, does not have a particularly easy time in courtship; none of the males in the world do. The first peahen, it turned out, was only faintly stirred by her suitor's beautiful train. She would often go quietly to sleep while he was whisking it around. The *Britannica* tells us that the peacock actually had to learn a certain little trick to wake her up and revive her interest: he had to learn to vibrate his quills so as to make a rustling sound. In ancient times man himself, observing the ways of the peacock, probably tried vibrating his whiskers to make a rustling sound; if so, it didn't get him anywhere. He had to go in for something else; so, among other things, he went in for gifts. It is not unlikely that he got this idea from certain flies and birds who were making no headway at all with rustling sounds.

One of the flies of the family Empidae, who had tried everything, finally hit on something pretty special. He contrived to make a glistening transparent balloon which was even larger than himself. Into this he would put sweetmeats and tidbits and he would carry the whole elaborate envelope through the air to the lady of his choice. This amused her for a time, but she finally got bored with it. She demanded silly little colorful presents, something that you couldn't eat but that would look nice around the house. So the male Empis had to go around gathering flower petals and pieces of bright paper to put into his balloon. On a courtship flight a male Empis cuts quite a figure now, but he can hardly be said to be happy. He never knows how soon the female will demand heavier presents, such as Roman coins and gold collar buttons. It seems probable that one day the courtship of the Empidae will fall down, as man's occasionally does, of its own weight.

The bowerbird is another creature that spends so much time courting the female that he never gets any work done. If all the male bowerbirds became nervous wrecks within the next ten or fifteen years, it would not surprise me. The female bowerbird insists that a playground be built for her with a specially constructed bower at the entrance. This bower is much more elaborate than an ordinary nest and is harder to build; it costs a lot more, too. The female will not come to the playground until the male has filled it up with a great many gifts: silvery leaves, red leaves, rose petals, shells, beads, berries, bones, dice, buttons, cigar bands, Christmas seals, and the Lord knows what else. When the female finally condescends to visit the playground, she is in a coy and silly mood and has to be chased in and out of the bower and up and down the playground before she will quit giggling and stand still long enough even to shake hands. The male bird is, of course, pretty well done in before the chase starts, because he has worn himself out hunting for eyeglass lenses and begonia blossoms. I imagine that many a bowerbird, after chasing a female for two or three hours, says the hell with it and goes home to bed. Next day, of course, he telephones someone else and the same trying ritual is gone through again. A male bowerbird is as exhausted as a night-club habitué before he is out of his twenties.

The male fiddler crab has a somewhat easier time, but it can hardly be said that he is sitting pretty. He has one enormously large and powerful claw, usually brilliantly colored, and you might suppose that all he had to do was reach out and grab some passing cutie. The very earliest fiddler crabs may have tried this, but, if so, they got slapped for their pains. A female crab will not tolerate any caveman stuff; she never has and she doesn't intend to start now. To attract a female, a fiddler crab has to stand on tiptoe and brandish his claw in the air. If any female in the neighborhood is interested— and you'd be surprised how many are not—she comes over and engages him in light badinage, for which he is not in the mood. As many as a hundred females may pass the time of day with him and go on about their business. By nightfall of an average courting day, a fiddler crab who has been standing on tiptoe for eight or ten hours waving a heavy claw in the air is in pretty sad shape. As in the case of the males of all species, however, he gets out of bed next morning, dashes some water on his face, and tries again.

The next time you encounter a male web-spinning spider, stop and reflect that he is too busy worrying about his love life to have any desire to bite you. Male web-spinning spiders have a tougher life than any other males in the animal kingdom. This is because the female web-spinning spiders have very poor eyesight. If a male lands on a female's web, she kills him before he has time to lay down his cane and gloves, mistaking him for a fly or a bumblebee who has tumbled into her trap. Before the species figured out what to do about this, millions of males were murdered by ladies they called on. It is the nature of spiders to perform a little dance in front of the female, but before a male spinner could get near enough for the female to see who he was and what he was up to, she would lash out at him with a flat-iron or a pair of garden shears. One night, nobody knows when, a very bright male spinner lay awake worrying about calling on a lady who had been killing suitors right and left. It came to him that this business of dancing as a love display wasn't getting anybody anywhere except the grave. He decided to go in for web-twitching, or strand-vibrating. The next day he tried it on one of the nearsighted girls. Instead of dropping in on her suddenly, he stayed outside the web and began monkeying with one of its strands. He twitched it up and down and in and out with such a lilting rhythm that the female was charmed. The serenade worked beautifully; the female let him live. The *Britannica*'s spider-watchers, however, report that this system is not always successful. Once in a while, even now, a female will fire three bullets into a suitor or run him through with a kitchen knife. She keeps threatening him from the moment he strikes the first low notes on the outside strings, but usually by the time he has got up to the high notes played around the center of the web, he is going to town and she spares his life.

Even the butterfly, as handsome a fellow as he is, can't always win a mate merely by fluttering around and showing off. Many butterflies have to have scent scales on their wings. Hepialus carries a powder puff in a perfumed pouch. He throws perfume at the ladies when they pass. The male tree cricket, Oecanthus, goes Hepialus one better by carrying a tiny bottle of wine with him and giving drinks to such doxies as he has designs on. One of the male snails throws darts to entertain the girls. So it goes, through the long list of animals, from the bristle worm and his rudimentary dance steps to man and his gift of diamonds and sapphires. The golden-eye drake raises a jet of water with his feet as he flies over a lake; Hepialus has his powder puff, Oecanthus his wine bottle, man his etchings. It is a bright and melancholy story, the age-old desire of the male for the female, the age-old desire of the female to be amused and entertained. Of all the creatures on earth, the only males who could be figured as putting any irony into their courtship are the grebes and certain other diving birds. Every now and then a courting grebe slips quietly down to the bottom of a lake and then, with a mighty "Whoosh!," pops out suddenly a few feet from his girl friend, splashing water all over her. She seems to be persuaded that this is a purely loving display, but I like to think that the grebe always has a faint hope of drowning her or scaring her to death.

I will close this investigation into the mournful burdens of the male with the *Britannica*'s story about a certain Argus pheasant. It appears that the Argus displays himself in front of a female who stands perfectly still without moving a feather. . . . The male Argus the *Britannica* tells about was confined in a cage with a female of another species, a female who kept moving around, emptying ash-trays and fussing with lampshades all the time the male was show-ing off his talents. Finally, in disgust, he stalked away and began displaying in front of his water trough. He reminds me of a certain male (Homo sapiens) of my acquaintance who one night after dinner asked his wife to put down her detective magazine so that he could read her a poem of which he was very fond. She sat quietly enough until he was well into the middle of the thing, intoning with great ardor and intensity. Then suddenly there came a sharp, disconcert-ing *slap!* It turned out that all during the male's display, the female had been intent on a circling mosquito and had finally trapped it between the palms of her hands. The male in this case did not stalk away and display in front of a water trough; he went over to Tim's and had a flock of drinks and recited the poem to the fellas. I am sure they all told bitter stories of their own about how their displays had been interrupted by females. I am also sure that they all ended up singing "Honey, Honey, Bless Your Heart." □

Exercises

1. Outline the structure of Thurber's essay. Identify Thurber's use of extended example and his use of multiple brief examples. Consider how he orders his examples. Why, for example, does he place the fiddler crab after the bowerbird and before the spider?

2. How many extended examples does Thurber use? Would more or fewer have been more effective?

3. How many examples are included in paragraph 7? How do these examples differ from those included before and after?

4. Write a paragraph in which you use examples to develop your point.

Make your first sentence a statement of this general point or idea. For example, your first sentence might be something like one of these:

> Animals have been known to aid men in a variety of ways.
> Fashion trends today are moving away from _____ and toward _____.
> Baseball is a game of inches.
> _____ is a game of _____.
> Best selling books (movies) (cars) appeal to one of _____things: _____, _____, and _____.

5. Write an essay in which you develop a generalization by means of exemplification. Decide how many examples to use, how extensively to present each, and what order to put them in. Some possible subjects:

> The importance of some invention or discovery
> The danger of or necessity for some change (in society, in your own life)
> A striking tendency in popular music or in current films
> Some important facet of education and learning
> A social problem

Comparison More complex than illustration, comparison requires seeing two things simultaneously—or seeing two aspects of a thing. When we compare, we set one thing off against another to gain a clearer picture of both. We compare partly because our minds are built to see things in relation to one another, partly because we have been taught to do so, and partly because comparison is a practical method for arriving at decisions (which college to attend, which car to buy, where to go for vacation). Comparison is thus both a natural and an efficient way for us to organize our thinking in writing.

In structuring an essay around a comparative analysis, you can proceed basically in one of two ways. You can discuss each of the two halves of the comparison separately, one after the other. Or you can discuss them alternately, moving back and forth between them. The first approach, called the block method, is simpler. It looks like this:

Introduction
Subject A

Subject B
Conclusion

The other organizational strategy for comparison, the alternating method, is set up generally like this:

Introduction
Point 1: Subjects A and B
Point 2: Subjects A and B
Point 3: Subjects A and B
Final point: Subjects A and B
Conclusion

Here is an example of the block method as exemplified by the historian Bruce Catton in a comparison of two Civil War generals, Robert E. Lee and Ulysses S. Grant.

Back of Robert E. Lee was the notion that the old aristocratic concept might somehow survive and be dominant in American life.

Lee was tidewater Virginia, and in his background were family, culture, and tradition . . . the age of chivalry transplanted to a New World which was making its own legends and its own myths. He embodied a way of life that had come down through the age of knighthood and the English country squire. America was a land that was beginning all over again, dedicated to nothing much more complicated than the rather hazy belief that all men had equal rights, and should have an equal chance in the world. In such a land Lee stood for the feeling that it was somehow of advantage to human society to have a pronounced inequality in the social structure. There should be a leisure class, backed by ownership of land; in turn, society itself should be keyed to the land as the chief source of wealth and influence. It would bring forth (according to this ideal) a class of men with a strong sense of obligation to the community; men who lived not to gain advantage for themselves, but to meet the solemn obligations which had been laid on them by the very fact that they were privileged. From them the country would get its leadership; to them it could look for the higher values—of thought, of conduct, of personal deportment—to give it strength and virtue.

Lee embodied the noblest elements of this aristocratic ideal. Through him, the landed nobility justified itself. For four years, the

Southern states had fought a desperate war to uphold the ideals for which Lee stood. In the end, it almost seemed as if the Confederacy fought for Lee; as if he himself was the Confederacy . . . the best thing that the way of life for which the Confederacy stood could ever have to offer. He had passed into legend before Appomattox. Thousands of tired, underfed, poorly clothed Confederate soldiers, long-since past the simple enthusiasm of the early days of the struggle, somehow considered Lee the symbol of everything for which they had been willing to die. But they could not quite put this feeling into words. If the Lost Cause, sanctified by so much heroism and so many deaths, had a living justification, its justification was General Lee.

Grant, the son of a tanner on the Western frontier, was everything Lee was not. He had come up the hard way, and embodied nothing in particular except the eternal toughness and sinewy fiber of the men who grew up beyond the mountains. He was one of a body of men who owed reverence and obeisance to no one, who were self-reliant to a fault, who cared hardly anything for the past but who had a sharp eye for the future.

These frontier men were the precise opposites of the tidewater aristocrats. Back of them, in the great surge that had taken people over the Alleghenies and into the opening Western country, there was a deep, implicit dissatisfaction with a past that had settled into grooves. They stood for democracy, not from any reasoned conclusion about the proper ordering of human society, but simply because they had grown up in the middle of democracy and knew how it worked. Their society might have privileges, but they would be privileges each man had won for himself. Forms and patterns meant nothing. No man was born to anything, except perhaps to a chance to show how far he could rise. Life was competition.

Yet along with this feeling had come a deep sense of belonging to a national community. The Westerner who developed a farm, opened a shop or set up in business as a trader, could hope to prosper only as his own community prospered—and his community ran from the Atlantic to the Pacific and from Canada down to Mexico. If the land was settled, with towns and highways and accessible markets, he could better himself. He saw his fate in terms of the nation's own destiny. As its horizons expanded, so did his. He had, in other words, an acute dollars-and-cents stake in the continued growth and development of his country.

And that, perhaps, is where the contrast between Grant and Lee becomes most striking. The Virginia aristocrat, inevitably, saw himself in relation to his own region. He lived in a static society which could endure almost anything except change. Instinctively, his first loyalty would go to the locality in which that society existed. He would fight to the limit of endurance to defend it, because in defending it he was defending everything that gave his own life its deepest meaning.

The Westerner, on the other hand, would fight with an equal tenacity for the broader concept of society. He fought so because everything he lived by was tied to growth, expansion, and a constantly widening horizon. What he lived by would survive or fall with the nation itself. He could not possibly stand by unmoved in the face of an attempt to destroy the Union. He would combat it with everything he had, because he could only see it as an effort to cut the ground out from under his feet.

So Grant and Lee were in complete contrast, representing two diametrically opposed elements in American life. Grant was the modern man emerging; beyond him, ready to come on the stage, was the great age of steel and machinery, of crowded cities and a restless, burgeoning vitality. Lee might have ridden down from the old age of chivalry, lance in hand, silken banner fluttering over his head. Each man was the perfect champion of his cause, drawing both his strengths and his weaknesses from the people he led. □

Notice how Catton first presents a large chunk of information about Lee, then follows with a similarly large chunk about Grant. Notice also how he clearly establishes the basis for the comparison (essentially a contrast since differences are paramount). Notice, too, how Catton continues the discussion by presenting additional briefer chunks of explanation about each general, first one then the other. And notice, finally, that Catton employs comparison/contrast as an organizational technique to make a point.

In the next example, John McPhee compares oranges from Florida with those from California. His procedure differs from Catton's: where Catton chunks his explanation, McPhee alternates his description in a sequence of points that refer to both Florida and California oranges.

An orange grown in Florida usually has a thin and tightly fitting skin, and it is also heavy with juice. Californians say that if you want to eat a Florida orange you have to get into a bathtub first. California oranges are light in weight and have thick skins that break easily and come off in hunks. The flesh inside is marvelously sweet, and the segments almost separate themselves. In Florida, it is said that you can run over a California orange with a ten-ton truck and not even wet the pavement. The differences from which these hyperboles arise will prevail in the two states even if the type of orange is the same. In arid climates, like California's, oranges develop a thick albedo, which is the white part of the skin. Florida is one of the two or three most rained-upon states in the United States. California uses the Colorado River and similarly impressive sources to irrigate its oranges, but of course irrigation can only do so much. The annual difference in rainfall between the Florida and California orange-growing areas is one million one hundred and forty thousand gallons per acre. For years, California was the leading orange growing state, but Florida surpassed California in 1942, and grows three times as many oranges now. California oranges, for their part, can safely be called three times as beautiful. □

Analogy   Analogy can be seen as a form of extended illustration but even more as a partial similarity or correspondence between two things. Analogy is a special form of comparison. The human heart, for example, can be compared with a pump; the Christian church with the human body; writing a book with building a house. In developing an analogy in a piece of writing, make sure that you clearly establish the basis for the analogy, and that you also specify the features shared by both elements of your comparison. Be careful of two of the major pitfalls of analogizing: pushing the analogy beyond the bounds of credibility and using the analogy as an instrument of argument rather than as an illustrative device. Study the following examples to see analogy at work.

A River Pilot's Knowledge
Mark Twain

There is one faculty which a [steamboat] pilot must incessantly cultivate until he has brought it to absolute perfection. Nothing

1. Edgar Degas. *The Bellelli Family.* 1859. Oil on canvas, 78¾ by 99½ inches. Musée d'Orsay, Paris. (Giraudon/Art Resource.)

2. Charles Willson Peale. *The Peale Family.* 1773 and 1809. Oil on canvas, 56½ by 88¾ inches. The New-York Historical Society, New York City.

3. George Tooker. *The Subway.* 1950. Egg tempera on composition board, 18⅛ by 36⅛ inches. Whitney Museum of American Art, New York. Juliana Force purchase.

4. Domenico Ghirlandaio. *Francesco Sassetti and His Son Teodoro.* 1472.
Tempera on wood, 29½ by 20½ inches. Metropolitan Museum of Art,
New York. The Jules S. Bache Collection, 1949.

5. Thomas Eakins. *Miss Van Buren.* About 1889–91. Oil on canvas, 45 by 32 inches. The Phillips Collection, Washington, D.C.

6. Peter Paul Rubens. *Susanna Fourment.* About 1620–25. Oil on panel, 31½ by 21½ inches. The National Gallery, London. (Scala/Art Resource.)

7. Pablo Picasso. *Three Musicians.* 1921. Oil on canvas, 79 by 87¾ inches. Museum of Modern Art, New York. (Giraudon/Art Resource/ARS NY/ Spadem, 1988.)

8. Berthe Morisot. *The Cradle.* 1833. Oil on canvas, 22 by 18⅛ inches. Musée d'Orsay, Paris. (Scala/Art Resource.)

9. Paul Cezanne. *Mont Sainte-Victoire.* 1902–04. Oil on canvas, 27½ by 35¼ inches. Philadelphia Museum of Art. Purchased by the George W. Elkins Collection.

10. Pierre Auguste Renoir. *Portrait of Madame Renoir.* About 1885. Oil on canvas, 25¾ by 21¼ inches. Philadelphia Museum of Art. W. P. Wilstach Collection.

short of perfection will do. That faculty is memory. He cannot stop with merely thinking a thing is so and so: he must *know* it; for this is eminently one of the "exact" sciences. With what scorn a pilot was looked upon, in the old times, if he ever ventured to deal in that feeble phrase "I think," instead of the vigorous one "I know!" One cannot easily realize what a tremendous thing it is to know every trivial detail of 1200 miles of river and know it with absolute exactness. If you will take the longest street in New York, and travel up and down it, conning its features patiently until you know every house and window and door and lamp-post and big and little sign by heart, and know them so accurately that you can instantly name the one you are abreast of when you are set down at random in that street in the middle of an inky black night, you will then have a tolerable notion of the amount and the exactness of a pilot's knowledge who carries the Mississippi River in his head. And then if you will go on until you know every street crossing, the character, size, and position of the crossing-stones, and the varying depth of mud in each of those numberless places, you will have some idea of what the pilot must know in order to keep a Mississippi steamer out of trouble. Next, if you will take half of the signs in that long street, and *change their places* once a month, and still manage to know their positions accurately on dark nights, and keep up with these repeated changes without making any mistakes, you will understand what is required of a pilot's peerless memory by the fickle Mississippi. □

Twain uses analogy to give us a sense of how good a pilot's memory has to be. To help us understand something unfamiliar, he compares it to something we already know about. Moreover, he extends the analogy far enough to successfully illustrate the scope of the pilot's problem. But he doesn't use the analogy as a form of argument, merely as an illustration to clarify the point.

In the next more elaborately developed example, Henry David Thoreau describes a confrontation between two species of ant. Notice how he sustains throughout his description an analogy between the ant battle and human warfare. Consider, as you read, what Thoreau is saying about both ants and men by means of his analogy.

The Battle of the Ants
Henry David Thoreau

One day when I went out to my wood-pile, or rather my pile of stumps, I observed two large ants, the one red, the other much larger, nearly half an inch long, and black, fiercely contending with one another. Having once got hold they never let go, but struggled and wrestled and rolled on the chips incessantly. Looking farther, I was surprised to find that the chips were covered with such combatants, that it was not a *duellum*, but a *bellum*, a war between two races of ants, the red always pitted against the black, and frequently two red ones to one black. The legions of these Myrmidons covered all the hills and vales in my woodyard, and the ground was already strewn with the dead and dying, both red and black. It was the only battle which I have ever witnessed, the only battle-field I ever trod while the battle was raging; internecine war; the red republicans on the one hand, the black imperialists on the other. On every side they were engaged in deadly combat, yet without any noise that I could hear, and human soldiers never fought so resolutely. I watched a couple that were fast locked in each other's embraces, in a little sunny valley amid the chips, now at noonday prepared to fight till the sun went down, or life went out. The smaller red champion had fastened himself like a vise to his adversary's front, and through all the tumblings on that field never for an instant ceased to gnaw at one of his feelers near the root, having already caused the other to go by the board; while the stronger black one dashed him from side to side, and, as I saw on looking nearer, had already divested him of several of his members. They fought with more pertinacity than bulldogs. Neither manifested the least disposition to retreat. It was evident that their battle-cry was "Conquer or die." In the meanwhile there came along a single red ant on the hillside of this valley, evidently full of excitement, who either had dispatched his foe, or had not yet taken part in the battle; probably the latter, for he had lost none of his limbs; whose mother had charged him to return with his shield or upon it. Or perchance he was some Achilles, who had nourished his wrath apart, and had now come to avenge or rescue his Patroclus. He saw this unequal combat from afar,—for the blacks were nearly twice the size of the red,—he drew near with rapid pace till he stood on his guard within half an inch of the combatants;

then, watching his opportunity, he sprang upon the black warrior, and commenced his operations near the root of his right fore leg, leaving the foe to select among his own members; and so there were three united for life, as if a new kind of attraction had been invented which put all other locks and cements to shame. I should not have wondered by this time to find that they had their respective musical bands stationed on some eminent chip, and playing their national airs the while, to excite the slow and cheer the dying combatants. I was myself excited somewhat even as if they had been men. The more you think of it, the less the difference. And certainly there is not the fight recorded in Concord history, at least, if in the history of America, that will bear a moment's comparison with this, whether for the numbers engaged in it, or for the patriotism and heroism displayed. For numbers and for carnage it was an Austerlitz or Dresden. Concord fight! Two killed on the patriot's side, and Luther Blanchard wounded! Why here every ant was a Buttrick,— "Fire, for God's sake fire!"—and thousands shared the fate of Davis and Hosmer. There was not one hireling there. I have no doubt that it was a principle they fought for, as much as our ancestors, and not to avoid a three-penny tax on their tea; and the results of this battle will be as important and memorable to those whom it concerns as those of the battle of Bunker Hill, at least.

I took up the chip on which the three I have particularly described were struggling, carried it into my house, and placed it under a tumbler on my window-sill, in order to see the issue. Holding a microscope to the first-mentioned red ant, I saw that, though he was assiduously gnawing at the near fore leg of his enemy, having severed his remaining feeler, his own breast was all torn away, exposing what vitals he had there to the jaws of the black warrior, whose breastplate was apparently too thick for him to pierce; and the dark carbuncles of the sufferer's eyes shone with ferocity such as war only could excite. They struggled half an hour longer under the tumbler, and when I looked again the black soldier had severed the heads of his foes from their bodies, and the still living heads were hanging on either side of him like ghastly trophies at his saddle-bow, still apparently as firmly fastened as ever, and he was endeavoring with feeble struggles, being without feelers and with only the remnant of a leg, and I know not how many other wounds, to divest himself of them; which at length, after half an hour more, he accomplished. I raised the glass, and he went off over the window-sill in that crippled state. Whether he finally survived that combat, and spent the remainder of his days in some Hôtel des Invalides, I do not know; but I thought that his industry would not be worth much thereafter. I never learned which party was victorious, nor the cause of the war; but I felt for the rest of that day as if I had had my feelings excited and harrowed by witnessing the struggle, the ferocity and carnage of a human battle before my door. □

Exercises

1. Write a paragraph comparing two things on the basis of one common feature. Stress the similarities. Examples: athletes and dancers; eating and learning; working and playing.

2. Write a paragraph contrasting two things. Stress their differences. Examples: the feeding habits of dogs and cats; the behavior of dogs and cats; training versus education; age and youth.

3. Write an essay using comparison/contrast to develop and organize your thinking about an idea. Decide whether to use the block or the alternating structure. Be sure to make a point. Some possible topics: your past and your future; two compact cars (or luxury or sports cars); two contact sports; two board games; two bosses you've worked for or two teachers you have had; two jobs you've had.

4. Write a paragraph developing an analogy between two different things that share one or more common features. Possible topics: crime and disease; education and work; education and play; love and madness; writing and running.

5. Write an essay grounded in an analogy that can be extensively developed.

Classification   Classification can be seen in relation to the other patterns of exposition. Like comparison, classification requires a close look at more than one thing or aspect of a thing. Like causal analysis, it requires the making of careful distinctions and the avoidance of oversimplified explanations.

To classify means to group or categorize. Classified ads organize goods for sale and services for hire. There you can find listings for houses and apartments for rent and sale; cars both new and used for sale or lease; jobs and merchandise. Each section of the classifieds is subdivided into smaller categories based on such things as location (for houses); size (for apartments); type of merchandise (cars: domestic/imported).

We ourselves can be classified in a variety of ways: according to sex, race, religion, socioeconomic status, body build, age, blood type, intellectual and emotional propensities, and so on. We are also familiar with classification as an act of mind by which we organize, construe, and make sense of our experience. That is, when we confront an unfamiliar event or situation, we make sense of it largely by classifying it. We see and understand things as types of something—or we don't understand and see them at all. We categorize according to the types or genres we are already familiar with. In sizing up a new film, for example, we classify it as an adventure movie, a comedy, a police drama, and so on.

Classification enables us to organize information, to order masses of data and experience that would otherwise overwhelm us with their volume and confuse us with their variety. Classification also enables us to divide and organize experience in more than one way. That is, the bases for organizing, categorizing, classifying are various, multiple, and fluid rather than fixed, determined, and static. We can classify cars, for example, according to size, speed, gas mileage, sex appeal, cost; we can classify sports according to their organization of time and space, their degree of physical contact, their use of equipment, their popularity.

Here's an example of classification at work in a paragraph.

The Three New Yorks
E. B. White

There are roughly three New Yorks. There is, first, the New York of the man or woman who was born here, who takes the city for granted and accepts its size and its turbulence as natural and inevitable. Second, there is the New York of the commuter—the city that is devoured by locusts each day and spat out each night. Third, there is a New York of the person who was born somewhere else and came to New York in quest of something. Of these three trembling cities the greatest is the last—the city of final destination, the city that is a goal. It is this third city that accounts for New York's high-strung disposition, its poetical deportment, its dedication to the arts, and its incomparable achievements. Commuters give the city its tidal restlessness, natives give it solidity and continuity, but the settlers give it passion. And whether it is a farmer arriving from Italy to set up a small grocery store in a slum, or a young girl arriving from a small town in Mississippi to escape the indignity of being observed by her neighbors, or a boy arriving from the Corn Belt with a manuscript in his suitcase and a pain in his heart, it makes no difference: each embraces New York with the intense excitement of first love, each absorbs New York with the fresh eyes of an adventurer, each generates heat and light to dwarf the Consolidated Edison Company. □

Notice how White opens his paragraph with a clear statement of his point: there are three New Yorks. And notice also how he follows by identifying each of these by number: first, second, third. Finally, notice how he devotes the bulk of the paragraph to the most important of the three groups he associates with his three versions of New York and their three distinctive contributions to the city.

For a more extensive and complex example of classification, read the following essay about types of people.

Can People Be Judged by Their Appearance?
Eric Berne

Everyone knows that a human being, like a chicken, comes from an egg. At a very early stage, the human embryo forms a three-layered tube, the inside layer of which grows into the stomach and lungs, the middle layer into bones, muscle, joints, and blood vessels, and the outside layer into the skin and nervous system.

Usually these three grow about equally, so that the average human being is a fair mixture of brains, muscles, and inward organs. In some eggs, however, one layer grows more than the others, and when the angels have finished putting the child together, he may have more gut than brain, or more brain than muscle. When this happens, the individual's activities will often be mostly with the overgrown layer.

We can thus say that while the average human being is a mixture, some people are mainly "digestion-minded," some "muscle-minded," and some "brain-minded," correspondingly digestion-bodied, muscle-bodied, or brain-bodied. The digestion-bodied people look thick; the muscle-bodied people look wide; and the brain-bodied people look long. This does not mean the taller a man is the brainier he will be. It means that if a man, even a short man, looks long rather than wide or thick, he will often be more concerned about what goes on in his mind than about what he does or what he eats; but the key factor is slenderness and not height. On the other hand, a man who gives the impression of being thick rather than long or wide will usually be more interested in a good steak than in a good idea or a good long walk.

Medical men use Greek words to describe these types of body-build. For the man whose body shape mostly depends on the inside layer of the egg, they use the word *endomorph*. If it depends mostly upon the middle layer, they call him a *mesomorph*. If it depends upon the outside layer they call him an *ectomorph*. We can see the same roots in our English words "enter," "medium," and "exit," which might just as easily have been spelled "ender," "mesium," and "ectit."

Since the inside skin of the human egg, or endoderm, forms the inner organs of the belly, the viscera, the endomorph is usually belly-minded; since the middle skin forms the body tissues, or soma, the mesomorph is usually muscle-minded; and since the outside skin forms the brain, or cerebrum, the ectomorph is usually brain-minded. Translating this into Greek, we have the viscerotonic endomorph, the somatotonic mesomorph, and the cerebrotonic ectomorph.

Words are beautiful things to a cerebrotonic, but a viscerotonic knows you cannot eat a menu no matter what language it is printed in, and a somatotonic knows you cannot increase your chest expansion by reading a dictionary. So it is advisable to leave these words and see what kinds of people they actually apply to, remembering again that most individuals are fairly equal mixtures and that what we have to say concerns only the extremes. Up to the present, these types have been thoroughly studied only in the male sex.

VISCEROTONIC ENDOMORPH

If a man is definitely a thick type rather than a broad or long type, he is likely to be round and soft, with a big chest but a bigger belly. He would rather eat than breathe comfortably. He is likely to have a wide face, short, thick neck, big thighs and upper arms, and small hands and feet. He has overdeveloped breasts and looks as though he were blown up a little like a balloon. His skin is soft and smooth, and when he gets bald, as he does usually quite early, he loses the hair in the middle of his head first.

The short, jolly, thickset, red-faced politician with a cigar in his mouth, who always looks as though he were about to have a stroke, is the best example of this type. The reason he often makes a good politician is that he likes people, banquets, baths, and sleep; he is easygoing, soothing, and his feelings are easy to understand.

His abdomen is big because he has lots of intestines. He likes to take in things. He likes to take in food, and affection and approval as well. Going to a banquet with people who like him is his idea of a fine time. It is important for a psychiatrist to understand the natures of such men when they come to him for advice.

SOMATOTONIC MESOMORPH

If a man is definitely a broad type rather than a thick or long type, he is likely to be rugged and have lots of muscle. He is apt to have big forearms and legs, and his chest and belly are well formed and firm, with the chest bigger than the belly. He would rather breathe than eat. He has a bony head, big shoulders, and a square jaw. His skin is thick, coarse, and elastic, and tans easily. If he gets bald, it usually starts on the front of the head.

Dick Tracy, Li'l Abner, and other men of action belong to this type. Such people make good lifeguards and construction workers. They like to put out energy. They have lots of muscles and they like to use them. They go in for adventure, exercise, fighting, and getting the upper hand. They are bold and unrestrained, and love to master the people and things around them. If the psychiatrist knows the things which give such people satisfaction, he is able to understand why they may be unhappy in certain situations.

CEREBROTONIC ECTOMORPH

The man who is definitely a long type is likely to have thin bones and muscles. His shoulders are apt to sag and he has a flat belly with a dropped stomach, and long, weak legs. His neck and fingers are long, and his face is shaped like a long egg. His skin is thin, dry, and pale, and he rarely gets bald. He looks like an absent-minded professor and often is one.

Though such people are jumpy, they like to keep their energy and don't fancy moving around much. They would rather sit quietly by themselves and keep out of difficulties. Trouble upsets them, and they run away from it. Their friends don't understand them very well. They move jerkily and feel jerkily. The psychiatrist who understands how easily they become anxious is often able to help them get along better in the sociable and aggressive world of endomorphs and mesomorphs.

In the special cases where people definitely belong to one type or another, then, one can tell a good deal about their personalities from their appearance. When the human mind is engaged in one of its struggles with itself or with the world outside, the individual's way of handling the struggle will be partly determined by his type. If he is a viscerotonic he will often want to go to a party where he can eat and drink and be in good company at a time when he might be better off attending to business; the somatotonic will want to go out and do something about it, master the situation, even if what he does is foolish and not properly figured out, while the cerebrotonic will go off by himself and think it over, when perhaps he would be better off doing something about it or seeking good company to try to forget it.

Since these personality characteristics depend on the growth of the layers of the little egg from which the person developed, they are very difficult to change. Nevertheless, it is important for the individual to know about these types, so that he can have at least an inkling of what to expect from those around him, and can make allowances for the different kinds of human nature, and so that he can become aware of and learn to control his own natural tendencies, which may sometimes guide him into making the same mistakes over and over again in handling his difficulties. □

In developing this typology of human character, Berne employs a number of techniques to make his classification system clear. First, he develops a series of triplet groupings that derive from the three-layered embryo. These include the inside, middle, and outside layers of the embryo; the gut, muscle, and brain that develop from them; the corresponding categories of people as digestion-bodied and minded; muscle-bodied and minded; and brain-bodied and minded. They also include the three corresponding appearances of the body as thick, wide, and long; and the inclination to favor a good steak, a good long walk, or a good idea. Finally, the tripartite divisions include the scientific categories viscerotonic endomorph, somatotonic mesomorph, and cerebrotonic ectomorph. Second, Berne illustrates the physical and psychological traits of his three classes, one at a time.

The advantage of using classification to organize and structure discourse is its clarity, order, and simplicity. The danger, however, is one of oversimplification. Is it true, for example, as Berne seems to suggest, that fat people like food more than they like ideas? (Can't an intellectual also be overweight? Or is it often the case that people with athletic bodies, conversely, are more adventurous than those with other body types?) Although it is useful to classify people physically and psychologically, it is also risky. Just how closely body type is related to psychological type is debatable.

Exercises

1. Classify three of the following: houses, books, men, women, ice cream, cookies, restaurants, actors, actresses, baseball (football, basketball, tennis) players, sports fans, cars, trucks, music, rock music. A list will be sufficient.

2. Reclassify the same three things, this time doing each another way. Explain the basis for both sets of categories for each of your three subjects.

3. Write an essay developing your ideas about one of the subjects you already classified. Organize by classification.

4. Write an essay in which you make use of two or more logical and

rhetorical patterns. You might combine, for example, comparison with classification; causal analysis with classification or comparison; causal analysis with problem–solution or before–after; or illustration with comparison or classification.

Form in Advertisement   An advertisement from one perspective is a two-part structure; it is most often composed of words and pictures. From another perspective, however, it can be seen as a four-part form composed of a picture, a headline, body copy, and a concluding tag line, or clincher.

Consider the ads on pages 186 and 187 from both standpoints. Identify the headline and clincher in each as you also notice the body copy and picture. As you study the advertisements consider why they were organized and arranged as they are.

Now look only at the picture in each ad. Notice how the picture in the Toyota ad falls into three parts: a main dominant image at the bottom center and two subsidiary smaller pictures appearing above. Notice too how the picture in the Pioneer ad provides an even more complex series of images. To the left, hanging on the back of a chair, is a military uniform accompanied by a sword, whose owner stands nearby dressed in eighteenth-century military attire. In the center is a picture of a Pioneer audio/video receiver; slightly above and to the right are a speaker and picture monitor that depict a revolutionary war marching unit.

These pictures, moreover, are supported by the language of each advertisement. The Toyota ad conveys the idea that the Celica is a powerful, comfortable, and exciting automobile. It suggests that in driving such a car you will feel like an airplane pilot. The ad accomplishes this largely by including words and phrases that suggest the language of flight: "flight plan"; "all systems, *go*"; and "take-off time." The Pioneer ad is both less playful with its language and more serious in tone. The ad conveys the idea that Pioneer audio/video equipment is "superior," because of the "revolutionary invention" in technology it represents. "The finest in the world," Pioneer equipment is described as "ultra-sophisticated," providing far more precision in sound and image (and user satisfaction) than what other brands may promise but are presumably unable to deliver.

The basic structure of the advertisements is the same. Each contains three verbal sections: a headline or introduction, an expla-

1987 Toyota Motor Sales, USA, Inc.

nation or body, and clincher or conclusion. In a well-constructed ad, the headline, body copy, and clincher should be consistent, well integrated, and mutually supportive parts of a unified whole. In addition, these verbal portions of the ad should further support the implications of the picture.

1986 Pioneer Electronics (USA), Inc.

Exercises

1. Examine each ad carefully first to see how the three text portions cohere, or hold together, and second to see how well picture and text fit together.

2. Select two advertisements from a magazine or newspaper and analyze their structure. Comment on the effectiveness of their organization.

3. Write the text for an ad, and either draw or describe the picture that should accompany it. Include headline, body copy, and clincher.

Revision and Form   We cannot leave the subject of form and structure without making one more important point: When we alter the form or shape of our writing, readers will experience that writing differently. It makes a difference when we are reading an essay or writing one whether a particular aspect of the subject is discussed first or last. It makes a difference if something is added or deleted, if a paragraph is moved from one position to another, if sentences are rearranged. Sometimes the difference will be one of clarity; it will be easier for readers to understand. Sometimes the difference will be a matter of emphasis; it will result in readers being struck more forcefully by what we are saying.

Perhaps the best way to understand the implications of this idea about structure is to work with one of your own essays. Take a paper written earlier in the semester—either a draft or a completed paper. Look back over it and consider some ways to alter its structure. Consider eliminating your opening paragraph, perhaps beginning with what is now your second or third paragraph. Consider eliminating the concluding paragraph(s) or sentence(s). Consider changing the order of the body paragraphs; combining details from different paragraphs; adding or deleting sentences.

The idea is to say to yourself: "What if I made this or that change in my paper's organization?" "What if I did it another way rather than my original way or my usual way?" "What if . . . ?"

If you need help, ask for it from a classmate who can offer suggestions—or from your instructor.

As further and final testimony to the effects of structural revision do the following exercises based on some brief American poems.

Exercises

1. Here is a little poem by Robert Frost:

Dust of Snow

The way a crow
Shook down on me
The dust of snow
From a hemlock tree

Has given my heart
A change of mood
And saved some part
Of a day I had rued.

First, eliminate the space between the stanzas, making the poem a
single eight-line stanza. What happens? Why do you think Frost
included the space between the stanzas? Second, write the poem out
as a single sentence across the page. What happened to the form of
the poem? How did that change affect your reading and
understanding of it?

2. Here are two more short poems for you to adjust. For each, alter the
    poem's structure either by combining lines and stanzas or by
    rearranging them. You can also combine lines to lengthen them or
    split them up to shorten them. Compare your versions with those of
    your classmates and with the originals.

When I Heard the Learn'd Astronomer
Walt Whitman

When I heard the learn'd astronomer,
When the proofs, the figures, were ranged in columns before me,
When I was shown the charts and diagrams, to add, divide, and
    measure them,
When I sitting heard the astronomer where he lectured with much
    applause in the lecture-room,
How soon unaccountable I became tired and sick,
Till rising and gliding out I wandered off by myself,
In the mystical moist night-air, and from time to time,
Looked up in perfect silence at the stars.

The Red Wheelbarrow
William Carlos Williams

so much depends
upon

a red wheel
barrow

glazed with rain
water

beside the white
chickens.

Form in Nature and Art   Unlike the forms of experience—
forms we impose and create—the forms of nature are already there.
Form exists in the natural world and is available for our discovery
and enjoyment. We don't have to look far to see the way nature
exhibits form and pattern. We don't have to be botanists to notice
the symmetry of a tulip or an oak leaf. All we need do is look carefully at trees and flowers, plants and animals, vegetables and min-
erals to discover the splendid geometry of nature.

Nor do we have to know that a snowflake exhibits precise and
perfect symmetry in its six-sided, or hexagonal, structure to notice
(if we can catch one before it melts) that form, perfect form, inheres
in it. And although it is an amazing fact that the growth of organ-
isms as different as the chambered nautilus and the common sun-
flower are governed by the mathematics of the Fibonacci sequence
(1, 2, 3, 5, 8, 13, 21, 34, 55, 89, . . .), we don't have to be mathe-
maticians to appreciate the formal properties of these remarkable
natural phenomena.

What is true of nature is true also of art—of painting, sculpture, architecture, photography, dance, and film. And although this
is not the place to discuss how form functions in any of these arts
(or in the natural world either for that matter), we do want to alert
you to the power and beauty of form throughout our environment
both natural and artificial. Everything exhibits form; in discerning
that form you come to know that thing—whatever it may be.

So we invite you to see and enjoy the forms of life and art all around you. And as one way to go about doing just that we present the following exercises as invitations to discover form.

Exercises

1. Identify two things in nature that are primarily circular or cylindrical; two things primarily linear or rectangular; two things that combine lines and circles or cylinders and rectangles.

2. Identify two things that exhibit triangular form.

3. Consider how the human body is composed of circles and rectangles. Identify as many as you can of each.

4. Consider also the body's stunning symmetry. Identify as many of its symmetries as you can.

5. In the photographs of nature on the following page, identify the forms found there by the photographer and framed for us to see.

6. Identify the painters' uses of line and volume, of circle and rectangle and triangle, in Cezanne's *Mont Sainte-Victoire* (Color Plate 9) and in Renoir's *Portrait of Madame Renoir* (Color Plate 10).

Ansel Adams. *The Tetons and the Snake River, Grand Teton National Park, Wyoming* (1942). Photograph by Ansel Adams. Courtesy of the Trustees of the Ansel Adams Publishing Rights Trust. All rights reserved.

Ansel Adams. *Helmet Rock, San Francisco, California* (c. 1953). Photograph by Ansel Adams. Courtesy of the Trustees of the Ansel Adams Publishing Rights Trust. All rights reserved.

CHAPTER 5

The Persuasive Voice

ARGUMENT AND PERSUASION

All arguments are statements that exist in some situation or context—linking a speaker or writer to an audience—for the purpose of making claims and justifying those claims. An effective argument has three basic parts:* (1) a *claim* that is probably true, (2) adequate and justified *support* for that claim, and (3) a *context* in which the argument takes place that helps determine its relevance and its reception.

Here is an argument, a statement by one student who took a political science course and passed it with an A to another who is taking the course at a later time and having difficulty with it: "You should buy *Political Science Made Simple*. It gives you all the information you need to pass the course and it's a lot easier to understand than the professor. What's more, it's really well written and has some great photos."

A claim has been made: "You should buy *Political Science Made Simple*." Support for that claim has been suggested: first, "It gives you all the information you need to pass the course"; second,

---

*Two of the following terms—claim and support—are adapted from Stephen Toulmin, *The Uses of Argument* (Cambridge: Cambridge University Press, 1958).

"it's a lot easier to understand than the professor"; third, "it's really well written and has some great photos." The context of the argument is a statement by a knowledgeable student to another student on the subject of a class both know something about.

There you have the bare bones of an argument—claim, support, context. Yet that summary does not do justice to all that is involved in making an effective argument. The *claim has to be reasonable; the support has to be adequate; the argument has to be appropriate within its context;* and above all, *the argument has to be persuasive.*

Let us start with the reasonableness of the claim. It is not unreasonable to ask someone to buy a book, given the context of the argument. But is the claim supported? The book is said to contain "all the information" someone might need to pass a specific course in political science. Furthermore, it is easy to understand, it is well written, and it has great photos.

But is the support adequate and justified? There a doubt might enter in: the quality of the writing is very relevant, but are you sure the book contains "all the information"? And why is there an emphasis on the photos? Do they help one to pass the course? Within the context, though, the argument seems quite strong because of the arguer's credibility. The first student has passed the course and both students would seem to share a feeling that the professor is difficult. The arguer also seems to know that the information in the book is enough to pass the course. (Of course, if the arguer had not actually taken the course, then the argument would be considerably weakened.)

Making and judging arguments is a complex business, for it is not just a matter of checking the logical connection between a claim and its support. An argument has to be persuasive for other reasons too. So what exactly is persuasion? Persuasion is the act of successfully convincing an audience that a claim is justified. Essentially, persuasion is a function of three things:

- How an argument *connects* its claims to its support—how it tries to prove something logically.

- How an argument *appeals* to an audience—how it motivates the reader or listener to accept its influence.

- How an argument is *relevant* within its context—how it speaks to a problem or issue and how clear, convincing, and strong the arguer's credibility and authority are.

The argument about the political science text does indeed make logical connections between its claims and its supporting evidence. The argument is also presented appealingly to its listener: It says to the listener "Look, I know what your problem is because I've had the problem too and this solution worked for me." Finally, the speaker has credibility because she does have personal knowledge of the course and has overcome the same problem the listener has— and has earned an A.

When we try to persuade someone of something, we try to prove a point *and* at the same time we try to get the reader or listener to see things the way we do. In persuasion, we are concerned with altering attitudes or behavior, usually by appealing to values or beliefs that we might all hold in common or that can be clearly justified. So you see, logic alone cannot help you to argue persuasively; your talent as a writer creating a dialogue with your reader through special appeals is equally important.

In this chapter we are concerned with writing persuasively, assuming that *all* effective written discourse is both argumentative *and* persuasive. It doesn't matter whether you are explaining or describing something or presenting a detailed argument; all writing tries to persuade a reader that a set of conditions either exists or should exist. All effective writing makes *reasonable claims* based on *adequate evidence* and with *justified motivational appeals* to an *audience* in a *context*.

To begin, though, we concentrate on writing that attempts to prove something. After all, we don't need to argue over facts; we argue over claims, issues, and interpretations, events that are in doubt. We also argue in situations. And we make claims that are either *probable* or *necessary*. In either case, the claims have to be *provable*. Reason plays a role, but so do any number of emotional appeals. We can't always differentiate between "pure reason" and all the emotional and psychological implications of what we say. We do not live in a world where all probable outcomes are provable. We live in a world where emotions play as large a part as reason, where the two are not easily separated, and where the art of persuasion is the art, above all, of creating a *dialogue* between a speaker and listener, a writer and a reader. Consider the following selection.

[handwritten: Suggest overall to zevon in intro.]

[handwritten: In America billions $ spent annually on enforcement annually on enforcement — many p. believe key to reducing violence by elim. prohib. in Amer. ?et yrs. = prohibition]

Drugs

Gore Vidal

[handwritten: No "I feel"]

[handwritten: Dangerous - people scared]

It is possible to stop most drug addiction in the United States within a very short time. Simply make all drugs available and sell them at cost. Label each drug with a precise description of what effect—good and bad—the drug will have on the taker. This will require heroic honesty. Don't say that marijuana is addictive or dangerous when it is neither, as millions of people know—unlike "speed," which kills most unpleasantly, or heroin, which is addictive and difficult to kick.

For the record, I have tried—once—almost every drug and liked none, disproving the popular Fu Manchu theory that a single whiff of opium will enslave the mind. Nevertheless many drugs are bad for certain people to take and they should be told why in a sensible way.

Along with exhortation and warning, it might be good for our citizens to recall (or learn for the first time) that the United States was the creation of men who believed that each man has the right to do what he wants with his own life as long as he does not interfere with his neighbor's pursuit of happiness (that his neighbor's idea of happiness is persecuting others does confuse matters a bit).

This is a startling notion to the current generation of Americans. They reflect a system of public education which has made the Bill of Rights, literally, unacceptable to a majority of high school graduates (see the annual Purdue reports) who now form the "silent majority"—a phrase which that underestimated wit Richard Nixon took from Homer who used it to describe the dead.

Now one can hear the warning rumble begin: if everyone is allowed to take drugs everyone will and the GNP will decrease, the Commies will stop us from making everyone free, and we shall end up a race of Zombies, passively murmuring "groovie" to one another. Alarming thought. Yet it seems most unlikely that any reasonably sane person will become a drug addict if he knows in advance what addiction is going to be like.

Is everyone reasonably sane? No. Some people will always become drug addicts just as some people will always become alcoholics, and it is just too bad. Every man, however, has the power

[handwritten: criminal side effects of prohibition eliminated. Violence Pushers, drug gangs. police raids]

crime reduced
Revenue- gov't (tax)
Regulated purity + potency

The Persuasive Voice   197

(and should have the legal right) to kill himself if he chooses. But since most men don't, they won't be mainliners either. Nevertheless, forbidding people things they like or think they might enjoy only makes them want those things all the more. This psychological insight is, for some mysterious reason, perennially denied our governors.

It is a lucky thing for the American moralist that our country has always existed in a kind of time-vacuum: we have no public memory of anything that happened before last Tuesday. No one in Washington today recalls what happened during the years alcohol was forbidden to the people by a Congress that thought it had a divine mission to stamp out Demon Rum—launching, in the process, the greatest crime wave in the country's history, causing thousands of deaths from bad alcohol, and creating a general (and persisting) contempt among the citizenry for the laws of the United States.

The same thing is happening today. But the government has learned nothing from past attempts at prohibition, not to mention repression.

Last year when the supply of Mexican marijuana was slightly curtailed by the Feds, the pushers got the kids hooked on heroin and deaths increased dramatically, particularly in New York. Whose fault? Evil men like the Mafiosi? Permissive Dr. Spock? Wild-eyed Dr. Leary? No.

The Government of the United States was responsible for those deaths. The bureaucratic machine has a vested interest in playing cops and robbers. Both the Bureau of Narcotics and the Mafia want strong laws against the sale and use of drugs because if drugs are sold at cost there would be no money in it for anyone.

If there was no money in it for the Mafia, there would be no friendly playground pushers, and addicts would not commit crimes to pay for the next fix. Finally, if there was no money in it, the Bureau of Narcotics would wither away, something they are not about to do without a struggle.

Will anything sensible be done? Of course not. The American people are as devoted to the idea of sin and its punishment as they are to making money—and fighting drugs is nearly as big a business as pushing them. Since the combination of sin and money is irresistible (particularly to the professional politician), the situation will only grow worse. □

over crowed prisons.

Exercises

In small groups answer these questions about Vidal's essay:

1. What claims are made? What support is offered for the claims? Do you think the support is adequate? What do you think is the context of the argument and how does that affect your reading of it?

2. Which parts of the text argue *emotionally* and which parts argue *rationally* and *logically*? Discuss this within your group, making sure you give clear reasons for your conclusions. Were you able to differentiate between the two "kinds" of argument clearly? If not, how did they mix and mingle in this passage?

Claims and Support   In the last chapter we explored various writing *forms* that can organize thinking in specific writing situations. We dealt with *causal analysis, process analysis, illustration, comparison and contrast, analogy,* and *classification.* In each case, effectively, a specific claim was linked to some kind of supporting information.

- In a *causal analysis* a situation derives from specific causes or certain causes lead to certain effects: "In a nuclear attack on New York, three quarters of its inhabitants would be killed because of the density of the population." The claim that "three quarters of the population would be killed" is supported by the information about the "density of the population." Our analysis or explanation is in effect an argument.

- In a *process analysis* something is done or a situation exists because it is a process that can be defined in its stages or parts. David Ogilvy argues, in effect, that there are ten aspects of a headline in an advertisement that can make it effective. His claim is that an effective headline results from the evidence that it functions in the ten different ways he lists (see pp. 158–160). The business of making an effective headline is really based on an argument about what constitutes an effective headline.

- In writing an *illustration* you *define* a subject by giving examples of it. The evidence on which you make a claim is based on providing further information in the form of examples, and you cannot give those examples without actually knowing what that something is. "A playboy is a 'wealthy, carefree man devoted to the pleasures of nightclubs, fast cars, and constantly changing female company.' Fred Bloggs is definitely a playboy."

- You frequently have to describe or explain a situation by using *comparison and contrast.* "When I flew to England last year, Airline A was right on time. This year I flew with Airline B and it was three hours late, so next year I'm going to use Airline A again." The claim is based on two sets of information which are compared and contrasted. Once more, you are really making an argument.

- Similarly, the use of forms of *analogy* involves making a claim that something is actually *like* something else. You are not just comparing the performance of two things or contrasting two situations; you are asserting that there is an intimate link between two things or two situations and further claims legitimately follow. "You and I are equally strong and fit, so if I can run a mile in five minutes, you can too."

- The last expository form you experimented with in Chapter 4 was *classification.* This form again involves a claim based on the fact that things are related in some way; they can be classified together. They are unlike other things which can be classified apart from the first group, and so on. Like illustration, classification depends on claims that rely on adequate definition of something or some situation.

As you can see from this quick review, your efforts at explanation and analysis in the last chapter were really efforts at *argument* as well. Remember *all* expository writing is argumentative and persuasive in some way because all writing involves linking a claim or assertion with supporting evidence. Advertisements provide a good example.

Managing Chemical Wastes

What the chemical industry is doing to improve waste-disposal methods

America's chemical companies have already invested hundreds of millions of dollars in safer, better waste-disposal methods. We'll spend over $2 *billion* more on waste-disposal facilities in the next two years. Here's how we're advancing the "state of the art":

1. Eliminating wasteful processes

We're redesigning manufacturing processes and improving efficiency. We're adding on-line treatment systems to neutralize, reduce the volume or change the nature of waste by-products. We're also using recovery techniques that let us recycle wastes back into the production process.

2. Building secure landfills

Secure landfills have a barrier that keeps wastes from seeping out into groundwater and keeps groundwater from migrating through the landfill. They may include facilities for recycling liquids, or a wastewater treatment unit to clean up liquids for safe disposal. Landfills—if *properly* designed, operated and monitored—are one of the best ways to dispose of certain kinds of solid wastes.

3. Continuing industry commitment

We were finding ways to manage solid wastes long before the nation recognized the need for better waste-disposal methods. In fact, we already had much of the required waste-disposal technology and remedial strategies in place—or being developed—when Congress passed the Resource Conservation and Recovery Act of 1976, which sets forth strict waste-disposal guidelines.

4. Sharing knowledge and new technology

As we develop new waste-disposal techniques, we share our knowledge with industry, government and the public. In 1979, the chemical industry began conducting a series of regional seminars that presented current techniques for solid-waste disposal. Individual chemical companies may use videotapes, visual aids or other techniques to train personnel in

waste-disposal methods.

5. Encouraging solid-waste exchanges

Sometimes one chemical company's wastes can become another company's raw material. So the chemical industry has encouraged the development of waste-exchange organizations, which develop and distribute lists of available wastes.

For more information, write to: Chemical Manufacturers Assn., Dept. FY-09, Box 363, Beltsville, MD 20705.

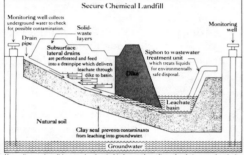

Secure Chemical Landfill

Monitoring well collects underground water to check for possible contamination.

Solid-waste layers

Drain pipe

Subsurface lateral drains are perforated and feed into a drainpipe which delivers leachate through dike to basin.

Siphon to wastewater treatment unit — which treats liquids for environmentally safe disposal.

Dike

Monitoring well

Leachate basin

Natural soil

Clay seal prevents contaminants from leaching into groundwater.

Groundwater

Depending on the solid waste, the chemical industry selects disposal techniques such as incineration, by-product recovery, stabilization or secure landfill design to protect the environment.

America's Chemical Industry
The member companies of the Chemical Manufacturers Association

---

Chemical Manufacturers Association.

It's Time To Start Feeling Good
About Yourself–*Really* Good!

"**P**RIDE goeth before a fall"—we've all heard it. But how **TRUE** is it?

It's mostly **BUNK**, agree today's top mental health experts.

William Plover
Dictionary Editor

do the extraordinary. Her novel <u>Frankenstein</u> was a classic celebration of a doctor's pride so great, it was larger than life itself.

Dr. Frankenstein's pride allowed him to create a human being—a task no fictional character had ever before accomplished.

Pride: the sin you can feel good about

You've heard all the bad-mouthing. At home. In Sunday school. In literary magazines. "Pride's a sin!" they proclaim. Well, don't you believe it.

"Pride's gotten a bad rap," says psychiatrist/ornithologist Bernard Warbler.

"It's time this country wakes up and faces facts. Pride, *to whatever extent*, is healthy and natural. The psychiatric community is in complete agreement on this point."

So stick out your chest, for heaven's sake. PRIDE—it's today's "buzz word" for mental health!

Henry VIII

Failure after romantic failure, it was Henry's pride that kept him searching for Mrs. Right. At 52, he finally found her—the lovely Catherine Parr.

The most misunderstood word in the English language?
"Hubris," or excessive pride, is a word that's quickly leaving our vocabulary. *Good riddance!* The concept of "excessive" pride no longer works—and people are taking notice.

<u>Dictionary editor William Plover</u>: "'Hubris,' of course, comes to us from ancient Greece, and most word-watchers think it's come far enough. It's quite clear, early translators misunderstood the sense of 'wellness' implied by the Greeks. Resulting in centuries of lexicological slander, if you will. To me, hubris is a rather pleasant word."

Next time you run across "hubris" in the dictionary, cross it out—or write a new definition. You'll feel better for doing so!

A poet celebrates pride

And on the pedestal these words appear:

My name is Ozymandias, king of kings:

Look on my works, ye Mighty, and despair!

—*Percy Bysshe Shelley,*
"Ozymandias"

Shelley was an early advocate of prideful living. His famous king Ozymandias wasn't afraid to put his words—or himself—up on a pedestal.

Shelley's wife, Mary Wollstonecraft Shelley, believed pride enabled men to

Putting yourself on a pedestal— it's never been more convenient

But how can *you* live more pridefully? It's easier than you think. We're the Pride Council. A trade association dedicated to bringing fine products— "Prouducts™"—to the American people. At prices that make pride easy to swallow.

ACT NOW! HERE'S HOW!

Just read the coupon below. You'll find carefully screened and selected companies that can help you design the look-down-your-nose lifestyle you've always dreamed of having.

Don't dally—send in your coupon today!

It would be a sin not to.

The Pride Council
Pride. It's not a sin anymore.™

PRIDE

Agency: Ogilvy & Mather. *Creative Director:* Jay Jasper. *Art Director:* Carrie Wieseneck. *Copywriter:* Jim Nolan. *Clients:* Hathaway, "The Man in the Hathaway Shirt"; American Express, "Don't Leave Home Without It"; Pepperidge Farm, "Pepperidge Farm Remembers."

Exercises

1. Consider the preceding advertisements.

   (a) List the *claims* each ad is making and the *evidence* on which each claim is based.

   (b) Describe their effects on you and whether or not you are persuaded by either advertisement. Is each claim successful? If so, why? If not, why not? Are there any fallacies in linking the claims to the evidence? Which advertisement do you think is more effective?

2. Read the selection below and answer the questions that follow.

Once Verboten, Now Chic

Ellen Goodman

The whole thing happened in one of those two-story planes they built to make you forget that you're five miles up in the air. I had just settled into a chair and opened a magazine when who should appear but Jo Jo White, standing half-naked in his little white cotton underpants with a towel wrapped around his neck.

Now, let me explain. I am not the sort of person who even fantasizes about encountering strange men in their underwear on planes, trains, etc. The one time I was sent to interview a houseful of nudists, I broke the *Guinness Book of Records* record for maintaining eye contact. I leave the rest to Erica Jong, who has a less conventional fear of flying than I do.

But Jo Jo was not alone. He was to the right of Denis Potvin and above Pete Rose, happily occupying a page in the middle of a respectable national newsweekly which was not called *Viva.* In short, there were eight male athletes posing in their little nothings for a Jockey ad over the cut-line that read: "Take Away Their Uniforms and Who Are They?"

Well, it seems that Ken Anderson is a Fun Top and Jim Hart is a Slim Guy Boxer. The only one who was fit to be seen in public was Jamaal Wilkes, who looked as if he were merely wearing a uniform of a different color. As for Jim Palmer's teeny-weeny green print bikini, his "Skants" were a scandal. Is it possible that he was not raised under the Eleventh Commandment: Thou Shalt Not Go Out of the House in Unseemly Undergarments Lest Thou Get in an Accident?

What were these jocks for Jockey doing—aside from earning a lifetime supply of undies? What were they doing wearing hockey gloves and blue-denim bikinis in front of millions of Americans?

They were being paid to convince the rest of the male population that it's OK to buy items they wouldn't have been caught dead in at fifteen. At that age, the average American male already had a conditioned response to anything that looked fancy or sexy, or smelled good. That response was to the single word imprinted in the playgrounds of their minds: *sissy.*

At the mere sound of sibilant *s*, strong men pulled their bodies into gray flannel like terrified turtles, shaved their heads to within an inch of their lives and learned how to remove each other's teeth with a single blow.

But over the past handful of years, men have been urged by women and assorted merchants to adopt a variety of products that were once *verboten*. The more questionable the origin of the product, the more they were sold as maler-than-male.

Pocketbooks were not, gasp, pocketbooks, but tote bags and carry-alls designed to look like saddle bags for the Marlboro Man's horse, or tackle boxes for the fisherman. Men wrote articles to each other about how to carry them—carefully—in a distinctively male over-the-shoulder fashion, as opposed to a female over-the-shoulder fashion.

It was obvious that if you wanted to sell men anything even vaguely neuter, you had to inject it with visual and verbal testosterone. Jewelry, for instance, could be sold either in the garrote-chain style or as medallions heavy enough to double as a mace. Rings were popular in the brass-knuckle fashion; bracelets that looked like recycled handcuffs were also all right.

Perfume—forgive me—Male Cologne, was repackaged and rebaptized. It became things like promise-him-anything-but-give-him—Hai Karate. And then came Macho, a perfume in a bottle the shape of which will never appear in this family newspaper.

But nothing has worked quite as well in the fight against sissy stuff as the jock. No one kicks sand in the face of a superstar. Dave Kopay's efforts notwithstanding, an athletic endorsement is as effective in fighting the old conditioned response as an Anita Bryant seal of approval.

Joe Namath sold pantyhose before he turned brute, or should I say, Brut. Pete Rose took to Aqua Velva before he stripped down to his Metre Briefs. (From the look of him in the briefs, I suspect he was drinking the Aqua Velva when he signed the modeling contract.)

The more things change in male decor, the more they stay the same in the ads. The more androgynous the product, the more macho the role-model. So progress inches forward, or downward, to the Tropez Brief. As a trend-watcher might suggest, it's only a matter of time before we have Doctor Julius Erving, the basketball superstar, selling eye-liner under the brand-name "Sado." In the meantime, I wish Jo Jo White's mother would cover the poor boy up. It must be cold in a Boeing 747 in just a pair of white briefs and a towel over your shoulder. □

> (a)   Assume that Goodman is *describing* a situation. State clearly what that situation is and list all its important aspects based on the information she gives you.
> (b)   Assume Goodman is *explaining* the same situation. Paraphrase her explanation.
> (c)   Assume Goodman is making an *argument* about this situation. What claim(s) is she making?
> (d)   Are Goodman's claims clearly linked to supporting evidence? Do you think her argument is successful?

TYPES OF ARGUMENTS

In writing any expository narrative, sooner or later you will make claims and therefore will rely on using *evidence*, on making *definitions*, and on creating *comparisons and contrasts*, not to mention *analogies*. You will invoke *authorities*, and you will try to make links between *causes and effects*. Let us briefly consider what happens when we try to link claims to their support in these ways.

Argument from Evidence   Whenever an argument is made using statistics, reports, or any kind of documentation, the writer is arguing from evidence. The "proof," as far as you know, is contained in the evidence, and you must, like judge and jury, evaluate the claim according to the nature of the evidence. It is important, then, to be sure that the evidence presented has the following characteristics:

- *Relevance.* Check all the details to make sure they relate to the conclusion and that nothing important has been left out.

- *Accuracy.* Make sure that the writer has presented facts and figures that can be checked if necessary. Are the sources clear?

- *Clear definition.* The facts should be presented without ambiguity.

- *Sufficiency.* The statistics and other data presented should be adequate to the claim. If you are trying to draw conclusions from statistics, you have to check to ascertain whether the statistics (the sampling procedure) are adequate and the statistical projections are reasonable. It is best not to try to draw conclusions from statistics unless you have had some kind of training in the art of such testing and understand the limits built into the various methods. A sound argument using statistics tries to justify its figures by giving clear percentages and even explaining in detail its statistical methods and margins of error.

We could say then that the following argument carries sufficient evidence:

Of the eight thousand students at this university, only fifty are minority students, so there is little doubt that, in spite of our scholarship program, we have not succeeded in attracting many of the five thousand black and Chicano young people in the area who have graduated from high school and are eligible to enter the university. Some three thousand graduating high school seniors who are black or Chicano were polled this year and over 75 percent gave high tuition costs as the main reason for not attending our university.

The following argument, however, plainly carries insufficient, unclear, and irrelevant evidence:

Of all the students at this university, very few are minority students. Most of them want to have little to do with us because we don't have a good student union. I have asked all my friends in our college what they think and they agree with me.

Argument from Definition When you come across a definition of a thing, person, institution, value, enterprise, or whatever, you should carefully examine it to see if it is adequate. There are, in traditional logic, several different kinds of definition governed by the writer's intention. Ask yourself which kind the writer seems to be using and the argument demands, and see if the definition serves the purpose:

- *New definitions.* If a writer is talking about a term or an event that has no previous history, the term has to be defined. *Space shuttle*, referring to the spaceship *Columbia*, had to be carefully described and defined when it first appeared in newspapers because few people knew what a space shuttle could do. A new definition should be adequate and clear.

- *Dictionary definitions.* A writer can explain clearly a term's meaning by referring to the meanings it already has. The dictionary, of course, is *the* sourcebook for every reader and writer since it lists what those meanings are. If a definition of a term or event does not fall under conventional usage, and there is no attempt made to explain what the new definition is, the argument is suspect. For example, if you were to argue from a definition of *democracy* as the right to do exactly what you want without explaining how that definition can be justified, your argument would be greatly weakened.

- *Precising definitions.* These are made by a writer who wants to use a term in a way that does not match ordinary usage. If you want to insist that reading *is* interpretation, you would have to offer a precising definition of the term *reading*. Check to see that a writer's definition is precise enough for the argument.

- *Persuasive definitions.* The reader has to be wary of these. There are as many definitions of *democracy, welfare*, and *communism* as there are politicians, and as many definitions of *love, marriage*, and *happiness* as there are psychologists, social scientists, and guidance counselors. What is more, writers often use special definitions of terms to carry their argument. So *democracy* might be defined as "a noncommunist way of life" by someone arguing against the Marxist line, and "love is a four-letter word" can be a definition used by someone who is trying to persuade by being cute.

Writers argue by using any of the foregoing defining techniques, and you should be aware of some of the common fallacies related to definition:

- *The fallacy of accident* occurs when an arguer takes an exception to be a general rule, or takes a general rule to be a universal one. For example, it is generally the case that to kill is a crime. If you argue that it is morally acceptable for the police to kill a homicidal maniac who is holed up in a building sniping at the public and cannot be disarmed, the general principle of the moral evil of killing is not disproved by this "accident" of an exceptional case.

- *The fallacy of converse accident* is commonly known as the *hasty generalization* and is simply the converse of the fallacy of accident. The fallacy is committed by generalizing on the basis of exceptional particular cases rather than on the basis of typical ones. If you define all roses as being scented because you know some of them are, you would be mistaken.

- *The fallacy of begging the question* commits the fallacy of a *circular* definition in which the conclusion of the argument is incorporated into the premise. This argument, for example, begs the question: "Nuclear disarmament is a necessity, and I know this is true because the people who believe in it are decent pacifists." If you want to prove that nuclear disarmament is a necessity, you need more evidence than the word of an avowed pacifist. One has to be careful not to preach to the converted or to present as evidence the conclusion you want to prove. Here is another circular argument: "Dallas will win the Super Bowl because it has the best team and the best coach and management. I know it has the best team and coach because it will win the Super Bowl. And it will win the Super Bowl because only the best team and the best coach deserve to do so. Besides, it's the outstanding team this year."

- *The fallacy of the complex question* is not strictly a definition but a question involving a controversial definition that the arguer is taking for granted: "Have you stopped lying to the press yet?" This has no simple yes or no answer that will not incriminate the responder. The complex question is similar to the circular argument in that the question asked incorporates a conclusion that has by no means been proved. So it has many popular forms: "When are those pro-abortion advocates going to stop breaking the law?" "Is this another pernicious supply-side economics theory?" "When are we going to stop those foreigners from interfering in the U.S. automobile market?"

- *The fallacy of composition* occurs when one reasons from the parts of a whole to the whole itself, or from individual members to a group. It is fallacious to argue, for example, that if every chapter in a book is an artistic masterpiece, then the whole book is an artistic masterpiece; or that if every item in a collection is inexpensive, then the whole collection must be too.

- *The fallacy of division* is the reverse of the fallacy of composition. It is fallacious to argue from the whole to the part. Thus one should not argue that if a motor car is heavy, all its individual parts must be heavy too.

Argument by Comparison and Contrast   This is perhaps the most common of all arguments found in advertising. Two or three versions of a razor blade or a painkiller are compared in action, and of course the winner is always the advertisement's sponsor. How convenient it would be if all comparisons could be so easily decided. The writer of an argument knows what the conclusion is going to be; the reader's job is to verify the relevance and correctness of the comparisons that are made.

- Is the comparison between two items that belong to the same class? You may compare planes and ships as modes of transatlantic transport, but not planes and cars. Comparing events of different classes is called *the fallacy of false comparison*.

- Has the writer compared enough important qualities of each item? Speed, cost, efficiency, comfort, and so on, make a comparison between planes and ships a useful one if you are planning to travel. The writer dealing with this theme comes to a conclusion about advantages and disadvantages.

- Has the writer's comparison proved the point? That is, is the comparison relevant to the conclusion?

Argument from Analogy   If you happen to like Brand X motor car, have owned three of them, and are trying to persuade someone to buy one, you would do so on the *analogy* that three of your cars have been great so this one probably will be, too. The argument, of course, has to be made carefully:

If a, b, c, d all have properties x and y
And a, b, c all have property z as well
Then d *probably* has property z.

If four models of Brand X motor car are efficient and economical, and three earlier models are powerful as well, the most recent model is likely to be powerful also. The argument from analogy, then, depends on several factors that determine the similarity between two or more things, and not just that a couple of items seem to look alike. For example, if you were arguing that someone should buy the new Brand X on the basis of your having liked the previous three, then the person you were trying to persuade would have every right to know what it was that you liked about the cars and what they had in common *with the new one.*

How do you judge an argument based on analogy for its degree of probability? There are five questions you can ask:

- *How many things are being compared?* Obviously, the greater the number of instances that are cited as evidence for doing something, the stronger the argument. If in the example above you had owned only one Brand X car, your argument would be less impressive. Note, however, that this does not mean that the person you are trying to persuade should be three times as impressed—or that the argument is three times stronger!

- *How many qualities do the items have in common?* It is more convincing if it can be shown that the car's new model has mileage, power, and styling the same as or better than the other three than if they are similar in one respect only.

- *How relevant is the evidence used?* If you were to argue that the latest model of Brand X is as good as the earlier ones because it has the same quality paint work, the same tires, tinted glass, and muffler, then clearly the argument is weaker than a comparison made between the engine capacity, the overall styling, and the mileage figures. It is important that the evidence used be directly related to the conclusion that is reached. Your major consideration in evaluating an argument by analogy is to question the relevance of the information cited in the premises.

- *How strong is the claim of the argument relative to the premises?* Say you argue that the statistics and car reviews show that the new model of Brand X car will definitely win a car-of-the-year award. The claim is based on statistics that are similar to those of previous models of the car, but none of the earlier models won the award. So the claim is not too strong and the argument is weak. But if the mileage of the car and its general performance will be no less than any of the earlier models (of similar capacity and design), and they did win awards, then the argument is considerably strengthened.

- *How dissimilar are the pieces of evidence used in the premises?* Plainly, you could list many similarities among the three earlier models of the Brand X car. But if it could be shown that the performance of each rated very highly and they were *different* cars in a number of respects (varying engine capacity, strong performance in both automatic and manual drive, and so on), then there would be a very strong argument for the generally high quality of the car. In short, *the more dissimilar the evidence cited, the stronger the argument.*

If any of these five requirements are not met, then *the fallacy of faulty analogy* occurs. This is the most common fallacy related to this kind of argument and it occurs when a claim is made on the basis of *irrelevant* evidence.

Argument from Authority   Authority can take different forms, the most usual being well-known people or well-known documentation. To argue effectively from authority, the arguer should quote from a genuinely authoritative source, one that is relevant and unprejudiced on the subject. Even though a military general may be a recognized authority on war tactics, he or she is not necessarily an authority on the question of science versus religion. And although an English teacher may be an authority on language and literature, he or she is not necessarily a reliable source on the subject of film.

When you encounter an argument that is even partly based on authority, ask these questions:

- *Is the argument by authority relevant at all?* Is anyone's opinion relevant when you are deciding which portable radio sounds best to you?

- *Is the authority really an authority on the subject?* Are all those people offering testimonials for products on television really experts on what they are talking about? Some are, but some are not, and you have to judge the value of the argument accordingly.

- *Is the authority truly unprejudiced?* Surely people touting products on television stand to gain something for their testimonial.

If you can answer these three questions affirmatively, the argument from authority is indeed convincing. But the problem with arguments that appeal to the weight and reputation of someone's opinion, or even to the "authority" of a common powerful human feeling, is that they often lead to fallacious reasoning. There are a few appeals common in argument that tend to make reasoning ineffective even while they seem to promote the persuasive effect of an argument. Note, though, that some of these appeals tend not to be clear-cut fallacies. We will discuss the pros and cons of each.

- *The appeal to an irrelevant or prejudiced authority.* This is a fallacy and usually occurs when an argument relies on the good reputation of a well-known figure to promote a cause or provide information that the figure is not an expert on. So a certain golfer advertising a tire because he knows how to drive a golf ball well is irrelevant to the value of the tire.

- *The appeal to the people.* This is not always a fallacy. You can appeal to popular feelings and patriotism quite reasonably. Various Allied leaders raised the spirits of many during the last world war for a reasonable patriotic cause. You always have to ask *why* the appeal is being made, and judge the argument for its effects rather than the logic of its appeal. For sometimes the appeal to the people covers up a motive that is selfish or undemocratic, and it may even involve the *fallacy of name calling.* So we find patriotic appeals being made all over the world in order to sell things, and national flags become emblems of commercial value. This constitutes a fallacy. Also it can be argued fallaciously that it is "un-American" to disagree with the president or "philistine" not to support your local symphony orchestra.

- *The appeal to pity.* This usually involves the argument that something should or should not take place because of pitiable circumstances. This is the appeal made in law courts when mitigating circumstances are offered. The judgment as to whether the appeal is relevant or not depends of course on the judge in each case, but we can say that in extreme cases the appeal to pity is fallacious because it is irrelevant to the charge. So there is a famous story of the mass murderer who claimed that he came from an unhappy home. Remember, however, that not all appeals to pity are fallacious, for we do rightly temper judgment with mercy.

- *The appeal to force.* This appeal commits the fallacy of arguing that "might is right," an argument we have all heard when reason breaks down. But it also covers more everyday occurrences. A would-be contributor to a political campaign might use the prospect of a large donation to gain a political favor.

- *The appeal to fear.* This is used as a cause for action: "You should side with those who want to ban the bomb or else you will surely die." There are more subtle and effective arguments for nuclear disarmament. The appeal to fear is an appeal to self-preservation without any rational inducement.

Argument from Cause to Effect, Effect to Cause   This is perhaps the most difficult kind of argument because it depends on the formulation of a hypothesis about an unknown factor, either cause or effect. Like many arguments by analogy, the argument from cause or effect predicts that something is or will be the case based on a prior or existing condition. That is, the writer is predicting a *relationship* between two events that is dependent on either an effect or a cause.

There are some obvious cause–effect relationships. If you thrust your hand in a fire, you will get burned. There is, you can assume, a necessary relationship between fire and burning. If you break the law, and you get caught, you can expect to be punished. That is perhaps not quite so highly probable, but there is a likely enough relationship between cause and effect. But most cause–effect relationships are difficult to prove. *You need a sufficient number of conditions in a cause before you can adequately predict what the effects will be.* You need to know, for example, the full theory behind an economic plan in order to guess what effect it will have on inflation. If you know only what the effects are, you can judge the cause only in terms of the necessary relationships between it and the effects. So if you see a heap of ashes, you can very reasonably assume that there has been a fire. But if you see someone driving carelessly all over the road, you are not sure what the cause is without more information.

There are, then, two important rules about cause-and-effect argument:

- You can infer cause from effect only through *necessary* conditions. If there appear to be several possible causes for an effect, you cannot make any reliable inference.

- You can infer effect from cause only through *sufficient* conditions.

So when an argument plainly depends on cause and effect, examine it closely to make sure that the writer has met one of these two conditions.

There are several kinds of fallacious thinking associated with assertions about cause, effect, and the circumstances of an event.

- *The fallacy of false cause.* This mistake occurs when we assume that one event is the cause of another when in fact their relationship is purely coincidental. The fallacy is also committed by oversimplifying a cause, or by choosing one possible cause over several others that would work as well. For example, if you insist that you recovered from a twisted ankle after resting it for a week because you wrapped it in a "miracle bandage," then you are committing the fallacy of false cause. The real cure was more likely the rest period.

- *The fallacy of arguing from ignorance.* This occurs when you assume that because no other cause is known to exist, a proposed cause must be the one. It is fallacious to argue that psychic phenomena cannot exist because they haven't been proven. Arguments that lead to the fallacy of arguing from ignorance usually arise because there is not enough information to argue one way or the other. Note, however, that under our law, an accused person is considered innocent until proven guilty, and if no evidence can be found to convict the accused, then that person goes free. That does not contradict this fallacy.

- *The genetic fallacy.* This fallacy is based on irrelevant statements about a person or thing. It is wrong to argue that Dylan Thomas is a bad poet because he seems to have been an alcoholic, or that a university president is impractical because he has been an academic.

- *The fallacy of the* ad hominem *argument.* (*Ad hominem* comes from the Latin, meaning literally "to the man.") This is a variety of the genetic fallacy and involves an argument to the circumstances of your opponent rather than to the issue itself. So you might argue, fallaciously, that a divorced person can't be an expert on marriage, or that a Frenchman should agree to unlimited imports of California wine into his own country because French people are known to like wine.

- *The* reductio ad absurdum *argument. (Again from Latin, meaning literally the "reduction to absurdity.")* In this argument, a possible consequence is described in extreme and oversimplified terms. For example: "The way I see it, Congress is nothing more than a group of businessmen who will lead us further into the murky depths of the capitalism they adhere to. We will eventually be ruled by giant corporations, and the Senate and Congress will be their power playground." It is also worth remembering, however, that some apparently absurd arguments have proven to be uncomfortably close to the truth, such as some predictions of economic decline made a few years ago.

- *Conspiracy theories.* These insist that a cause must always be plural and have perhaps more to do with those uneasily walking the corridors of power than with the average citizen. But again, since the assassination of John F. Kennedy and the conspiracy of Watergate, it has not been unusual to see conspiracies everywhere from the kindergarten lunchroom to the university president's office. Uncovered conspiracies will always remind us that it is naive to assume that people do not gang together for special ends. But it is equally naive to assume that any wrongdoing is *necessarily* the creation of more than one person. Before you claim conspiracy, you should be able to prove your case beyond a reasonable doubt.

As you can imagine, evaluating and avoiding these fallacies is not easy to do. The scientist—who is perhaps our most scrupulous hypothesizer—must do so in order to produce a theory that will earn the respect of fellow scientists. You do not have to be a scientist, however, to realize that every hypothesis that demands to be taken seriously should meet these conditions. And you do not have to be a scientist to be able to interpret cause–effect arguments.

Exercise

Here are a number of short arguments. With each, comment on whether the argument is correct or not, giving reasons and naming any fallacies involved:

(a) Of course, we have a very fine student body. One of our seniors won a Rhodes Scholarship this year, and we have several honors societies.

(b) Undoubtedly the Republican candidate will get the nomination. She's the best qualified and we know that because she said so in her speech. Furthermore, the Republicans are the stronger party this year.

(c) You eat the flesh of cows and lambs, don't you? Then don't complain about me because I go hunting.

(d) It's insane to think that a small group of people can have any effect on government policy. If we continue to protest, we'll be singled out and carefully eliminated. I know. I've seen what governments can do when they want to.

(e) When a famous scientist tells me how the second law of thermodynamics works, I believe him. When a famous author tells me that Shakespeare is our greatest writer, I believe him, too. So when the president tells me that my country wants me to save lots of money, I think it's my reasonable duty to do so. After all, if the president can't be trusted, who can?

(f) It is written that thou shalt not covet they neighbor's wife. Well, my neighbor Frank died last year of a heart attack and I've been seeing a lot of his widow Louise. In fact, we're getting married soon. So I guess that commandment is no longer valid.

(g) There is no evidence that the fee raise was decided by the chancellor alone. The athletics' director and the head of the research institute had to have something to do with it, because everyone knows they always want more money in order to siphon off funds to visibly "prestige" causes at the university.

(h) When Lena got bad tennis elbow, we took her to three doctors who treated her with various support devices. They seemed to work for a while, but then someone told us about this Australian tennis champion who had been cured by soaking in mineral spings in the Rockies. So we took her there and she recovered perfectly after about two weeks.

(i) Cruelty to animals is not confined to streets and homes. It goes on in every science laboratory, too.

(j) If a, b, c, d, e, and f all have properties p and q, and a, b, c, and d all have property r, and e has property s, then f probably has property r and s, too.

(k) I have asked my colleagues this question over and over again, and I've yet to hear a reasonable answer: When will the Democrats give up their losing ways in Congress? Never, I say, so long as we refuse to develop a sound economic theory.

(l) My favorite ice skater is Mary Smith. She has won the world championship twice in a row now, and she said on television the other day that she managed to keep fit on "No-eat" diet candy and little else. So I'm going on the Mary Smith graceful fitness plan, and you should, too.

(m) How much longer do we have to spend on this problem? Consider how many people could possibly have taken the money. Only Brown, Jones, and Smith are known to have gone into the locker room. Jones and Smith couldn't have done it because they are both wealthy, which leaves Brown. Let's just confront him with it now.

(n) All you ladies out there will love "Lye-a-wile," the crafty new washing powder from Myrtle Industries. Now washing is truly relaxing for it takes only one teaspoon per washing load in your machine to remove all—yes, *all*— stains from your family's clothes in less than four minutes!

(o) We can't avoid losing all the rest of the matches in the women's basketball season. Three of the top players are out with injuries, and the remainder of our matches are away games. So we won't even have the advantage of a home court.

(p) The fruit trees in my garden have all given bumper crops in the last two years: big, juicy apples, plums, peaches, and pears. I'm sure they'll all produce as well again this year.

Now consider Sallie Tisdale's "We Do Abortions Here."

We Do Abortions Here: A Nurse's Story
Sallie Tisdale

We do abortions here; that is all we do. There are weary, grim moments when I think I cannot bear another basin of bloody remains, utter another kind phrase of reassurance. So I leave the procedure room in the back and reach for a new chart. Soon I am talking to an eighteen-year-old woman pregnant for the fourth time. I push up her sleeve to check her blood pressure and find row upon row of needle marks, neat and parallel and discolored. She has been so hungry for her drug for so long that she has taken to using the loose skin of her upper arms; her elbows are already a permanent ruin of bruises. She is surprised to find herself nearly four months pregnant. I suspect she is often surprised, in a mild way, by the blows she is dealt. I prepare myself for another basin, another brief and chafing loss.

"How can you stand it?" Even the clients ask. They see the machine, the strange instruments, the blood, the final stroke that wipes away the promise of pregnancy. Sometimes I see that too: I watch a woman's swollen abdomen sink to softness in a few stuttering moments and my own belly flip-flops with sorrow. But all it takes for me to catch my breath is another interview, one more story that sounds so much like the last one. There is a numbing sameness lurking in this job: the same questions, the same answers, even the same trembling tone in the voices. The worst is the sameness of human failure, of inadequacy in the face of each day's dull demands.

In describing this work, I find it difficult to explain how much I enjoy it most of the time. We laugh a lot here, as friends and professional peers. It's nice to be with women all day. I like the sudden, transient bonds I forge with some clients: moments when I am in my strength, remembering weakness, and a woman in weakness reaches out for my strength. What I offer is not power, but solidness, offered almost eagerly. Certain clients waken in me every tender urge I have—others make me wince and bite my tongue. Both challenge me to find a balance. It is a sweet brutality we practice here, a stark and loving dispassion.

I look at abortion as if I am standing on a cliff with a telescope, gazing at some great vista. I can sweep the horizon with both eyes, survey the scene in all its distance and size. Or I can put my eye to the lens and focus on the small details, suddenly so close. In abortion the absolute must always be tempered by the contextual, because both are real, both valid, both hard. How can we do this? How can we refuse? Each abortion is a measure of our failure to protect, to nourish our own. Each basin I empty is a promise—but a promise broken a long time ago.

I grew up on the great promise of birth control. Like many women my age, I took the pill as soon as I was sexually active. To risk pregnancy when it was so easy to avoid seemed stupid, and my contraceptive success, as it were, was part of the promise of social enlightenment. But birth control fails, far more frequently than our laboratory trials predict. Many of our clients take the pill; its failure to protect them is a shocking realization. We have clients who have been sterilized, whose husbands have had vasectomies; each one is a statistical misfit, fine print come to life. The anger and shame of these women I hold in one hand, and the basin in the other. The distance between the two, the length I pace and try to measure, is the size of an abortion.

The procedure is disarmingly simple. Women are surprised, as though the mystery of conception, a dark and hidden genesis, requires an elaborate finale. In the first trimester of pregnancy, it's a mere few minutes of vacuuming, a neat tidying up. I give a woman a small yellow Valium, and when it has begun to relax her, I lead her into the back, into bareness, the stirrups. The doctor reaches in her, opening the narrow tunnel to the uterus with a succession of slim, smooth bars of steel. He inserts a plastic tube and hooks it to a hose on the machine. The woman is framed against white paper that crackles as she moves, the light bright in her eyes. Then the machine rumbles low and loud in the small windowless room; the doctor moves the tube back and forth with an efficient rhythm, and the long tail of it fills with blood that spurts and stumbles along into a jar. He is usually finished in a few minutes. They are long minutes for the woman; her uterus frequently reacts to its abrupt emptying with a powerful, unceasing cramp, which cuts off the blood vessels and enfolds the irritated, bleeding tissue.

I am learning to recognize the shadows that cross the faces of the women I hold. While the doctor works between her spread legs, the paper drape hiding his intent expression, I stand beside the table. I hold the woman's hands in mine, resting them just below her ribs. I watch her eyes, finger her necklace, stroke her hair. I ask about her job, her family; in a haze she answers me; we chatter, faces close, eyes meeting and sliding apart.

I watch the shadows that creep up unnoticed and suddenly darken her face as she screws up her features and pushes a tear out each side to slide down her cheeks. I have learned to anticipate the quiver of chin, the rapid intake of breath and the surprising sobs that rise soon after the machine starts to drum. I know this is when the cramp deepens, and the tears are partly the tears that follow pain— the sharp, childish crying when one bumps one's head on a cabinet door. But a well of woe seems to open beneath many women when they hear that thumping sound. The anticipation of the moment has finally come to fruit; the moment has arrived when the loss is no longer an imagined one. It has come true.

I am struck by the sameness and I am struck every day by the variety here—how this commonplace dilemma can so display the differences of women. A twenty-one-year-old woman, unemployed, uneducated, without family, in the fifth month of her fifth pregnancy. A forty-two-year-old mother of teenagers, shocked by her condition, refusing to tell her husband. A twenty-three-year-old mother of two having her seventh abortion, and many women in their thirties having their first. Some are stoic, some hysterical, a few giggle uncontrollably, many cry.

I talk to a sixteen-year-old uneducated girl who was raped. She has gonorrhea. She describes blinding headaches, attacks of breathlessness, nausea. "Sometimes I feel like two different people," she tells me with a calm smile, "and I talk to myself."

I pull out my plastic models. She listens patiently for a time, and then holds her hands wide in front of her stomach.

"When's the baby going to go up into my stomach?" she asks. I blink. "What do you mean?"

"Well," she says, still smiling, "when women get so big, isn't the baby in your stomach? Doesn't it hatch out of an egg there?"

My first question in an interview is always the same. As I walk down the hall with the woman, as we get settled in chairs and I glance through her files, I am trying to gauge her, to get a sense of the words, and the tone, I should use. With some I joke, with others I chat, sometimes I fall into a brisk, business-like patter. But I ask every woman, "Are you sure you want to have an abortion?" Most nod with grim knowing smiles. "Oh, yes," they sigh. Some seek forgiveness, offer excuses. Occasionally a woman will flinch and say, "Please don't use that word."

Later I describe the procedure to come, using care with my language. I don't say "pain" any more than I would say "baby." So many are afraid to ask how much it will hurt. "My sister told me—" I hear. "A friend of mine said—" and the dire expectations unravel. I prick the index finger of a woman for a drop of blood to test, and as the tiny lancet approaches the skin she averts her eyes, holding her trembling hand out to me and jumping at my touch.

It is when I am holding a plastic uterus in one hand, a suction tube in the other, moving them together in imitation of the scrubbing to come, that women ask the most secret question. I am speaking in a matter-of-fact voice about "the tissue" and "the contents" when the woman suddenly catches my eye and asks, "How big is the baby now?" These words suggest a quiet need for a definition of the boundaries being drawn. It isn't so odd, after all, that she feels relief when I describe the growing bud's bulbous shape, its miniature nature. Again I gauge, and sometimes lie a little, weaseling around its infantile features until its clinging power slackens.

But when I look in the basin, among the curdlike blood clots, I see an elfin thorax, attenuated, its pencilline ribs all in parallel rows with tiny knobs of spine rounding upwards. A translucent arm and hand swim beside.

A sleepy-eyed girl, just fourteen, watched me with a slight and goofy smile all through her abortion. "Does it have little feet and little fingers and all?" she'd asked earlier. When the suction was over she sat up woozily at the end of the table and murmured, "Can I see it?" I shook my head firmly.

"It's not allowed," I told her sternly, because I knew she didn't really want to see what was left. She accepted this statement of authority, and a shadow of confused relief crossed her plain, pale face.

Privately, even grudgingly, my colleagues might admit the power of abortion to provoke emotion. But they seem to prefer the broad view and disdain the telescope. Abortion is a matter of choice, privacy, control. Its uncertainty lies in specific cases: retarded women and girls too young to give consent for surgery, women who are ill or hostile or psychotic. Such common dilemmas are met with both compassion and impatience: they slow things down. We are too busy to chew over ethics. One person might discuss certain concerns, behind closed doors, or describe a particularly disturbing dream. But generally there is to be no ambivalence.

Every day I take calls from women who are annoyed that we cannot see them, cannot do their abortion today, this morning, now. They argue the price, demand that we stay after hours to accommodate their job or class schedule. Abortion is so routine that one expects it to be like a manicure: quick, cheap, and painless.

Still, I've cultivated a certain disregard. It isn't negligence, but I don't always pay attention. I couldn't be here if I tried to judge each case on its merits; after all, we do over a hundred abortions a week. At some point each individual in this line of work draws a boundary and adheres to it. For one physician the boundary is a particular week of gestation; for another, it is a certain number of repeated abortions. But these boundaries can be fluid too: one physician overruled his own limit to abort a mature but severely malformed fetus. For me, the limit is allowing my clients to carry their own burden, shoulder the responsibility themselves. I shoulder the burden of trying not to judge them.

This city has several "crisis pregnancy centers" advertised in the Yellow Pages. They are small offices staffed by volunteers, and they offer free pregnancy testing, glossy photos of dead fetuses, and movies. I had a client recently whose mother is active in the anti-abortion movement. The young woman went to the local crisis center and was told that the doctor would make her touch her dismembered baby, that the pain would be the most horrible she could imagine, and that she might, after an abortion, never be able to have children. All lies. They called her at home and at work, over and over and over, but she had been wise enough to give a false name.

She came to us a fugitive. We who do abortions are marked, by some, as impure. It's dirty work.

When a deliveryman comes to the sliding glass window by the reception desk and tilts a box toward me, I hesitate. I read the packing slip, assess the shape and weight of the box in light of its supposed contents. We request familiar faces. The doors are carefully locked; I have learned to half glance around at bags and boxes, looking for a telltale sign. I register with security when I arrive, and I am careful not to bang a door. We are all a little on edge here.

Concern about size and shape seem to be natural, and so is the relief that follows. We make the powerful assumption that the fetus is different from us, and even when we admit the similarities, it is too simplistic to be seduced by form alone. But the form is enormously potent—humanoid, powerless, palm-sized, and pure, it evokes an almost fierce tenderness when viewed simply as what it appears to be. But appearance, and even potential, aren't enough. The fetus, in becoming itself, can ruin others; its utter dependence has a sinister side. When I am struck in the moment by the contents in the basin, I am careful to remember the context, to note the tearful teenager and the woman sighing with something more than relief. One kind of question, though, I find considerably trickier. "Can you tell what it is?" I am asked, and this means gender. This question is asked by couples, not women alone. Always couples would abort a girl and keep a boy. I have been asked about twins, and even if I could tell what race the father was.

An eighteen-year-old woman with three daughters brought her husband to the interview. He glared first at me, then at his wife, as he sank lower and lower in the chair, picking his teeth with a toothpick. He interrupted a conversation with his wife to ask if I could tell whether the baby would be a boy or girl. I told him I could not.

"Good," he replied in a slow and strangely malevolent voice, "'cause if it was a boy I'd wring her neck."

In a literal sense, abortion exists because we are able to ask such questions, able to assign a value to the fetus which can shift with changing circumstances. If the human bond to a child were as primitive and unflinchingly narrow as that of other animals, there would be no abortion. There would be no abortion because there would be nothing more important than caring for the young and perpetuating the species, no reason for sex but to make babies. I sense this sometimes, this wordless organic duty, when I do ultrasounds.

We do ultrasound, a sound-wave test that paints a faint, gray picture of the fetus, whenever we're uncertain of gestation. Age is measured by the width of the skull and confirmed by the length of the femur or thighbone; we speak of a pregnancy as being a certain "femur length" in weeks. The usual concern is whether a pregnancy is within the legal limit for an abortion. Women this far along have bellies which swell out round and tight like trim muscles. When they lie flat, the mound rises softly above the hips, pressing the umbilicus upward.

It takes practice to read an ultrasound picture, which is grainy and etched as though in strokes of charcoal. But suddenly a rapid rhythmic motion appears—the beating heart. Nearby is a soft oval, scratched with lines—the skull. The leg is harder to find, and then suddenly the fetus moves, bobbing in the surf. The skull turns away, an arm slides across the screen, the torso rolls. I know the weight of a baby's head on my shoulder; the whisper of lips on ears, the delicate curve of a fragile spine in my hand. I know how heavy and correct a newborn cradled feels. The creature I watch in secret requires nothing from me but to be left alone, and that is precisely what won't be done.

These inadvertently made beings are caught in a twisting web of motive and desire. They are at least inconvenient, sometimes quite literally dangerous in the womb, but most often they fall somewhere in between—consequences never quite believed in come to roost. Their virtue rises and falls outside their own nature: they become only what we make them. A fetus created by accident is the most absolute kind of surprise. Whether the blame lies in a failed IUD, a slipped condom, or a false impression of safety, that fetus is a thing whose creation has been actively worked against. Its existence is an error. I think this is why so few women, even late in a pregnancy, will consider giving a baby up for adoption. To do so means making the fetus real—imagining it as something whole and outside oneself. The decision to terminate a pregnancy is sometimes so difficult and confounding that it creates an enormous demand for immediate action. The decision is a rejection; the pregnancy has become something to be rid of, a condition to be ended. It is a burden, a weight, a thing separate.

Women have abortions because they are too old, and too young, too poor, and too rich, too stupid, and too smart. I see women who berate themselves with violent emotions for their first and only abortion, and others who return three times, five times, hauling two or three children, who cannot remember to take a pill or where they put the diaphragm. We talk glibly about choice. But the choice for what? I see all the broken promises in lives lived like a series of impromptu obstacles. There are the sweet, light promises of love and intimacy, the glittering promise of education and progress, the warm promise of safe families, long years of innocence and community. And there is the promise of freedom: freedom from failure, from faithlessness. Freedom from biology. The early feminist defense of abortion asked many questions, but the one I remember is this: Is biology destiny? And the answer is yes, sometimes it is. Women who have the fewest choices of all exercise their right to abortion the most.

Oh, the ignorance. I take a woman to the back room and ask her to undress; a few minutes later I return and find her positioned discreetly behind a drape, still wearing underpants. "Do I have to take these off too?" she asks, a little shocked. Some swear they have not had sex, many do not know what a uterus is, how sperm and egg meet, how sex makes babies. Some late seekers do not believe themselves pregnant; they believe themselves *impregnable.* I was chastised when I began this job for referring to some clients as girls: it is a feminist heresy. They come so young, snapping gum, sockless and sneakered, and their shakily applied eyeliner smears when they cry. I call them girls with maternal benignity. I cannot imagine them as mothers.

The doctor seats himself between the woman's thighs and reaches into the dilated opening of a five-month pregnant uterus. Quickly he grabs and crushes the fetus in several places, and the room is filled with a low clatter and snap of forceps, the click of the tanaculum, and a pulling, sucking sound. The paper crinkles as the drugged and sleepy woman shifts, the nurse's low, honey-brown voice explains each step in delicate words.

I have fetus dreams, we all do here: dreams of abortions one after the other; of buckets of blood splashed on the walls; trees full of crawling fetuses. I dreamed that two men grabbed me and began to drag me away. "Let's do an abortion," they said with a sickening leer, and I began to scream, plunged into a vision of sucking, scraping pain, of being spread and torn by impartial instruments that do only what they are bidden. I woke from this dream barely able to breathe and thought of kitchen tables and coat hangers, knitting needles striped with blood, and women all alone clutching a pillow in their teeth to keep the screams from piercing the apartment-house walls. Abortion is the narrowest edge between kindness and cruelty. Done as well as it can be, it is still violence—merciful violence, like putting a suffering animal to death.

Maggie, one of the nurses, received a call at midnight not long ago. It was a woman in her twentieth week of pregnancy; the necessarily gradual process of cervical dilation begun the day before had stimulated labor, as it sometimes does. Maggie and one of the doctors met the woman at the office in the night. Maggie helped her onto the table, and as she lay down the fetus was delivered into Maggie's hands. When Maggie told me about it the next day, she cupped her hands into a small bowl—"It was just like a little kitten," she said softly, wonderingly. "Everything was still attached."

At the end of the day I clean out the suction jars, pouring blood into the sink, splashing the sides with flecks of tissue. From the sink rises a rich and humid smell, hot, earthy, and moldering; it is the smell of something recently alive beginning to decay. I take care of the plastic tub on the floor, filled with pieces too big to be trusted to the trash. The law defines the contents of the bucket I hold protectively against my chest as "tissue." Some would say my complicity in filling that bucket gives me no right to call it anything else. I slip the tissue gently into a bag and place it in the freezer, to be burned at another time. Abortion requires of me an entirely new set of assumptions. It requires a willingness to live with conflict, fearlessness, and grief. As I close the freezer door, I imagine a world where this won't be necessary, and then return to the world where it is. □

Exercises

1. Briefly summarize Tisdale's essay.

2. What claims do you think Tisdale is making in this essay?

3. How does she support them? Do you think she supports them adequately?

4. Describe what you think Tisdale takes her audience to be. How, would you assume, has that affected her writing?

5. Write a response to Tisdale, either agreeing or disagreeing with her
    position and making sure that you support your claims.

BEING PERSUADED

Clear logic and reasonable claims are not the only way we can
be persuaded. As you will remember from Chapter 1, a reader is
someone who *wants* to be persuaded. You read because you want
to make meaning and you expect to be able to do so. For that reason
you may very well find yourself influenced in ways that have more
to do with your needs, your likes, and your dislikes than with the
purity of fine reasoning.

For one thing, as a reader or a listener, you can be persuaded
of something—rationally or otherwise—only if you are involved in
it and if some or all of the following activities take place:

- You develop responses and find yourself reacting to a text or thinking creatively or critically along with it.

- You find yourself reflected in some way in what is being said; you
  can relate a text to your own experience.

- You sense you are the listener the speaker has in mind. You can
  create a dialogue with the text, and perhaps even its writer. You
  identify with something in the writing; your expectations are
  raised and satisfied.

- You help make the meaning of the text by filling in gaps and making connections, accumulating information in sequences or clusters
  of related facts.

- You are influenced by appeals to your reason, your emotions, your
  sense of importance and need for power, your respect for authority, your aesthetic sense (or sense of the beautiful), and values that
  you hold dear.

The following speech was given in Stockholm by William
Faulkner as he received the Nobel Prize for literature.

I feel that this award was not made to me as a man, but to my
work—a life's work in all the agony and sweat of the human spirit,

not for glory and least of all for profit, but to create out of the materials of the human spirit something which did not exist before. So this award is only mine in trust. It will not be difficult to find a dedication for the money part of it commensurate with the purpose and significance of its origin. But I would like to do the same with the acclaim too, by using this moment as a pinnacle from which I might be listened to by the young men and women already dedicated to the same anguish and travail, among whom is already that one who will some day stand here where I am standing.

Our tragedy today is a general and universal physical fear so long sustained by now that we can even bear it. There are no longer problems of the spirit. There is only the question: "When will I be blown up?" Because of this, the young man or woman writing today has forgotten the problems of the human heart in conflict with itself which alone can make good writing because only that is worth writing about, worth the agony and the sweat.

He must learn them again. He must teach himself that the basest of all things is to be afraid; and, teaching himself that, forget it forever, leaving no room in his workshop for anything but the old verities and truths of the heart, the old universal truths lacking which any story is ephemeral and doomed—love and honor and pity and pride and compassion and sacrifice. Until he does so, he labors under a curse. He writes not of love but of lust, of defeats in which nobody loses anything of value, of victories without hope and, worse of all, without pity or compassion. His griefs grieve on no universal bones, leaving no scars. He writes not of the heart but of the glands.

Until he relearns these things, he will write as though he stood among and watched the end of man. I decline to accept the end of man. It is easy enough to say that man is immortal simply because he will endure; that when the last ding-dong of doom has clanged and faded from the last worthless rock hanging tideless in the last red and dying evening, that even then there will still be one more sound: that of his puny inexhaustible voice, still talking. I refuse to accept this. I believe that man will not merely endure: he will prevail. He is immortal, not because he alone among creatures has an inexhaustible voice, but because he has a soul, a spirit capable of compassion and sacrifice and endurance. The poet's, the writer's, duty is to write about these things. It is his privilege to help man endure by lifting his heart, by reminding him of the courage and honor and hope and pride and compassion and pity and sacrifice which have been the glory of his past. The poet's voice need not merely be the record of man, it can be one of the props, the pillars to help him endure and prevail. □

Exercises

1. Form small groups and discuss the speech. After writing down your reactions, discuss whether the speech is persuasive. During the discussion, each group member should also note the major reactions of others in the group.

2. After the discussion of Faulkner's speech has taken place, write a one-page summary of how you think the passage and the opinions expressed by various people influenced the group you are in, noting similar and different reactions. You can use the short list of reading activities above (p. 225) as a basis for your discussion.

3. Write about one page in which you try to persuade someone that Faulkner's ideas are either right or wrong.

Responding Critically   You read by

- Listening to the voices of the text
- Interacting with them, adapting information to your personal experience
- Having your expectations raised and satisfied
- Accumulating information through sequences and clusters of related facts
- Questioning the text
- Reading and rereading to build on your initial experience of the text

All appeals a text makes to you—to your reason, values, opinions, need for power and respect, sense of beauty, emotions, and love of authority—all these appeals are literally "read" by you as you read the text. Your ability to identify with the writer and your admiration for him or her plays an especially important role. Your identity themes—those images you have of yourself—determine not only your behavior but also your susceptibility to influence. You will at first stubbornly resist Faulkner if you are impatient with the "old" virtues. You will agree with Frye if you believe in the necessity for learning to handle English well in order to achieve free speech.

You tend to select information that reinforces your attitudes and behavior. You like literature, films, political speeches, and so on, that are easily assimilated into your own value systems. The *beliefs* you base on those values are not quite so stubborn, but they are hard to budge nonetheless. Would Faulkner's speech alter an opinion that nuclear power is good? Then there are your *attitudes*—your moods, dispositions, feelings—which are based on your self-image, your beliefs, and your values but which, unlike these, can be changed with relative ease. This is where you are most susceptible to influence.

Moods, as we know, swing. We act sometimes for quite impulsive reasons. Politicians and advertisers, for example, will prey heavily on our desires, self-images, values, and beliefs in order to change our attitudes. They rarely try to alter anything more important: They want our vote or they want us to buy; they don't want our souls. They know, for example, that most of us will vote for the most "American" party and that we will agree that we should not buy foreign cars for patriotic reasons. When we do buy foreign cars, it is because they are cheap and economical to drive, or expensive and prestigious—both part of the American value systems. Foreign car advertisers emphasize these values and beliefs in order to change our predisposition to buy American, even while they play up the fact that we are doing ourselves a good turn and not really harming the American economy—we're saving gas and money. They leave our patriotic values intact but alter our moods and dispositions. Thus our attitudes can be changed without changing our value systems.

So what is important about your response to persuasion? One thing only: that you must go to the trouble to *interpret* what is placed before you.

- Get the information clear by asking who? what? when? where? how? and why?

- Listen carefully to the voices you hear and be aware of conflicting comments.

- Examine your personal reactions as closely as you can.

- Consider if your expectations have been satisfied.

- Check carefully to see which facts relate and which don't.

- Do not ignore problem passages, places where the meaning is unclear.

- Try to discover the social implications of the text for you and for a general audience.

- Examine the relationship between a claim and its support.

In other words, when you are obviously in the presence of persuasive writing, more than ever you need to read critically.

Say you are reading Faulkner's speech and have responded to his words as those of an authority figure. You are moved by the passion of his sentiments, but you are not sure about the appeal he makes to the fear of a nuclear holocaust: "When will I be blown up?" Something jars in you at that point, so you look carefully into the reasons why. Admittedly, the speech was given some years ago, but was the question ever really appropriate? You may think so; if you do, you can be persuaded by his belief that humanity "will prevail" and perhaps accept his reasons for it.

But say you are not sure that the situation is quite so black and white: lust versus love, contemporary writing of "victories without hope and, worst of all, without pity and compassion" versus the "old" literature of "universal truths." You may sense that there is some dramatic oversimplifying going on here, that Faulkner is presenting a rather dubious either–or argument—either embrace the old virtues or wallow in lust. Maybe he is even promoting his own writing, rich in just these universal values.

There is no need for a cynical reading, of course. Faulkner's is still a stirring speech and the call to arms is beautifully made, if somewhat overstated. You may still find your values reinforced; you respond to the images of courage under fire; your belief in the essential optimism of the human spirit remains firm. But you may want to qualify your enthusiasm a little. For certainly, the values Faulkner speaks of are enduring, and certainly, much of the literature is about "the human heart in conflict," but does that mean that that is the *only* kind of writing that can counter our malaise? Aren't some of the old virtues like "pride," "honor," and "sacrifice" a little suspect themselves? Might not they, too, have caused some of our problems, been among the causes of war? You need not diminish the grandeur of the prose or the power of the message, but you can still read critically, tempering persuasion with a little careful thought.

Exercises

1. Read the next three selections and carefully answer the following
    questions for each:

    (a) How does each text try to influence you?
    (b) Do you hear any conflicting voices in the text? Are there passages
    where the meaning is unclear? Why?
    (c) What conflicting voices do you find in your own responses?
    (d) Can you honestly unify your response to each text without
    oversimplifying both your response and the text? Explain your opinion
    carefully.
    (e) What do you think are the *implications* of each text for society at
    large?

2. Choose one of the extracts as an inspiration for a short essay that
    persuasively develops a claim made in the extract—either for or
    against that claim.

The Educated Imagination
Northrop Frye

You see, freedom has nothing to do with lack of training; it
can only be the product of training. You're not free to move unless
you've learned to walk, and not free to play the piano unless you
practice. Nobody is capable of free speech unless he knows how to
use a language, and such knowledge is not a gift: it has to be learned
and worked at. The only exceptions, and they are exceptions that
prove the rule, are people who, in some crisis, show that they have
a social imagination strong and mature enough to stand out against
a mob. In the row over desegregation in New Orleans, there was
one mother who gave her reasons for sending her children to an
integrated school with such dignity and precision that the reporters
couldn't understand how a woman who never got past grade six
learned to talk like the Declaration of Independence. Such people
already have what literature tries to give. For most of us, free speech
is cultivated speech, but cultivating speech is not just a skill, like
playing chess. You can't cultivate speech, beyond a certain point,
unless you have something to say, and the basis of what you have

to say is your vision of society. So while free speech may be, at least at present, important only to a very small minority, that very small minority is what makes the difference between living here and living in East Berlin or South Africa. ☐

Autobiography
Benjamin Franklin

I believe I have omitted mentioning that in my first Voyage from Boston, being becalm'd off Block Island, our People set about catching Cod and hawl'd up a great many. Hitherto I had stuck to my Resolution of not eating animal Food; and on this Occasion, I consider'd with my Master Tryon, the taking every Fish as a kind of unprovok'd Murder, since none of them had or ever could do us any injury that might justify the slaughter. All this seemed very reasonable. But I had formerly been a great Lover of Fish, and when this came hot out of the Frying Pan, it smelt admirably well. I balanc'd some time between Principle and Inclination: till I recollected, that when the Fish were opened, I saw smaller Fish taken out of their Stomachs: Then thought I, if you eat one another, I don't see why we mayn't eat you. So I din'd upon Cod very heartily and continu'd to eat with other People, returning only now and then occasionally to a vegetable Diet. So convenient a thing it is to be a *reasonable Creature*, since it enables one to find or make a Reason for every thing one has a mind to do. ☐

Night
Elie Wiesel

They found a trail. It eventually led to the Dutch Oberkapo. And there, after a search, they found an important stock of arms.

The Oberkapo was arrested immediately. He was tortured for a period of weeks, but in vain. He would not give a single name. He was transferred to Auschwitz. We never heard of him again.

But his little servant had been left behind in the camp in prison. Also put to torture, he too would not speak. Then the SS sentenced him to death, with two other prisoners who had been discovered with arms.

One day when we came back from work, we saw three gallows rearing up in the assembly place, three black crows. Roll call. SS all round us, machine guns trained: the traditional ceremony. Three victims in chains—and one of them, the little servant, the sad-eyed angel.

The SS seemed more preoccupied, more disturbed than usual. To hang a young boy in front of thousands of spectators was no light matter. The head of the camp read the verdict. All eyes were on the child. He was lividly pale, almost calm, biting his lips. The gallows threw its shadow over him.

This time the Lagerkapo refused to act as executioner. Three SS replaced him.

The three victims mounted together onto the chairs.

The three necks were placed at the same moment within the nooses.

"Long live liberty!" cried the two adults.

But the child was silent.

"Where is God? Where is He?" someone behind me asked.

At a sign from the head of the camp, the three chairs tipped over.

Total silence throughout the camp. On the horizon, the sun was setting.

"Bare your heads!" yelled the head of the camp. His voice was raucous. We were weeping.

"Cover your heads!"

Then the march past began. The two adults were no longer alive. Their tongues hung swollen, blue tinged. But the third rope was still moving; being so light, the child was still alive. . . .

For more than half an hour he stayed there, struggling between life and death, dying in slow agony under our eyes. And we had to look him full in the face. He was still alive when I passed in front of him. His tongue was still red, his eyes were not yet glazed.

Behind me, I heard the same man asking:

"Where is God now?"

And I heard a voice within me answer him:

"Where is He? Here He is—He is hanging here on this gallows. . . . "

That night the soup tasted of corpses. □

Persuasion and Ethics   Not all persuasion is either logical or good. Here we consider briefly the question of whether there is a definable relationship between persuasion and ethics.

Those who believe that advertising and political rhetoric are based on a kind of lying have little trouble in asserting the unethical nature of the two. Lies, as we know, can be amazingly persuasive. Hitler's arguments for race differences between "Aryans" and Jews were illogical to the extreme, but they were frighteningly persuasive for reasons that continue to fascinate researchers and that seem to have had something to do with the social, political, and economic conditions of the time in Germany and Europe. That was a case of persuasion used for demented reasons, but advertising, we know, is somewhat less consequential even if it creates a pervasive environment. Many think that there is little point in being "moralistic" about advertising, for it is overseen by the Federal Trade Commission and by and large does not get out of control.

It is up to you to decide how seriously you want to take the impact of advertising on your life. There have been *just* complaints that advertising employs sexual and race stereotyping, raises prices, tries to dump inferior products on an unsuspecting public, and generally disseminates a banal and boring image of life. But then so do other media events. Short of a rigid aesthetic as well as moral censorship, we have no option but to fall back on the old saying: "buyer beware." Our choices are constantly conditioned by family, religion, education, and the media in general, not just by advertising. The question of influence extends beyond advertising and propaganda and raises the issue of the *personal responsibility we all have not to be led to unethical decisions by poor interpretations.*

It is much easier to describe unethical than ethical persuasion, but even this is controversial. You may ask why ethics becomes a question at all. "If people are foolish enough to buy this product, then that's their fault," is a statement that is often heard. Well, that is in part true, but it is also true that some of us are more susceptible than others to arguments and need "to be saved from ourselves." Even more important, every statement and claim is a social act. Since the statements are made publicly, whoever makes them must bear responsibility. Whatever is said in public has moral consequences.

So if a persuader *intentionally makes untrue statements,* and *intentionally aims to mislead an audience by not giving all the facts or by presenting them ambiguously,* then the persuasion is *unethical.* Product advertising is regulated for these characteristics. You may remember a recent case when a leading mouthwash manufacturer had to change its advertising and delete the statement that its product "killed" certain "germs" because it could not prove that it did. Advertisements, however, still walk the fine line between the ethical and the unethical, *insinuating claims* even if they are unable to prove them. "In *some* cases," runs a familiar ad, "your gas mileage *may* be higher."

You should, of course, interpret very closely every piece of important persuasion you come across. You should always begin your analysis by asking

Are the statements untrue?
Is the persuader trying to mislead me?

If you can answer yes to either of these questions and can substantiate your reaction, you have found a case of unethical persuasion.

Ethical Codes   There is a large area of ethical judgment that is more personal than public. You may think it unethical for a politician to defend the sale of arms to certain countries that in your opinion will use them to prop up a corrupt government. On the other hand, someone else may say that it is ethical to do so, for that government provides the only stable control in the region and is staving off civil and regional war in which many more people would be killed. What are judgments based on, then? They are based on a code of ethics that may be yours and yours alone but that you want to justify and make as general as possible.

How do you judge ethical codes and questionable persuasive appeals? There are plenty of suggestions available from philosophers, but try these simple questions: Does the code by which you judge appeal to universal values? Will it have good effects? This brings us back to the old question: How do we define *good?* That argument is often more philosophical than it need be for everyday terms. In the social arena, we have long associated *good* with the rights of personal freedoms, government for and by the people, and values that represent the greatest happiness for the greatest number. Obviously this casts doubt on any code that asserts that there are no universal standards, that every situation requires individual judgment (situational ethics). It also casts doubt on the notion that all universal standards should free us to pursue our own course of happiness entirely (individual ethics).

Again, you have to decide on the nature of the good, and no discussion as short as this one can possibly hope to provide you with conclusive guidance. For morality is a cumulative, changing set of values defined sometimes by the influence of the few on the many, and sometimes by the many on the few. But persuasion does have ethical implications. Interpretation leads to evaluation, and in your own interests at least, you should be prepared to

- *Examine the evidence on which claims are made.* Is it relevant? True? Unambiguously presented? Choose the best set of standards you know and judge according to it. Do not merely react.

- *Examine the argument based on the evidence.* Is it clear? Does it falsify the evidence? Does it use correct, logical reasoning?

- *Examine the claim that results from the argument.* Is it justified, given the evidence and the argument?

- *Examine the appeals the argument makes to you.* Are they reasonable and fair?

You will notice that discussing persuasion leads us inevitably to ethics, and that in turn leads us to the question of judging arguments, which we discuss in the next section. But first consider ethics in advertising. Read the following selection and the accompanying advertisements. Remember these are not "real" advertisements in the sense that they are trying to promote something commercial. Real advertising companies were commissioned to use their skills to promote "the seven deadly sins." Only three of those sins are reproduced here (along with "Pride" earlier in this chapter).

You Can Have It All!

The recent public debate on our nation's scandals exposes a fundamental irony. Amid the moralizing columns of pundits and

The only emotion powerful enough both to start a war — and stop one.

WRATH

Agency: Saatchi & Saatchi DFS Compton. *Creative Director:* Dick Lopez. *Copywriter:* Jeff Frye. *Clients:* Toyota, "Who Could Ask for Anything More? Toyota"; PaineWebber, "Thank You, PaineWebber"; Wendy's, "Where's the Beef?"

IF THE ORIGINAL SIN HAD BEEN SLOTH, WE'D STILL BE IN PARADISE.

SLOTH

Agency: J. Walter Thompson. *Art Director:* Jean Marcellino. *Copywriter:* Chuck Hoffman. *Clients:* Ford, "Have You Driven a Ford Lately?" Pepsi Slice, "We Got the Juice"; U.S. Marine Corps, "We're Looking for a Few Good Men."

two-minute homilies by newscasters warning "Thou Shalt Not" fall the whispers of advertisers: "Who Says You Can't Have It All?" and "Obsession" and "You Deserve a Break Today" and "The Pride Is Back!"

With sweet words, Madison Avenue seeks to profit from our longing to lead ourselves into temptation. The schizophrenia of public puritanism and private libertinism creates a host of charming—and uniquely American—effects. Ivan Boesky cloisters himself with the Torah. The President publicly offers his urine for official inspection. Mafia bosses make a public show of attending church. Preachers swear off adultery.

In the interest of moral instruction and clarification, *Harper's Magazine* asked leading advertising agencies to develop a campaign *promoting* the seven deadly sins: Wrath, Lust, Avarice, Gluttony, Sloth, Envy, and Pride. Each agency pitted in-house teams against one another to perform this public service, to provide grist for tomorrow's sermonizers and to reconcile God and Mammon. ☐

Exercises

1. For each of the advertisements, explain the main persuasive appeals.

2. Write an essay explaining the "moral instruction and clarification" you find in these advertisements. Specifically answer this question: What ethical issues concerning advertising do these "advertisements" raise?

WRITING PERSUASIVELY

When writing for a general reader, each of us has in mind some idea of whom we are writing for. Sometimes this mythical person flits in and out of consciousness and is hard to pin down. Sometimes we choose a well-rounded, well-educated, rational person who likes many of the things we happen to like and could be one of our peers. That may seem a somewhat narrow way of "imagining the reader." It is also a somewhat idealized portrait of a reader, for none of us is really so predictable, nor do we all look and think like one another. But if we model our reader on someone we think we are like in our best (and most relaxed) moments—or someone we want to be like—then we will probably do well in getting our point across by assuming we are talking to such a person.

Such a reader need not just be us in our most private moments, but may be us when we feel at one with society and friends, when we are confident about the way we fit in. Such a reader is also someone we can assume will be able to connect the claims we make with the support we offer for them, and will understand the context of our argument, providing we have carefully fulfilled our obligations to make those connections and the context as clear as possible.

The art directors and copywriters of the advertisements for "You Can Have It All" tried to appeal to a generic reader like that, specifically to what we all are supposed to secretly *want:* to live in a world without taboos where sins are not sins at all. And the advertisements are strangely effective because they *argue* for this, they try to justify the seven deadly sins, by using conventional ways of promoting commercial products. It is all very ironic, of course. Somehow, a part of us wants to be persuaded that sinning is all right. But part of the irony is that we do not *have* to go off and sin; we can like the advertisement without actually buying the product.

That is how persuasive writing works too. It talks to people at large; it draws in the reader because its argument seems generally plausible and its writer seems credible. It creates a powerful situation and clearly contextualizes its arguments. It makes readers feel as though they are *there* and *experiencing* something.

Your success as a persuasive writer therefore depends on a number of things:

- The reasonableness of your claims and the adequacy and clarity of your support.

- The relevance of your claims to experience that can be shared with others.

- Your credibility and the common humanity you express to a reader.

How you treat the reader and how you treat your material are equally crucial. If you appear to present a genuine and *earned* opinion, and not simply a bias or an oversimplification, you stand a chance of persuading a reader that you might just be right about something. If you support your claims, show both sides of the question, dwell on common interests, make a reasoned analysis, appeal to common values, and avoid biased language, the reader may be prepared to give you the benefit of the doubt. There is no guarantee, of course. There is no predicting the mood or powers of concentration of the reader when he or she reads your work. But the more detailed and reasonable the context of an argument, the more concrete the situation, and the more justified the opinions, the better your chances are.

Consider the following situation. Sean Manly is a television celebrity and he receives many letters a week, far too many to answer individually. So he decides to write a form letter that will go out to all but the very few correspondents to whom he wants to write personally:

> Dear Friend:
>
> Many thanks for your letter. I'm afraid that so many of you write in that I cannot respond to you all personally. It takes me too long to prepare for my show and unfortunately the producers don't give me a secretary—or several secretaries—which I badly need. But I am happy you watch my show and for some reason or other want to write to me. Excuse the impersonality of this letter . . . and keep your TV tuned to me!
>
> Yours,
> Sean Manly

What sort of effect do you think a letter like this will have on a reader? It reads as though Manly wants to be pleasant, but it suggests both his frustration and his egotism. He does not want to lose viewers, but he may very well realize that unless he is Bruce Springsteen and allows a sweat stain to fall on the page, thereby making it a valuable memento, it is unlikely that his reader will be impressed by this note.

Exercises

1. Put yourself in Manly's place and ask yourself: How can I touch *every* reader who writes to me? How can I persuade them that I am sincere? Write a paragraph describing what you should do.

2. Rewrite Sean Manly's letter to make it more effective.

3. Now read the accompanying letter sent out by Andy Rooney, a commentator on the CBS News show *60 Minutes*. Write a paragraph on the effectiveness of Rooney's writing—or its lack of effectiveness.

Memo to Letter Writers from Andy Rooney

There are good things and bad things about this recent well-knownness of mine. The money's good but there are problems. One of the problems is mail. I simply don't know what to do about it. I hate to think of all the people I've offended by not answering a letter they've sent me but I'm often getting as many as 100 letters a day. I hate answering letters anyway but even if I liked doing it, I couldn't answer 100 a day and do anything else.

This may be the most formless form letter you ever got but I'll tell you something I've thought about my mail for a couple of years now. We all make friends in different sections of our lives. We make them in grade school, high school, and maybe college. We graduate, get married, take a job or move to another town and we make a whole new group of friends. We still like our old friends but our paths have diverged and we lose each other. We don't see our good old friends anymore. We make new friends and eventually part with them too. Our lives are compartmented and we have different friends in each compartment. No one can be friends all the time with all the friends he or she has made. Very often we lose track of them completely and can't even send them a Christmas card.

One of the best things about being in the public eye—and believe me, there aren't many good things about it—is that my old friends can find me and write me. Them I write back. Everyone else who writes me a good letter makes me feel terrible because I have to send them this.

Forgive me,
Andy Rooney

4. Imitating Rooney's style, write a letter to a girlfriend or boyfriend breaking off your relationship.

The Writer's Credibility   In persuasive writing, our feelings often run high—sometimes too high to allow us to present a lucid, well-argued position. Other times we have no real feelings at all on a topic and are merely going through the motions of presenting an "argument." In both cases, it is important that you not start writing until after you have gone through the initial stages of the writing process: finding a topic, opening up the topic, limiting the topic, and, by playing off opposites reaching a conclusion about the topic. Only then will too strong or weak feelings be remedied. The question then becomes: *How do you present your case?*

Your basic aim is to present yourself as a writer with as much credibility as possible. You know what kind of writing impresses you: writing in which the writer is talking to *you* and doing so in a way that leads you to trust the writer. So your credibility depends above all on your developing a trustworthy voice, your own voice. Your credibility does not emerge from either showing off or being self-effacing, from refusing to listen to other points of view, or from listing your credentials. It arises from your handling of the topic: your motives and competences and your values as implied by your relationship to the topic.

There are some general points to remember, and perhaps the most important is that credibility arises from your *being in control of your material.* Let it be known that you know what you want to say and can express it in a qualified and committed tone.

- You want to appear *rational,* but not overrational. A reasoned justification lies in the direct presentation of the argument, not in long-winded defenses or uncertain repetitions.

- You might appear genuinely *angry* and *ironic,* but beware of blind rage and sarcasm, for sarcasm is not irony. The persuasive essay is not a slap in the reader's face but an attempt to change attitudes.

- You want to *express ideas* and show the implications of your topic. You are not mouthing slogans or glibly passing judgments. To the extent that you show a dynamic relationship between facts, you will entice a reader in.

- You want to *discuss and dramatize a topic,* not merely repeat points about it. The topic is not a list of qualities but, again, a whole network of facts.

- You want to reveal a genuine, substantiated *opinion,* not a bias. In other words, your point of view must be clear and justified. Your tone should be committed but qualified.

- You want to show that you have listened well and can understand an opponent's argument, or can think at least of what the arguments of your potential opposition might be.

Read the following passage and think about the writer's credibility as you do so:

The Case for Christianity
C. S. Lewis

And, of course, that raises a very big question. If a good God made the world why has it gone wrong? And for many years I simply wouldn't listen to the Christian answers to this question, because I kept on feeling "whatever you say, and however clever your arguments are, isn't it much simpler and easier to say that the world was *not* made by any intelligent power? Aren't all your arguments simply a complicated attempt to avoid the obvious?". . .

My argument against God was that the universe seemed so cruel and unjust. But how had I got this idea of *just* and *unjust*? A man doesn't call a line crooked unless he has some idea of a straight line. What was I comparing this universe with when I called it unjust? If the whole show was bad and senseless from A to Z, so to speak, why did I, who was supposed to be part of the show, find myself in such violent reaction against it? A man feels wet when he falls into water, because man isn't a water animal: a fish wouldn't feel wet. Of course I could have given up my idea of justice by saying it was nothing but a private idea of my own. But if I did that then my argument against God collapsed too—for the argument depended on saying that the world was really unjust, not that it just didn't happen to please my private fancies. Thus in the very act of trying to prove that God didn't exist—in other words, that the whole of reality was senseless—I found I was forced to assume that one part of reality—namely my idea of justice—was full of sense. Consequently atheism turns out to be too simple. If the whole universe has no meaning, we should never have found out that it has no meaning: just as if there were no light in the universe and therefore no creatures with eyes we should never know it was dark. *Dark* would be a word without meaning.

Very well then, atheism is too simple. And I'll tell you another view that is also too simple. It's the view I call Christianity-and-water, the view that just says there's a good God in Heaven and

everything is all right—leaving out all the difficult and terrible doc-
trines about sin and hell and the devil, and the redemption. Both
these are boys' philosophies.

It is no good asking for a simple religion. After all, real things
aren't simple. They *look* simple, but they're not. The table I'm sitting
at looks simple: but ask a scientist to tell you what it's really made
of—all about the atoms and how the light waves rebound from
them and hit my eye and what they do to the optic nerve and what
it does to my brain—and, of course, you find that what we call
"seeing a table" lands you in mysteries and complications which
you can hardly get to the end of. A child, saying a child's prayer,
looks simple. And if you're content to stop here, well and good. But
if you're not—and the modern world usually isn't—if you want to
go on and ask what's really happening—then you must be prepared
for something difficult. If we ask for something more than simplicity, it's silly then to complain that the something more isn't simple.
Another thing I've noticed about reality is that, besides being difficult, it's odd: it isn't neat, it isn't what you expect, I mean, when you
grasped that the earth and the other planets all go round the sun,
you'd naturally expect that all the planets were made to match—all
at equal distances from each other, say, or distances that regularly
increased, or all the same size, or else getting bigger or smaller as
you go further from the sun. In fact, you find no rhyme or reason
(that we can see) about either the sizes or the distances; and some
of them have one moon, one has four, one has two, some have none,
and one has a ring.

Reality, in fact, is always something you couldn't have
guessed. That's one of the reasons I believe Christianity. It's a religion you couldn't have guessed. If it offered us just the kind of universe we'd always expected, I'd feel we were making it up. But, in
fact, it's not the sort of thing anyone would have made up. It has
just the queer twist about it that real things have. So let's leave
behind all these boys' philosophies—these over-simple answers.
The problem isn't simple and the answer isn't going to be simple
either. □

Now it does not matter whether you believe in God or not or
whether you are a Christian or not—those are not the issues here.
The question is: Is Lewis convincing? Do you listen to Lewis because
he sounds credible? He is at least low-keyed and rational. Unlike so

many writers on religion, he does not *rationalize* pre-existing belief but works via a series of problems and solutions. He points out that a simple religion or a simple opposition to religion will not work. There is no defensiveness in his position. He implies that the enemy to belief lies in part within each of us, in our natural skepticism. So he presents the argument against belief but does so with care, for atheism and skepticism are not necessarily the same thing. Atheism runs into a problem if it claims that the world is unjust and meaningless because even meaninglessness has a meaning: "If the whole universe has no meaning, we should never have found out that it has no meaning."

Not only does Lewis present a strong but quietly stated rational appeal that takes account of the opposite view, but he seems confident in his opinions. He is thinking his way through his argument and not stumbling about. He offers no slogans or strident claims, nor does he glibly pass judgment or pretend to be in possession of the whole truth. Religious belief cannot be simple because it has to contend with a whole network of facts, some of which are unpredictable in their function: like the nature of God as good and the presence of so much unhappiness on earth.

Lewis discusses his topic; he does not simply preach. He wants to reveal a genuine opinion, not a formulated bias. There is no doubt that his tone is committed, but it allows qualification, the major qualification being that religion is not easy. So credibility is built up slowly, modestly, competently, and rationally, with a strong sense of conveying values the writer does believe in. The writer's motive here is not simply to proselytize, but to explain reasonably and persuasively. Does he persuade you? Can you find any problems with his argument?

Persuasive writing can serve less lofty purposes, as you will see in the following selection.

I Married Alexis

Excerpted from the "Declaration of Peter Holm in Support of Respondent's Request for Spousal Support," filed in California Superior Court on March 27, 1987. Joan Collins

*filed for divorce from Holm in December, after thirteen
months of marriage.*

STANDARD OF LIVING OF THE PARTIES PRIOR TO THE MARRIAGE

One afternoon in July 1983, I met Joan Collins. She noticed me and, through a third party, invited me to escort her that evening to the world premier of the film *Superman.* We shared a wonderful evening. After the screening, we went to the most famous and chic London discothèque, TRAMPS, where we danced together all through the night. This was the evening in which I fell in love with Joan. We had both fallen in love. Joan left that following morning for Los Angeles. We parted, and the final words Joan said to me—after giving me her phone number and address in Beverly Hills—were: "Please come and visit me in Los Angeles." I was greatly affected by that wonderful evening, for it was the first time I had fallen in love. A couple of days later, I telephoned Joan in America. I was missing her terribly. Joan asked me when I would be visiting America, so that we might see each other again. I made arrangements immediately to take a plane at the end of the week.

I arrived in Los Angeles, where Joan's driver picked me up at the airport and took me to the house at Bowmont Drive. I was surprised that Joan's main car was a ten-year-old Mercedes. I said to myself that Joan should have a brand new Rolls-Royce. It was a happy and loving reunion. That evening Joan and I dined at MA MAISON and attended a party at Hugh Hefner's PLAYBOY MANSION. Once again Joan and I danced into the early hours of the morning. We fell even more in love. That night, in consideration of Joan's daughter, Katy, I slept in a guest room at Bowmont. I had only taken one week's holiday, but the time was flying away as we spent every minute we could together. Joan had to work at the studio on the *Dynasty* set, which I visited just to be close to her. When the week's holiday was up, I extended my holiday for another two weeks. Joan and I were together all of this time. We enjoyed and loved each other. We made love for the first time, and we got to know each other more and more. Then, unfortunately, I had to return to England to attend to my businesses. After only a week away from each other, Joan flew over to England to be with me. It was during this week that we decided we wanted to be together, wherever that was. Joan had to be in L.A. because of her work, so I decided to join her. We flew back to Los Angeles together, and I lived with her at Bowmont Drive. My businesses in England suffered greatly as a result of this move, and finally I had no option but to sell them in order that I might spend my time with Joan.

As the days went by, I had to comfort Joan, as she had so many financial and business problems that were making her unhappy. It seems that Joan wasn't capable of being an actress and a business-woman at the same time. It became clear to me when I asked Joan if she knew how much money she was spending and earning, that Joan needed help. As she didn't know, I decided to help Joan in whatever way I could. I couldn't stand to see my sweetheart being unhappy.

Christmas 1984, Joan and I became engaged. I proposed marriage to Joan because we were living together and I was happy in my own mind that we would always be together. It would be my first marriage. I proposed to Joan on the island of Antigua, in the Caribbean. I gave Joan a five-carat diamond solitaire ring. Almost a year later, Joan and I married in Las Vegas on November 6, 1985. It proved an exciting week for both of us. Not only did we fly by private jet to Las Vegas and get married, but later that week, in Florida, we met and danced with Prince Charles and Lady Diana.

I felt that Joan had such great talent and good taste that I thought we should jointly produce television movies. I initiated and negotiated the seven-hour CBS miniseries called *Sins*, which had production costs of $14,000,000. During the production we stayed in a six-room suite at the RITZ in PARIS, the world's most exclusive and expensive hotel. We stayed there for three months at a cost of approximately $200,000, which was paid for by the production company. The project was very profitable for Joan and myself, and was also a great ratings success. Together, we were the executive producers. From the initial idea to the completed project, Joan and I worked happily and proudly together. It was the ideal situation for two people so in love.

During all these years, Joan and I were inseparable. When Joan was in Europe, I was with her. Every social function, private function, business function, we were always together. I am pleased that our relationship has not only been wonderful and romantic but also that our joint efforts have resulted in a gross income in excess of $5,200,000 during our marriage, up until December 8, 1986.

STANDARDS OF LIVING OF THE PARTIES DURING THE COURSE OF THE MARRIAGE

The Petitioner and I have always traveled extensively during our marriage. Many of the expenses were paid for by other entities. However, we have paid for a good portion of our travel expenses during the marriage. For example, we have two houses in Beverly Hills and two houses in the south of France. I travel to the south of France frequently.

We both have friends and business acquaintances throughout Europe and the United States. We have been entertained by PRESIDENT REAGAN and were invited on December 4, 1984, to the White House.

During the summer of 1986, while visiting LONDON, we enjoyed the company of HER ROYAL HIGHNESS, QUEEN ELIZABETH II, PRINCE CHARLES and LADY DIANA, and SIR GORDON WHITE at the famous ASCOT RACES.

During the summer of 1986, I attended a private cocktail party with PRINCESS CAROLINE and PRINCE ALBERT—at the ROYAL PALACE in MONTE CARLO. Unfortunately, the Petitioner could not join us.

We dined out at restaurants on an average of five or six nights per week, at an average cost of $100 per person.

RESTAURANTS IN EUROPE

Annabel's, Connaught Hotel, Harry's Bar, Langan's Brasserie, Mr. Chow, Mr. Kai, San Lorenzo, Trader Vic's, Tramps, White Elephant, Maxim's

RESTAURANTS IN CALIFORNIA

Bistro Garden, Bombay Palace, Chasen's, La Scala, La Serre, Ma Maison, Mr. Chow, Morton's, Nicky Blair, Nipper's, Pastel, Scandia, Spago, Studio Grill, Tramps, Trumps

We were always part of the local HOLLYWOOD party scene and attended parties at the homes of, or with: Johnny Carson, Roger Moore, Linda Evans, Jackie Bisset, Sammy Cahn, Michael Caine, Dyan Cannon, Allan Carr, Barbara Carrera, Diahann Carroll, Chris Cazanove, Marvin Davis, Sammy Davis Jr., Kirk Douglas, Timothy Dalton, Morgan Fairchild, James Farentino, Freddie Fields, John Forsythe, Eva Gabor, Zsa Zsa Gabor, Regine, Larry Hagman, George Hamilton, David Hasselhoff, Hugh Hefner, Lauren Hutton, Julio

Iglesias, John James, Don Johnson, Gene Kelly, Irving Lazar, Michele Lee, Liza Minnelli, Michael Nader, Catherine Oxenburg, Ryan O'Neal, Farrah Fawcett, Gregory Peck, Joanna Poitier, Stefanie Powers, Norman Parkinson, Jean-Pierre Aumont, Jane Seymour, Robert Wagner, Esther Williams, Raquel Welch, Joan Rivers, Harold Robbins, Adnan Khashoggi.

Because of this life style we always had to wear very expensive designer clothing and jewelry, and use limousine services, luxury cars, and private drivers.

We entertained in our Bowmont home on average once every ten days and held a major event every month. We employed extra staff—caterers, car valets, and extra security—for these parties. We catered to our friends' expensive tastes. Provisions included Russian caviar, smoked salmon, and champagne, vintage wines, and liquor by the crate.

I currently enjoy the use of two luxury automobiles, a custom-built and -designed Spartan (purchased at approximately $40,000) and a BMW 635CSI. However, the latter vehicle was removed from my control and possession by the Petitioner and hidden from me despite the court order of February 17, 1987, which stated that I should have exclusive temporary use of my BMW 635CSI. In order to maintain properly both vehicles, the cost is approximately $2,800 per month, due to their luxury nature.

During our marriage we purchased a second family home, located at 1196 Cabrillo Drive, Beverly Hills, for $1,950,000 cash, which we paid for with some funds earned during our marriage. The home comprises 13,000 square feet of living space, including a huge master bedroom suite, a separate guest house, and numerous other amenities—including room to park twenty cars, a large pool and fountains, an extensive lawn, and terraced walks throughout the estate.

In order to maintain my current life style I have begun looking for a permanent residence in the area. I realize that to live in a property like the Cabrillo residence may be unrealistic for me at this time. However, I have looked at residences about half the size of the Cabrillo property that would be suitable to me and find that the monthly rent is $16,500.

Throughout our marriage I have dressed stylishly. I have spent large sums updating my wardrobe to enhance my wife's and my public image. I spent approximately $20,000 per month on clothing and accessories. I purchased an extensive amount of clothing while

I traveled (always first class) in Europe during our marriage. In fact, during our marriage we withdrew over $600,000 in cash for these kinds of expenditures.

Shopping was one of our favorite pastimes and we patronized such places as RODEO DRIVE in Beverly Hills. We both have expensive tastes in our choice of wardrobes. Our life style demands that we wear quality clothing at all times, including expensive leather and fur jackets, ties, watches, shoes, and silk shirts. For instance, I wear $2,000 leather jackets, $400 crocodile shoes, and tens of thousands of dollars worth of jewelry.

While our income and expenses may seem extraordinary to the average person, the fact of the matter is that to us, it is our normal way of life and is typical of those depicted in the television series *Lifestyles of the Rich and Famous*, on which we have been featured several times.

Because I am presently unemployed, and all savings during the marriage were invested in our Cabrillo home, my cash flow is, at present, zero. Therefore, I am requesting $80,000 per month *pendente lite* support in order that I can maintain my standard of living which I have enjoyed previous to and during our marriage. Petitioner's income is more than sufficient to support my request for temporary support while maintaining her life style and standard of living. □

Exhibit A

The following estimates of my present monthly expenses are based on actual expenses for the calendar year 1986.

Projected new residence:

Rent	$16,500.00
Household Salaries	7,000.00
Payroll Taxes	1,400.00
Household Cash	300.00
Household Supplies	
General	700.00
Groceries	1,900.00
Hardware, etc.	200.00
Miscellaneous	500.00
Maintenance	500.00

(continued)

Utilities	600.00
Telephone	1,300.00
TV Cable and Video Supplies	670.00
Dry Cleaning	100.00
Insurance	300.00
Security—Bel Air Patrol	200.00
TOTAL	32,170.00

Car expenses:

Leasing of 1984 BMW	3,910.00
Gas	160.00
Repairs and Maintenance	1,300.00
Depreciation	1,500.00
Insurance	400.00
Registration	25.00
TOTAL	7,295.00

Other:

Club Membership and Dues	400.00
Newspapers and Magazines	100.00
Personal Grooming	200.00
Medical Expenses	250.00
Gifts	1,650.00
Audio Supplies	400.00
Computer Equipment and Supplies	3,000.00
Freight and Messengers	100.00
Office Expenses	1,125.00
Books	280.00
Clothing and Accessories	12,000.00
Photos and Supplies	800.00
Subscriptions	36.00
Maintenance and Taxes (Port Grimaud)	1,500.00
Advertising	250.00
Entertainment	6,000.00
Cash Draws	8,000.00
Travel and Lodging	4,000.00
Limousine Expenses	500.00
TOTAL	40,591.00

GRAND TOTAL	$80,056.00

Exercises

1. How credible do you think the preceding writer has made himself through his writing? Write about a page in which you carefully consider how the writer presents and supports his claims. Discuss the kinds of appeals he makes.

2. Assume the role of someone arguing the case *against* Christianity (see the C. S. Lewis passage on page 244–245), or of the defendant in the Joan Collins–Peter Holm case (i.e., Miss Collins). Write a statement that makes claims, supports them adequately, appeals to a general audience, and tries to establish your credibility as clearly as possible.

Handling Controversy When you write on a controversial topic, refute an argument, or present an unpopular point of view, what can you do to be persuasive?

An immediate interest in dealing with a controversial topic is to *avoid conflict*, but this does not mean that you have to offer immediate compromises. Instead, engage the opposition. When you locate opposing interpretations as you brainstorm your topic, you are locating the arguments that might be made against you. In persuasive writing, you can anticipate what the opposition might be.

- State both sides of the question clearly.

- Show you understand the opposition's argument.

- Discuss the strengths as well as the weaknesses of the other side.

- Account for your own weaknesses as well as strengths.

- Compare opposing interpretations and settle on as many common interests as possible. Aim for dialogue and *cooperation*.

- Analyze a potentially hostile or skeptical audience carefully for age, sex, group membership, level of education, level of income, and religious and political affiliations. It is not always possible to do this in detail, of course, but when it is relevant—that is, when you are speaking to a specific audience—your avoidance of unnecessary conflict sometimes depends on your understanding of your opposition's values and beliefs.

- Explain carefully the *contexts* in which the opposite arguments exist. No argument takes place in a vacuum, and you want to uncover the common influences and even the common fate of your argument and your opponent's. Ask yourself what both your arguments have in common in terms of influence. Does the same set of conditions create both your arguments? You may find that you have a common enemy. You may, for example, be arguing for a day care center in your university and your opponent may want the funds to be used for library books. Both are worthy causes and your common enemy may be an administration official who insists that neither is important and that a new dean of janitorial affairs is needed. Maybe you should join your rival.

- Try to get your reader to identify with your position by making a careful, reasoned explanation and analysis of the problem underlying the argument—not just your opinion of it.

- Avoid biased language, name calling, or stacking the cards against your opponent. Build up your credibility by expressing a genuine opinion in a committed but rational argument.

- Appeal to reason and to common values, justifying your decision as one that is based on a valid code of ethics which your opponent might share. Remember that no argument is without ethical implications.

Now read the following selections with these points in mind.

Execution Eve
William F. Buckley, Jr.

(1) The business about the poor and the black suffering excessively from capital punishment is no argument against capital punishment. It is an argument against the *administration* of justice, not against the penalty. Any punishment can be unfairly or unjustly applied. Go ahead and reform the processes by which capital punishment is inflicted, if you wish; but don't confuse maladministration with the merits of capital punishment.

(2) The argument that the death penalty is "unusual" is circular. Capital punishment continues on the books of a majority of states, the people continue to sanction the concept of capital punishment, and indeed capital sentences are routinely handed down. What has made capital punishment "unusual" is that the courts and, primarily, governors have intervened in the process so as to collab-

orate in the frustration of the execution of the law. To argue that capital punishment is unusual, when in fact it has been made unusual by extralegislative authority, is an argument to expedite, not eliminate, executions. □

Through the Looking Glass
Lewis Carroll

"What a beautiful belt you've got on!" Alice suddenly remarked. (They had had quite enough of the subject of age, she thought: and, if they really were to take turns in choosing subjects, it was *her* turn now.) "At least," she corrected herself on second thoughts, "a beautiful cravat, I should have said—no, a belt, I mean—I beg your pardon!" she added in dismay, for Humpty Dumpty looked thoroughly offended, and she began to wish she hadn't chosen that subject. "If only I knew," she thought to herself, "which was neck and which was waist!"

Evidently Humpty Dumpty was very angry, though he said nothing for a minute or two. When he *did* speak again, it was in a deep growl.

"It is a—*most*—*provoking*—thing," he said at last, "when a person doesn't know a cravat from a belt!"

"I know it's very ignorant of me," Alice said, in so humble a tone that Humpty Dumpty relented.

"It's a cravat, child, and a beautiful one, as you say. It's a present from the White King and Queen. There now!"

"It is really?" said Alice, quite pleased to find that she *had* chosen a good subject after all.

"They gave it me," Humpty Dumpty continued thoughtfully as he crossed one knee over the other and clasped his hands round it, "they gave it me—for an un-birthday present."

"I beg your pardon?" Alice said with a puzzled air.

"I'm not offended," said Humpty Dumpty.

"I mean, what *is* an un-birthday present?"

"A present given when it isn't your birthday, of course."

Alice considered a little. "I like birthday presents best," she said at last.

"You don't know what you're talking about!" cried Humpty Dumpty. "How many days are there in a year?"

"Three hundred and sixty-five," said Alice.

"And how many birthdays have you?"

"One."

"And if you take one from three hundred and sixty-five what remains?"

"Three hundred and sixty-four, of course."

Humpty Dumpty looked doubtful. "I'd rather see that done on paper," he said.

Alice couldn't help smiling as she took out her memorandum-book, and worked the sum for him:

$$\begin{array}{r} 365 \\ \underline{1} \\ 364 \end{array}$$

Humpty Dumpty took the book and looked at it carefully. "That seems to be done right—" he began.

"You're holding it upside down!" Alice interrupted.

"To be sure I was!" Humpty Dumpty said gaily as she turned it round for him. "I thought it looked a little queer. As I was saying, that *seems* to be done right—though I haven't time to look it over thoroughly just now—and that shows that there are three hundred and sixty-four days when you might get un-birthday presents—"

"Certainly," said Alice.

"And only *one* for birthday presents, you know. There's glory for you!"

"I don't know what you mean by 'glory,'" Alice said.

Humpty Dumpty smiled contemptuously. "Of course you don't—till I tell you. I meant 'there's a nice knock-down argument for you!'"

"But 'glory' doesn't mean 'a nice knock-down argument,'" Alice objected.

"When I use a word," Humpty Dumpty said, in a rather scornful tone, "it means just what I choose it to mean—neither more or less."

"The question is," said Alice, "whether you *can* make words mean so many different things."

"The question is," said Humpty Dumpty, "which is to be master—that's all." □

The Phantom Captain
R. Buckminster Fuller

Man?
A self-balancing, 28-jointed adapter-base biped; an electro-chemical reduction-plant, integral with segregated stowages of special energy extracts in storage batteries, for subsequent actuation of thousands of hydraulic and pneumatic pumps, with motors attached; 62,000 miles of capillaries; millions of warning signals, railroad and conveyor systems; crushers and cranes (of which the arms are magnificent 23-jointed affairs with self-surfacing and lubricating systems, and a universally distributed telephone system needing no service for 70 years if well managed); the whole, extraordinarily complex mechanism guided with exquisite precision from a turret in which are located telescopic and microscopic self-registering and recording range finders, a spectroscope, *et cetera*, the turret control being closely allied with an air conditioning intake-and-exhaust, and a main fuel intake. ☐

The Medium, the Mystic, and the Physicist
L. Le Shan

In the Hasidic tradition it is repeated over and over that if the Zaddick, the wise man, serves only God and not the people, he will descend from whatever "rung of the ladder of perfection" he has ascended to. "If the Zaddick serves God," typically wrote Rabbi Nahman of Bratislav, "but does not take the trouble to teach the multitude, he will descend from his rung."

The great mystics have understood this, and functioned strongly in both worlds. W. R. Inge, a scholar of the subject, has pointed out that "all the great [Western] mystics have been energetic and influential, and their business capacity is specially noted in a curiously large number of cases." The lives of St. John of the Cross, St. Teresa of Avila, Kabir, Vivekananda, and many others show this understanding, concern, and active involvement with the world of multiplicity. In her usual incisive way, St. Teresa once stated the situation clearly. At dinner, a dish of roast partridges had been served, and she was eating with great gusto and enjoyment. Someone reproached her that it was unseemly for a bride of Christ to have such zest for and participation in the mundane aspects of the world. St. Teresa replied, "When it's prayer time, pray; when it's partridge time, partridge!" □

Exercises

For each of the preceding selections

1. Discuss how the controversy is handled.

2. Comment on the credibility of the writer.

3. Write a critical statement taking up any of the issues discussed in any of the extracts and offering a strong opinion of your own.

CHAPTER 6

Writing and Revising

As words spill out of our minds during the rush of creativity, we hurriedly record our thoughts, not worrying about misspellings, repetitive sentences, poor word choices, or fragments. Later, when we have time, we revise with our readers in mind, rethinking our words and considering their effects on our readers.

Although revision occurs in virtually every step of the writing process, the most extensive kind of revision occurs after you have written one, two, or three drafts or when you sense you have reached a satisfactory conclusion to your work. In the final revisions of a paper you fine-tune your ideas, clarify your thoughts, and arrange your words for your readers' understanding.

This chapter explores ways to make your ideas more accessible and persuasive. By increasing your awareness of style, especially its effects on readers, you will be able to revise your writing for clarity and increased reader interest. By means of thoughtful revision we encourage readers to continue with us until we are ready to end the dialogue. We increase our chances they will do just that.

WHAT IS STYLE?

Style is the verbal identity of a writer, as unmistakable as his or her face or voice. All the habitual choices a writer makes—of word and phrase, of sentence pattern and length, of structure and organization, of voice and tone—all these and more constitute style. A writer's style reflects an individual way of seeing the world, and as such is something far greater than the sum of the identifiable parts within a sentence or a paragraph.

Some characteristics of a writer's style are more striking than others. And some aspects of a writer's style are more appealing than others. We respond favorably to writers largely because we enjoy in some measure their style. Sometimes, in fact, we may like one author because his or her style reminds us of another writer we admire or enjoy. The similarities we may detect in the kinds of sentences or vocabularies the two writers use may be part of what they share in style. The more important and less immediately identifiable aspect of style that we respond to with equal enthusiasm, however, may be less a matter of words or sentences than of vision. In responding to a writer's style, we respond to his or her way of seeing the world.

Exercises

1. Write a few paragraphs comparing the styles of one of the following pairs of public figures: Bruce Springsteen and John Cougar Mellencamp; Whitney Houston and Madonna; Whoopi Goldberg and Joan Rivers; Robin Williams and Eddie Murphy; Roger Clemens and Dwight Gooden; Oprah Winfrey and Geraldo Rivera; Jesse Jackson and Pat Robertson; Michael Jordan and Magic Johnson. How much do you feel a person's style contributes to his or her success? Is it possible to like a person's style but dislike what he or she represents or thinks?

2. Analyze at least two pages of your own writing to discover your stylistic habits. Pay particular attention to the patterns you frequently use. The following questions will guide you through your self-analysis.

   How many sentences did you write in your two-page sample?
   What is the average word count of your sentences?
   How do you usually begin sentences? End them?
   Is there any word or phrase you use quite often?
   How many times did you use each of the following verbs: am, is, are, was, were, seems?
   How many times did you use a verb containing more than one word?
   How many times did you use a word that your readers will have to look up in a dictionary?

STYLISTIC EFFECTS

The following excerpt illustrates how an author's style affects us in different ways. The passage describes its author's personal encounter with native Alaskans. During your first reading of the excerpt, underline passages that strongly affect you, that make you want to stop or read further. As you read it the second time, list specific words and phrases that engaged you.

Arctic Dreams
Barry Lopez

The mountain in the distance is called Sevuokuk. It marks the northwest cape of Saint Lawrence Island in the Bering Sea. From where we are on the ice, this eminence defines the water and the sky to the east as far as we can look. Its western face, a steep wall of snow-streaked basalt, rises above a beach of dark cobbles, riven, ice-polished, ocean-rolled chips of Sevuokuk itself. The village of Gambell is there, the place I have come from with the Yup'ik men, to hunt walrus in the spring ice.

We are, I believe, in Russian waters; and also, by a definition to them even more arbitrary, in "tomorrow," on the other side of the international date line. Whatever political impropriety might be involved is of little importance to the Yup'ik, especially while they are hunting. From where blood soaks the snow, then, and piles of meat and slabs of fat and walrus skin are accumulating, from where ivory tusks have been collected together like exotic kindling, I stare toward the high Russian coast. The mental categories, specific desires, and understanding of history among the people living there are, I reflect, nearly as different from my own as mine are from my Yup'ik companions'.

I am not entirely comfortable on the sea ice butchering walrus like this. The harshness of the landscape, the vulnerability of the boat, and the great size and power of the hunted animal combine to increase my sense of danger. The killing jars me, in spite of my regard for the simple elements of human survival here.

We finish loading the boats. One of the crews has rescued two dogs that have either run off from one of the Russian villages or been abandoned out here on the ice. Several boats gather gunnel to gunnel to look over the dogs. They have surprisingly short hair and seem undersize to draw a sled, smaller than Siberian huskies. But the men assure me these are typical Russian sled dogs.

We take our bearing from the far prominence of Sevuokuk and turn home, laden with walrus meat, with walrus hides and a few seals, with crested auklets and thick-billed murres, with ivory and Russian dogs. When we reach shore, the four of us put our shoulders to the boat to bring it high up on the beach. A young man in the family I am staying with packs a sled with what we have brought back. He pulls it away across the snow behind his Honda three-wheeler, toward the house. Our meals. The guns and gear, the harpoons and floats and lines, the extra clothing and portable radios are all secured and taken away. I am one of the last to leave the beach, still turning over images of the hunt.

No matter what sophistication of mind you bring to such events, no matter what breadth of anthropological understanding, no matter your fondness for the food, your desire to participate, you have still seen an animal killed. You have met the intertwined issues—What is an animal? What is death?—in those large moments of blood, violent exhalation, and thrashing water, with the acrid odor of burned powder in the fetid corral smells of a walrus haul-out. The moments are astounding, cacophonous, also serene. The sight of men letting bits of meat slip away into the dark green water with mumbled benedictions is as stark in my memory as the sud-denly widening eyes of the huge, startled animals.

I walk up over the crest of the beach and toward the village, following a set of sled tracks. There is a narrow trail of fresh blood in the snow between the runners. The trail runs out at a latticework of drying racks for meat and skins. The blood in the snow is a sign of life going on, of other life going on. Its presence is too often con-fused with cruelty.

I rest my gloved fingers on the driftwood meat rack. It is easy to develop an affection for the Yup'ik people, especially when you are invited to participate in events still defined largely by their own traditions. The entire event—leaving to hunt, hunting, coming home, the food shared in a family setting—creates a sense of well-being easy to share. Viewed in this way, the people seem fully capa-ble beings, correct in what they do. When you travel with them, their voluminous and accurate knowledge, their spiritual and technical confidence, expose what is insipid and groundless in your own culture.

I brood often about hunting. It is the most spectacular and succinct expression of the Eskimo's relationship with the land, yet one of the most perplexing and disturbing for the outsider to consider. With the compelling pressures of a cash-based economy to contend with, and the ready availability of modern weapons, hunting practices have changed. Many families still take much of their food from the land, but they do it differently now. "Inauthentic" is the criticism most often made of their methods, as though years ago time had stopped for the Yup'ik.

But I worry over hunting for another reason—the endless reconciliation that must be made of Jacob with his brother Esau. The anguish of Gilgamesh at the death of his companion Enkidu. We do not know how exactly to bridge this gap between civilized man and the society of the hunter. The Afrikaner writer Laurens van der Post, long familiar with Kalahari hunting peoples as archetypal victims of our prejudice, calls the gap between us "an abyss of deceit and murder" we have created. The existence of such a society alarms us. In part this is a trouble we have with writing out our history. We adjust our histories in order to elevate ourselves in the creation that surrounds us; we cut ourselves off from our hunting ancestors, who make us uncomfortable. They seem too closely aligned with insolent, violent predatory animals. The hunting cultures are too barbaric for us. In condemning them, we see it as "inevitable" that their ways are being eclipsed. Yet, from the testimony of sensitive visitors among them, such as van der Post and others I have mentioned in the Arctic, we know that something of value resides with these people.

I think of the Eskimos compassionately as *hibakusha*—the Japanese word for "explosion-affected people," those who continue to suffer the effects of Hiroshima and Nagasaki. Eskimos are trapped in a long, slow detonation. What they know about a good way to live is disintegrating. The sophisticated, ironic voice of civilization insists that their insights are only trivial, but they are not.

I remember looking into a herd of walrus that day and thinking: do human beings make the walrus more human to make it comprehensible or to assuage loneliness? What is it to be estranged in this land?

It is in the land, I once thought, that one searches out and eventually finds what is beautiful. And an edge of this deep and rarefied beauty is the acceptance of complex paradox and the forgiveness of others. It means you will not die alone. ☐

In the excerpt from *Arctic Dreams* Barry Lopez writes about a walrus hunt and his personal, philosophical reaction to it. He creates an intimacy with us through his use of the first-person narrator. In effect, he talks directly about his experience, as we would do if we were conversing with someone face-to-face. Even so, Lopez's words are not those of casual conversation; he does not use slang, contractions, or snippets of dialogue as we would expect in a friendly, intimate conversation. If we read his words aloud, we hear a formal tone, the sound of someone we hardly know telling us about a meaningful experience he had.

Lopez prevents himself from getting too intimate with us because he wants us to think about the meaning of the experience, not about his personal encounters in Alaska. He focuses on the larger significance of the hunt by diverting us from the "bits of meat slip[ping] away into the dark green water" and directing us to the political innocence of the Yup'ik and the precariousness of their lifestyle. Through a series of analogies—Jacob and Esau, Gilgamesh and Enkidu, the Kalahari hunters, and the *hibakusha*—he converts the walrus hunt from a single event to one with historical reverberations.

Lopez also deemphasizes his personal experience at the hunt through his vocabulary. He selects words we seldom use in sustained, everyday conversation—words like *eminence, impropriety, prominence, exhalation, cacophonous, voluminous, reconciliation, archetypal, assuage,* and *paradox.* His vocabulary elevates the tone of his writing, moving it beyond observation and into interpretation. By means of particular stylistic decisions—the use of particular analogies, the creation of tone and mood through careful word choices—Lopez reinforces his content and underscores his main idea.

In the following excerpt Joe McGinniss describes his stay with Olive Cook and her family and his realization that he is witness to a dying culture. Like Lopez, he writes in the first person, but the tone he creates is far different.

Going to Extremes
Joe McGinniss

In the distance, I saw a figure walking slowly up the river. A bulky figure, in a parka, maybe about a hundred yards away. The figure waved an arm. I waved back. This was Olive Cook, I assumed. She had heard the plane—in the village, you could not help but hear the plane—and had come out to see if I was on it. I picked up my duffel bag by one end, and, dragging the other end through the snow, I headed toward her.

"Hey, you crazy guy, you really nuts, you know that? I never thought you would come. How long you staying anyway? It's very crowded here for the Slavic. I think you just be in the way." Then she laughed. A bit hysterically, I thought.

"Look at that bag. What you got in there? You got presents for me, I sure hope. I don't know where you going to put a big bag like that. We don't have no extra space in our house. When you going back? When you tell that pilot to come for you? Oh boy, you crazy guy, I don't know what you are doing here."

We walked down the river to her house. Most of the village had been built on the east bank of the river. The Cook family, and one or two others, lived on the west bank, so in summer to pick up their mail, or to use the telephone, or simply to go out and visit, they would have to cross the river in a boat. In winter, of course, it made no difference. The river was like a six-lane highway right through town.

The house was an unpainted wooden shack. Olive pushed open the door and we stepped inside, accompanied by billows of steam.

"Take off your boots, you!" This was Olive's mother. Glaring at me, and pointing to a pile of boots by the door. In my socks, I stepped into the room that served as kitchen, living room, and dining room, and as bedroom for Olive's younger brothers and her cousin.

The room contained a wood-burning stove, a big table, and a couch that folded out to be a bed. There was a basin to wash in. Water was obtained by melting ice. There was a small storage closet, separated from the kitchen by a curtain. At the rear of the storage closet there was a bucket. This bucket was the Cook family's toilet. Every couple of days, they dumped it outside and started again. In spring, when breakup came—when the snow melted and the ground thawed and the river started flowing—the winter's waste pile would gradually disappear. As would all the other waste piles around the village.

There was a second, smaller room. With a bed in one corner for the parents, a bunk bed next to it, a bunk bed at the other end, and a cot pushed up against a wall. Normally, five people slept in this room. The parents, Olive, her sister, who was fourteen years old, and a male relative who lived with the family much of the time.

Olive's father was sitting cross-legged by the stove, working intently with a knife. A bald and bloody carcass lay beside him. He looked up, nodded once, went back to work.

"What's the matter?" Olive said. "You never seen anybody skin a fox?"

There was fur, blood, gristle, and bones all over the floor. Olive's father worked silently, with head bowed. He was a short man, of medium build, with a crew cut. Her mother was taller, lighter in color, less Asiatic looking.

"Hey, what do you think?" her mother said. "This is some kind of hotel? What you come here for with that big bag?"

"It's not so big."

"Yeah, where you think we gonna put it? We don't have no space in here."

"Hey, goddamn you," Olive said. "I sure hope you brought us some vegetables."

But no, I had not brought vegetables. I should have. I had thought of buying vegetables and fruit in Anchorage. But then I had been in a rush to catch my plane.

Olive's father put down his knife, wiped his bloody hands on his pants, and sat down at the table to eat lunch. Olive's mother put a bowl in front of me. She filled it with a light brown, pasty substance. There was a plate of pilot bread—thick, flat crackers—to go with it.

"I hope you like moose soup," Olive said. "That's all we eat here in the winter."

Actually, this was not quite true. That night, for dinner, following an afternoon during which Olive took me on a walking tour of the village, there was moose stew. The difference was, moose stew had gristly joints of moose in it, while the soup was just moose-flavored gruel.

As soon as the evening meal was over, Olive's father went back to the floor, where, now that he was finished skinning fox, he had started to build a blackfish trap.

Blackfish were oily little fish that swam all winter long in the river that flowed through the village. To catch them, you lowered the trap into the water through a hole in the ice, and pulled it out the next day. The trap was made of freshly cut wood, which was peeled, cut into strips, and then woven together to make a basket. A cone was placed over the open end. The fish would swim into the basket but then would be unable to get out.

It was a painstaking, intricate process, but Olive's father worked quickly, with total concentration, his sharp knife flashing, his stubby, worn fingers handling the wood the way a professional blackjack dealer handles cards.

The children had disappeared right after dinner into the other room of the house. Olive was helping her mother wash some clothes. They had an old-fashioned washtub, with a wringer that had to be cranked by hand.

By 9 p.m. Olive's father had almost finished the trap. Just two or three more strips to weave into place. His breathing was steady and rhythmic. He sat with head bowed, legs crossed, nothing moving but the masterful hands. To watch him work was to see not just the heart of a separate culture, but, it seemed, the essence of a dying age. *would do that anymore & saw hay contrast*

All over Alaska, Eskimos were giving up, moving to the cities, signing on for government aid. Taking jobs on the pipeline, or staying home and cashing welfare checks. Some, the more adaptable, had begun going to school to learn white men's trades: real estate, construction, and other forms of profitable entrepreneurship.

But here, in the village, was Al Cook. A survivor. Impervious to the assaults of time and progress upon the sacred traditions of his people.

His expression had not changed; he had not uttered a sound for more than an hour. The blackfish trap had come to seem an extension of himself. Then, suddenly, Olive's eight-year-old brother ran in from the back room.

"Papa, Papa!" the boy shouted. "Hurry up! Hurry up! 'Six Million Dollar Man' on TV!"

Al Cook dropped his knife. He tossed the almost completed blackfish trap aside. He jumped to his feet, his face animated for the first time all day. Grinning and chattering and rubbing his hands in anticipation, he hurried toward the other room, following his son.

"Oh boy," he said. "Hurry up." Motioning for me to accompany him. "'Six Million Dollar Man' on TV." □

Through numerous details and transcriptions of casual conversation, McGinniss invites us into his narrative and lets us experience the Cook household. We hear the apprehension in Olive's voice and see her father wipe fox blood on his pants before eating. We feel Al Cook's concentration as he cuts and weaves wooden strips for a blackfish trap, and we experience his joy as he leaves to watch *The Six Million Dollar Man*.

By carefully listening to McGinniss's words, we can hear him talking to us, almost as if we are sitting with him in a booth at a corner café. His vocabulary, simple and direct, focuses more on the events he describes and less on their implications. Our familiarity with his vocabulary allows us to share his experience and appreciate the moment as he describes it.

In contrast to Lopez, who through analogy places the plight of the Yup'ik into a historical context, McGinniss rivets our thoughts and emotions on the contemporary lifestyle of the Cooks. By deepening our understanding of the Cooks' daily lives, he encourages us to compare our lives with theirs, thereby increasing the impact of his words. He depicts a hybrid culture where sacred customs and high technology coexist, and he lets us decide the efficacy of progress.

Exercises

1. Write a two- or three-page paper explaining which writer you liked better. In your essay discuss *how* the writer's tone and language influenced your opinion of his work. (That is, point out specific words and phrases you found effective and explain how they created a particular response in you.)

2. Read over the following excerpt written by a Vietnam War correspondent. As you read, jot down in the margins specific techniques the writer employs. Pinpoint aspects of the writing that create interest and make you want to continue.

Dispatches
Michael Herr

There was a song by the Mothers of Invention called "Trouble Comin' Every Day" that became a kind of anthem among a group of around twenty young correspondents. We'd play it often during those long night gatherings in Saigon, the ashtrays heaped over, ice buckets full of warm water, bottles empty, the grass all gone, the words running, "You know I watch that rotten box until my head begin to hurt, From checkin' out the way the newsmen say they get the dirt" (bitter funny looks passing around the room), "And if another woman driver gets machine-gunned from her seat, They'll send some joker with a Brownie and you'll see it all complete" (lip-biting, flinching, nervous laughter), "And if the place blows up, we'll be the first to tell, 'Cause the boys we got downtown are workin' hard and doin' swell . . . " That wasn't really about *us*, no, we were *so* hip, and we'd laugh and wince every time we heard it, all of us, wire-service photographers and senior correspondents from the networks and special-assignment types like myself, all grinning together because of what we knew together, that in back of every column of print you read about Vietnam there was a dripping, laughing death-face; it hid there in the newspapers and magazines and held to your television screens for hours after the set was turned off for the night, an after-image that simply wanted to tell you at last what somehow had not been told.

On an afternoon shortly before the New Year, a few weeks before Tet, a special briefing was held in Saigon to announce the latest revisions in the hamlet-rating system of the Pacification program, the A-B-C-D profiling of the country's security and, by heavy inference, of the government's popular support "in the country-side," which meant any place outside of Saigon, the boonies. A lot of correspondents went, many because they had to, and I spent the time with a couple of photographers in one of the bars on Tu Do, talking to some soldiers from the 1st Infantry Division who had come down from their headquarters at Lai Khe for the day. One of them was saying that Americans treated the Vietnamese like animals.

"How's that?" someone asked.

"Well, you know what we do to animals . . . kill 'em and hurt 'em and beat on 'em so's we can train 'em. Shit, we don't treat the Dinks no different than that."

And we knew that he was telling the truth. You only had to look at his face to see that he really knew what he was talking about. He wasn't judging it, I don't think that he was even particularly upset about it, it was just something he'd observed. We mentioned it later to some people who'd been at the Pacification briefing, someone from the *Times* and someone from the AP, and they both agreed that the kid from the Big Red One had said more about the Hearts-and-Minds program than they'd heard in over an hour of statistics, but their bureaus couldn't use his story, they wanted Ambassador Komer's. And they got it and you got it. □

SOME ELEMENTS OF STYLE

As you have seen so far in this chapter, some elements of style are inseparable from others. Voice, tone, and vocabulary work together to form a coherent text that produces particular effects on readers. Your awareness of the interrelationships of voice, tone, and vocabulary allows you to revise your writing for its overall impact on your readers.

Voice   As we mentioned in Chapter 1, the voice behind our words sends our readers strong signals about us and about our feelings toward our subject. Our voices reflect the role we cast ourselves in: an excited participant in a sport, an objective witness to a wreck, a knowledgeable gardener, a thoughtful moviegoer, a concerned citizen. The roles we take in writing are as crucial as those we assume in conversation. Our readers will respond to us according to the role we assume and the image of ourselves our writing projects.

Our readers expect us to observe social conventions and use a voice appropriate to the occasion and suitable for our audience. When we read the following information from a telephone directory, we do not expect to hear an individual behind the words:

> In order to ensure prompt and effective handling of all customer problems, a detailed complaint procedure is on file and may be reviewed in each of our local Public Offices and at the State Corporation Commission in Richmond.

Custom and experience tell us we will hear a "corporate voice," the sound of a large, faceless organization. And from the organization's point of view it is probably good that we cannot identify a particular person to hold responsible, for our demands on that individual would be enormous. Even so, we make judgments about the business based on our interpretation of the corporate voice, just as we evaluate a writer's credibility based on his or her use of language. If the writing confuses or intimidates us, we might think a company or a writer is "trying to put one over on us." Conversely, if we know a company's reputation or feel the voice is objective, clear, and honest, we might be more inclined to do business with it.

Sometimes our voices shout out at our readers, regardless of conventional expectations, because our topic really interests or excites us on many levels; our voices are identifiable, even behind the logo of a company or the anonymity of group authorship. Notice how the voice of the writer or writers reverberates behind the directions to the game "Out of Context."

"Out of Context" Rules

THE RIGHT EQUIPMENT

"Out of Context" contains one box of REAL QUOTES and the names of the famous people being quoted (500 cards), six boxes of BLUFF QUOTES (150 cards each), a Card Frame, Special Marker, and a score pad.

STARTING OFF

Each Player or Team of Players selects a box of color-coded BLUFF QUOTE cards. (Players should resist the temptation to glance through the cards or take them out of the box, as this can cause severe headaches and disorientation.)

One Player agrees to start the game as the Dealer. He (or she, of course) sets aside his box of BLUFF QUOTES for that round and selects the first card in the REAL QUOTE box. (The Dealer should avoid peeking at any of the other cards in the REAL QUOTE box, as this would be unfair to the other Players, truly a "raw deal.")

Each Player (except, of course, the Dealer) selects six cards from the front of their BLUFF QUOTE box, holding the cards so that the other Players cannot see them. None of the BLUFF QUOTES are the same as the REAL QUOTE being used. That's why they're called BLUFF QUOTES.

Cards should always be taken from the front of the boxes and returned to the back to avoid seeing the same cards too often.

The Dealer for the round checks the NAME on the first card in the REAL QUOTE box and announces the NAME of the person being quoted for that round.

The Players then review their BLUFF QUOTES, selecting the candidate that is most likely to fool the other Players and attract their votes. (Any similarity between "Out of Context" and the political process is purely coincidental.)

Players pass their selected BLUFF QUOTES to the Dealer, who (after receiving *all* of the BLUFF QUOTES) randomly inserts them, along with the REAL QUOTE card, into the slots in the open Card Frame. The Card Frame is then closed so that no one can see the color stripes and/or detect the REAL QUOTE.

The Dealer now repeats the NAME aloud, followed by the first quote showing. He then repeats the NAME, followed by the second quote. And so on, until all the quotes have been read aloud. (It is important to repeat the NAME before each quote and to be careful to read the REAL QUOTE in the same manner as the BLUFF QUOTES. One more thing: DO NOT PASS THE CARD FRAME AROUND OR SHOW IT TO THE OTHER PLAYERS. (They can't be trusted.)

It may be necessary to read through the quotes a second, and possibly, a third time. (Requests for a fourth reading, however, are manifestations of spineless indecision and should not be tolerated.) After the first reading paraphrasing should be adequate.

THE MOMENT OF TRUTH

Now it's time to vote. Starting with the Player to the Dealer's left, each Player announces which quote he believes is the REAL QUOTE. As each vote is cast, the Dealer makes a check mark on the appropriate Voting Slate on the Card Frame, using the Special Marker.

When everyone has voted, the Dealer turns the Card Frame so it faces the Players and, with appropriate theatrical flourish, opens the Card Frame to reveal the REAL QUOTE—which he triumphantly reads aloud. (Anyone who slaps their forehead and claims that they were going to vote for the REAL QUOTE all along, but changed their mind at the last minute, loses one point.)

SCORING

Each vote cast for a BLUFF QUOTE is worth one pair to the Player who submitted it. (The color stripes on the top of each card make it easy to give points to the right Player.)

Each vote cast for the REAL QUOTE is worth THREE POINTS to the voter.

Clearly, it makes sense to vote for the REAL QUOTE. But inasmuch as the REAL QUOTE is an elusive commodity, Players have been known to don their poker faces and vote for their own BLUFF QUOTE—sacrificing their chance for three points in hopes the other Players will jump on the bandwagon.

The Dealer may double as scorekeeper. However, it is more efficient to have the Dealer read the scores aloud while another Player records them. It is also more embarrassing.

The first Player to score 25 points wins the game.

MOVING ON

At the end of each round, the Dealer removes all of the cards from the Card Frame and lays them face-down in a pile. (You can have fun putting all the cards back in their appropriate boxes.)

At the end of each round each Player or Team draws one card from the front of their BLUFF QUOTE box to replace the card they just used.

At this point, any Players who are unhappy with their selection of BLUFF QUOTES may elect to discard up to two cards and exchange them for fresh ones. Discards should be placed at the back of the box and fresh cards drawn from the front. This provides variety. You decide if you want to draw replacement cards before or after the next name is announced.

The Dealer then wipes the Voting Slates clean and passes the Card Frame to the Player on his left, who now becomes the Dealer.

The new Dealer pulls the first card from the REAL QUOTE box and the game plays on. □

Exercises

1. Briefly describe the voice of the writer(s) in "Out of Context." How do you feel about the writer(s), the game, and the directions? What specifically did the writer(s) say that evoked your reaction to them?

2. Do you think the voice or voices you heard in these directions are appropriate for a company? If you were a production manager for the game, would you have approved these directions? Why or why not?

3. Rewrite a portion of the rules for "Out of Context," changing the voice to an objective, impersonal one.

Tone   Our written voice conveys a tone and creates a mood just as it does in conversation. While we usually cannot point to one word or group of words that create tone in a piece of writing, we can point to a complex network of words, phrases, and nuances that express our attitude toward our subject. The tone of your voice might be humorous, sad, serious, playful, sincere, or sarcastic. Regardless of the emotion you feel, your attitude comes through your words, just as a feeling of sadness or joy comes through the notes in a piece of music.

Tone is an important element of style because it tells us how to interpret a writer's attitude toward his or her subject. If we do not believe what we are writing about, why should anyone else believe us? Our feelings toward a subject send a very clear message to our readers, although we cannot often isolate one specific sentence that expresses those feelings.

In the following newspaper editorial, Carl Hiassen, a syndicated columnist for Knight-Ridder Newspapers, discusses the Southland Corporation's decision to remove sexually explicit material from its shelves to protect its customers. As you read the article, write your reactions in the margins, underline sentences where Hiassen clearly reveals his attitude toward the company's new policy, and decide whether he is making a serious point about the corporation's actions or about something else.

Anything Goes for Magazines about Violence

Carl Hiassen

What a pleasure to report that it's safe again for all God-fearing citizens to venture into 7-Eleven for their boysenberry Slurpees.

The parent company of 7-Eleven, Southland Corp. of Dallas, has responded to the Meese Commission by hastily removing from its stores the twin evil influences of *Playboy* and *Penthouse* magazines.

This is a relief for all us parents who harbored a dread that our sons might someday, in a frenzy, vault the counter to sneak a peek at Miss July. Now Mr. Jere W. Thompson, president of Southland, has banished such publications because of "a possible connection between adult magazines and crime, violence and child abuse."

I was so relieved by Mr. Thompson's display of civic concern that I dropped by two of his convenience stores last week to sample some of the approved newspapers and magazines. Guess what— scarcely a breast, bosom or buttock to be found! Well done, Thompson, you old smut buster.

Thanks to your vigilance, the shelves of 7-Eleven are once more a rich trove of wholesome family reading. Take a look:

- GLAMOUR BOYS OF CARNAGE!—A psychological ode to sex killers Ted Bundy and Christopher Wilder, featured in the August issue of *Front Page Detective*.

On Page 26, you'll also see a police photograph of a nude murdered man in a bathtub full of blood—but don't worry, Mom and Dad, there's not a naked female breast in the whole magazine.

- WHITE SLAVERS KIDNAP U.S. GIRLS IN EUROPE—Valuable travel tips from the July 15 issue of the *Sun* tabloid, including an account of "perverted intrigue" and an actual photograph of a "raped and drugged" female tourist.

- HAVE FUN WITH GUNS!—From *The Basic Guide to Guns and Shooting*, an impassioned firearms instructor reveals: "The modern repeating handgun . . . is the answer to social predation."
  Brings a lump to your throat, doesn't it?

- MANIAC MADE THE BRUNETTE DIE 3 TIMES!—From the July issue of *Inside Detective*, a quaint torture tale to share around the family hearth. Don't miss the tasteful photo on Page 32: A young stabbing victim strung up to a tree.

- Q&A WITH SGT. SLAUGHTER—From the September issue of *The Wrestler* magazine, an interview with one of wrestling's leading intellectuals ("I love a knock-down, drag-out brawl as much as the next man!"), plus a photograph of our hero gouging an opponent's bloody face with a two-pronged ice pick.
  And who says there are no role models for kids today!

- LOVELY MEXICAN GIRLS—A recurrent ad in the staples of 7-Eleven's magazine rack: "Hundreds of attractive young Mexican girls offer friendship, love and marriage to men of all ages. Personal service!" What a nice idea, sort of like the Campfire Girls, I guess.

- CRIMSON FOOTPRINTS BESIDE THE BATTERED NUDE!—Whoa, parents, don't be scared off by the caption. This issue of *Inside Detective* contains no offensive photos of nudes, just one measly decomposed corpse on Page 32.

- MOM & BOYFRIEND KILL BABY BY POURING PEPPER DOWN ITS THROAT—More unusual home recipes, courtesy of the *Sun*.

- THE GAY HUSTLERS THOUGHT MURDER WAS A LAUGHING MATTER!—A little something to amuse the kids on that long bus ride to summer camp. This tale is bannered in the August issue of *True Detective*. As a bonus for science buffs, the same issue shows a dead body crawling with—how shall we put this—fly larvae.

- FITNESS RECIPES FOR BETTER BREASTS—Wait a second, how did this rubbish slip by? From the July issue of *New Woman* magazine, an illustrated article about special exercises for you-know-what. Oh geez, what's that—a picture of a topless woman! Aaaggh! And bare buttocks on both Pages 38 and 39!

Get Dallas on the phone, pronto. Thompson! Quick, send the Magazine Purification Squad—yeah, there's still trouble in the 7-Elevens. I know, I know. Today a breast, tomorrow a sex massacre. Read all about it. ☐

For most of us, Hiassen's details and phrases create a humorous pattern that encourages us to smile, although perhaps a bit self-righteously, at the well-meaning intentions of the company. Through exaggeration he establishes a tone of disbelief and underscores for us the absurdity and the irony of the situation—the discrepancy between the reality and the intent of the Southland Corporation's decision, which oversimplifies the disputed relationship between criminality and sexuality.

Exercises

1. Briefly explain the main point of Hiassen's essay. Do you feel his tone weakens or strengthens the point he is trying to make?

2. Are your expectations of tone different for editorials and news articles? Why and how are they different? Rewrite Hiassen's column as a news article written by a reporter.

3. Write a paragraph analyzing the specific stylistic changes that took place when you rewrote Hiassen's editorial in Exercise 2.

Vocabulary and Details Your word choice reinforces your voice and tone, telling your readers a great deal about your relationship to your topic. The authors' vocabularies in some of the previous readings drew us immediately into their works, either from an emotional or intellectual perspective. In the excerpt from *Dispatches* Michael Herr pulls us into his personal world of the war correspondent, a world of deceptive words, by means of the ordinary vocabulary of daily life. Through his selection of everyday details and casual conversations he counterpoints the realities of war with the interpretations given it by the journalist, the soldier, and the general public. Song lyrics, ashtrays, empty bottles, direct quotes, and a common vocabulary—all focus our minds and emotions on the discrepancy between what the young writer knew was happening in Vietnam and what the public was told.

The tone, voice, and vocabulary of our writing must be compatible, working together to achieve an overall effect on our readers. When conflict exists among these elements, we create a dissonance, an unpleasant sound, like the wrong musical note in our favorite song, and risk losing our readers' attention.

Exercises

1. The following passage is a "dewritten" version of E. L. Doctorow's novel *Welcome to Hard Times*. All of the interesting details, sentence structures, and vocabulary have been deleted. Rewrite the passage, emphasizing voice and tone. For example, you might want to create a mysterious, humorous, gothic, or evil atmosphere through your word choices. Here's the stripped-down passage—see what you can do with it.

    > Dusk came over the town. Men stood around. Anger lay on the dust in the air. From inside the saloon came the sound of one man's laugh. Tied up at the railing was a nag.
    > Looking over the doors, I could see only his shoulders and his hat. Then he raised his head, and there was his dark reflection in the saloon mirror.
    > "Hey, who's the boss here," he called out.
    > No one moved. The saloon was silent. The man laughed. Then he stood up to his full height. He had caught sight of me.

2. Describe the speaker in the following monologue. How much can you tell about him or her through the use of vocabulary, detail, tone, and voice?

Potemkin Village
Aden Ross

I don't know why people get so pissed when they call me up and ask to talk to Frank, and I say, "Frank isn't home," and then they start to leave some important message, and I say, "Actually I am Frank" so I can get the message. Then they ask if I really am Frank or if I'm lying, and I say I was lying before but I'm not lying now. What's the big deal? Is this a low tolerance for ambiguity, or what? Americans are so effing pathological about "honesty." The George Washington bit is no fluke.

My Russian friend Nick says lying is a national pastime in Russia. I'm not calling anybody Commie-Pinko-Fag, but Russians do love to lie. Like that guy in Dostoevsky who says a whole bunch of stuff, then adds, "I was lying just now." Well, you wonder, when did "now" start. Nick is always saying incredible things like his brother just died, and we both saw his brother yesterday. Or that he's written a book called *Computer Analysis of Gas Chromotography*. I mean, Nick couldn't pass home ec, let alone chemistry.

Nick says the Russians have sixteen different words for lying. May not be true, but he should know. One phrase means "feeling especially inclined to lie." Don't you have days like that? Not because you're in trouble or you're a sickie, but because something about the day *demands* a lie? Russian also has a verb that means "to lie yourself into a trance." Like when your mouth blurts out something utterly fantastic, which needs back-up, which then needs more back-up? And before you know it, you're on a roll. Nick says Russians consider lying an exercise of the imagination.

When Catherine the Great was touring Siberia, her Secretary of State, Potemkin, knew reality would be a real downer. So he constructed a pretend village with all these false fronts and kept moving it. I mean, wherever Catherine went, she saw the same fake blue store and the same white picket fence and the same cut fir trees. She loved it. Besides, in Russia it's bad manners to mention you notice a lie. Talk about civilized.

Nick's taught me a lot. But I hope our politicians know all this; it'd be terrible if only Americans told the truth. Actually, I'm not sure Nick is Russian. He said once he was Austrian—descended from some famous composer like Chopin or Beethoven.

Now that I think about it, did they have kids? □

IMITATING STYLES

You might at first find it difficult to believe that you have a style because you are concentrating your energies on deciding what to write about and then simply on finding the right words to communicate your thoughts, attitudes, and feelings. Stylistic revisions are major reconsiderations of our writing, ways of unifying the language we use into a coherent whole. When our style is effective, it offers our readers consistency in vocabulary, tone, and voice as well as clarity in thought. Initially, at least, you can alert yourself to the kinds of stylistic options authors use by imitating the styles of others. Imitation offers you an in-depth look at another writer's choices, particularly the verbal techniques he or she uses to convey thought and express feeling.

Carefully study the following passages, one by James Boswell, an eighteenth-century Scottish biographer, and the other by Ian Frazier, a contemporary American writer. In his imitation, Frazier pays close attention to Boswell's sentence length and variety, as well as vocabulary and tone. Frazier parodies Boswell's style, imitating his verbal choices to the point of exaggeration. Nevertheless, he pays close attention to his original source and teaches us something about Boswell's writing.

The Boswell excerpt is from *The Life of Johnson*, a biography of the famous Dr. Samuel Johnson. In this selection, Boswell describes the first time he ever met the revered Johnson. As you read, study Boswell's vocabulary, formality, selection of details (including dialogue), sentence length, and punctuation. And notice, too, his penchant for interrupting his text to talk about himself. In actuality, Boswell's biography of Johnson is as much Boswell's own autobiography as the story of Johnson's life.

The Life of Samuel Johnson, LL.D.
James Boswell

To write the Life of him who excelled all mankind in writing the lives of others, and who, whether we consider his extraordinary endowments, or his various works, has been equalled by few in any age, is an arduous, and may be reckoned in me a presumptuous task.

Had Dr. Johnson written his own life, in conformity with the opinion which he has given, that every man's life may be best written by himself; had he employed in the preservation of his own history, that clearness of narration and elegance of language in which he has embalmed so many eminent persons, the world would probably have had the most perfect example of biography that was ever exhibited. But although he at different times, in a desultory manner, committed to writing many particulars of the progress of his mind and fortunes, he never had persevering diligence enough to form them into a regular composition. Of these memorials a few have been preserved; but the greater part was consigned by him to the flames, a few days before his death.

. . .

Samuel Johnson was born at Lichfield, in Staffordshire, on the 18th of September, N.S., 1709; and his initiation into the Christian Church was not delayed; for his baptism is recorded, in the register of St. Mary's parish in that city, to have been performed on the day of his birth. His father is there stiled *Gentleman,* a circumstance of which an ignorant panegyrist has praised him for not being proud; when the truth is, that the appellation of Gentleman, though now lost in the indiscriminate assumption of *Esquire,* was commonly taken by those who could not boast of gentility. His father was Michael Johnson, a native of Derbyshire, of obscure extraction, who settled in Lichfield as a bookseller and stationer. His mother was Sarah Ford, descended of an ancient race of substantial yeomanry in Warwickshire. They were well advanced in years when they married, and never had more than two children, both sons; Samuel, their first born, who lived to be the illustrious character whose various excellence I am to endeavour to record, and Nathanael, who died in his twenty-fifth year.

. . .

At last, on Monday the 16th of May, when I was sitting in Mr. Davies's back-parlour, after having drunk tea with him and Mrs. Davies, Johnson unexpectedly came into the shop; and Mr. Davies having perceived him through the glass-door in the room in which we were sitting, advancing toward us,—he announced his aweful approach to me, somewhat in the manner of an actor in the part of Horatio, when he addresses Hamlet on the appearance of his father's ghost, "Look, my Lord, it comes." I found that I had a very perfect idea of Johnson's figure, from the portrait of him painted by Sir Joshua Reynolds soon after he had published his *Dictionary,* in the attitude of sitting in his easy chair in deep meditation, which was the first picture his friend did for him, which Sir Joshua very kindly presented to me, and from which an engraving has been made for this work. Mr. Davies mentioned my name, and respectfully introduced me to him. I was much agitated; and recollecting his prejudice against the Scotch, of which I had heard much, I said to Davies, "Don't tell where I come from."—"From Scotland," cried Davies roguishly. "Mr. Johnson, (said I) I do indeed come from Scotland, but I cannot help it." I am willing to flatter myself that I meant this as light pleasantry to sooth and conciliate him, and not as an humiliating abasement at the expence of my country. But however that might be, this speech was somewhat unlucky; for with that quickness of wit for which he was so remarkable, he seized the expression "come from Scotland," which I used in the sense of being of that country, and, as if I had said that I had come away from it, or left it, retorted, "That, Sir, I find, is what a very great many of your countrymen cannot help." This stroke stunned me a good deal; and when we had sat down, I felt myself not a little embarrassed, and apprehensive of what might come next. He then addressed himself to Davies: "What do you think of Garrick? He has refused me an order for the play for Miss Williams, because he knows the house will be full, and that an order would be worth three shillings." Eager to take any opening to get into conversation with him, I ventured to say, "O, Sir, I cannot think Mr. Garrick would grudge such a trifle to you." "Sir, (said he, with a stern look,) I have known David Garrick longer than you have done: and I know no right you have to talk to me on this subject." Perhaps I deserved this check; for it was rather presumptuous in me, an entire stranger, to express any doubt of the justice of his animadversion upon his old acquaintance and pupil. I now felt myself much mortified, and began to think that the hope which I had long indulged of obtaining his acquaintance was blasted. And, in truth, had not my ardour been uncommonly strong, and my resolution uncommonly persevering, so rough a reception might have deterred me for ever from making any further attempts. Fortunately, however, I remained upon the field not wholly discomfited; and was soon rewarded by hearing some of his conversation, of which I preserved the following short minute, without marking the questions and observations by which it was produced. □

In his imitation, Ian Frazier parodies Boswell's style, emphasizing his manner of phrasing words, his lengthy sentences, and his constant self-referential prose. Frazier gives himself away with his title, "Boswell's Life of Don Johnson." As you read Frazier, you might consider whether Boswell or Don Johnson, heartthrob and star of *Miami Vice*, is the object of the parody.

Boswell's Life of Don Johnson
Ian Frazier

To attempt to preserve for posterity one whose wit and understanding outsped the swiftest minds in his business, and who knew better than any other the temper of his age and time slot, is a task for which any honest man must declare himself unfit. That Don Johnson should receive no chronicler approaching himself in stature is, I fear, a condition necessarily imposed by the eminence of his person. On my behalf, I present as credentials only a lively affection for my subject, coupled with a respect for the lofty qualities of his imagination—inclinations grown many times greater in the course of an intimacy that endured, to my gratification, through a period of several weeks' time.

As a young man raised in Scotland, and later (after a reversal in my family's fortunes) in a Thrifty Scot motel, I longed for the intellectual pleasures of the metropolis. Like many others throughout Europe and the Americas whose interest in the arts and sciences no provincial seat could satisfy, I filled my leisure hours with fancies of Miami, Florida. And, naturally, with every thought of Miami came thoughts of Don Johnson, whose name with Miami's shall be forever linked, and whose reputation shines as the brightest ornament of the location where he tapes. Accordingly, when I attained my majority I removed to that city, and settled myself in rented beachfront lodgings within walking distance of the Seaquarium.

My friend having but little interest in reviewing for me the smaller details of his birth and upbringing, I must rely for this account upon remarks that I think I heard him make at one meeting or another. Don Johnson was born near the midpoint of his century to a couple who also lived in that time. Like many young boys, Don Johnson was inclined to mischief. His parents either wished him to

read law at university in preparation for a career at the bar or else
they did not wish it or else they had no thoughts on the matter. For
his own part, when his schooling was finished, or earlier, Don Johnson strengthened his resolve to brave the uncertainties of a player's
life. Toward this end, he changed his probable Christian name,
"Donald," to the better and more dramatic "Don."

My own introduction to Don Johnson was an occasion of such
moment that I refrain from entrusting it to memory's leaky barque.
Instead, I refer to an entry made shortly afterward in my daily
breviary:

> March 11
>   Dined this evening in company at Enrique's Little Havana, an
> eating place (with dancing). Of a sudden, came a measure of stirring
> music, and through the door strode a man of good figure and erect
> carriage, wearing a light-colored nankeen suit and spectacles of a tint
> so opaque as to hide the eyes within. Instantly, I recognized the cel-
> ebrated Don Johnson—this despite his stature, which was in appear-
> ance somewhat shorter than in the portrait at the National Gallery.
> At the first opportunity, I took leave of my party, made my way to
> his table, and, emboldened by the warmth of my sentiment, clasped
> him by the hand. Conveying to him my admiration in the strongest
> terms, I added that I had many questions that I hoped one day to
> discuss with him, and inquired whether I might call upon him some
> afternoon at his trailer. In the silence that ensued, my heart raced in
> anticipation of another of Don Johnson's famed epigrams, when, with
> a look at his companions at table, Don Johnson replied, "Hey. Who
> *is* this wing nut?"

Later, I was to learn that my friend's abruptness bespoke no
hidden depths of ill-humor but only the natural impatience of a spirited intellect checked by society's custom. Indeed, when next we
met, and I, blushing crimson and stammering out my words, yet
managed to ask of him whether he did all his own stunts, he
responded most willingly. I then followed by inquiring how he contrived to juggle his fame with his personal life, and so began a conversation that continued late into the evening.

To those several critics who, with but the most superficial
knowledge, accuse Don Johnson of haughty and peremptory behavior, I reply that my friend has long suffered from a recurring melancholia, brought on by the exigencies of a career that no critic could

ever sustain. In addition, I submit that Don Johnson became (through no fault of his own) a man of painfully divided loyalties: on the one hand, he belonged to the city, while, on the other hand, he belonged to the night. We can only imagine the agonies of doubt this must have occasioned within him, as his mind turned first toward the one indebtedness, and then toward the other. Moreover, Don Johnson has been troubled at irregular intervals by a very rare disorder whereby the reflections of street lamps cross the lenses of his spectacles in dizzying succession and deafening airs from popular operettas fill his ears. That he has managed even the smallest degree of civility in the face of such impediments I consider a remarkable feat.

Recently, I found among my papers the text of a hymn that, though unsigned, shows the unmistakable evidence of Don Johnson's authorship. As I recall, it was composed as a tribute to his friend Lord Cranwyck, of Ayles, Lincolnshire, in celebration of the latter's marriage to a mutual friend. It reads, in part:

> You did it, pal—hey, it's a lock.
> You got legs, Mister; you can walk
> The gig's a tough one, understand?
> Count on it, buddy—ask the man.
> Pal, get the wax out of your ears.
> We're lookin' at at least ten years.
> The only thing I'm gonna say—
> Hey, read my lips: "Flight's cancelled, Ray."

Were Don Johnson's detractors only aware of this and many other proofs of devotion which he showed repeatedly to those cherished in his affection, I am certain they would revise their opinions.

On the subject of women, Don Johnson is perhaps best known for his remark that whereas one cannot, assuredly, live with them, one cannot, by equal measure, live without them. Of his own version of marriage, to a daughter of the French-sounding D'Arbanville family, I shall speak more at a later time. Suffice it to say that Don Johnson had the wisdom to choose for a companion an actress whose beauty, charm, talent, and sense of fun all vie with each other for preference in the eye of the observer, and one who can do an excellent imitation of a person coughing. I seem to recall hearing recently that Don Johnson and Patti had moved to separate dwellings; however, I believe someone else possibly informed me (more recently yet) that they were once again together, which later report I hope may be fact, inasmuch as I think she is nice. □

From your study of these two pieces, what specifically did you learn about Boswell's style? Do you feel Frazier's parody helps you understand Boswell's style better than you would have without having it as a comparison? Why or why not? And do you think Frazier captures the spirit of Boswell's style? Why or why not?

Exercises

1. Write a brief paper evaluating the quality of Frazier's parody. Do you feel he writes an effective stylistic parody, or do you feel he has strained his imitation too far? Explain.

2. Write a one- or two-page description of a famous landmark in your community using the style of your favorite author. Be as faithful as you can to the stylistic techniques your author uses.

REVISING FOR CLARITY

Although style is not something you add to or take away from your writing, it appears in the verbal choices—words, phrases, and sentences—you habitually make as a writer. In the imitations you wrote and read above, you learned you can consciously imitate another writer's style. And if you are really astute, you can, as Frazier does, imitate a writer's voice and tone.

As you revise your writing, you can change words, phrases, and sentence lengths to achieve clarity and observe social conventions. Although no foolproof method exists for achieving a clear style, a few revision strategies can help you eliminate some wordy or ambiguous phrases that often confuse your readers.

As you read the following sections, remember that revisions occur in context. As you revise one word, phrase, or sentence, you often affect the context surrounding your revision. One simple revision can set off a chain of alterations that forces you to reconsider words and sentences that come before and after your revision.

Exercise

Return to your rewriting of the passage from Doctorow's *Welcome to Hard Times* (page 278). Revise one sentence to emphasize an atmosphere different from the one you wrote earlier. How does this change affect your original draft?

Revising Subjects and Verbs   Subjects and verbs form a unique relationship in a sentence by making an assertion, asking a question, or stating a fact. As you revise, you can reduce the likelihood of your readers' misunderstanding the main thrust of your ideas by clarifying the relationship between the subjects (actors) and verbs (actions) in each sentence. A clear subject–verb relationship directs your readers' attention to the main idea of a sentence, connecting a particular actor with a specific action and establishing the necessary basis for the understanding of your writing.

As we hasten to capture the essence of an idea in our first drafts, we often fail to identify an actor or subject in a sentence. We assume a subject capable of performing whatever action the sentence calls for, but we forget to tell our readers what we have in mind.

Notice the ambiguity caused by the unspecified subject in each of the following sentences taken from student papers:

1. It has been proven that long-term and concentrated use of the eyes on small figures and movements can cause eyestrain.

2. Blacks, Hispanics, and Anglos, along with other minorities, are shown working together for one common cause.

Although each of these sentences lacks a context, we can still see the readers' difficulty in interpreting the writer's intent. Who is the "it" in sentence 1, and what specifically does "it" do? If the writer means "something" causes eyestrain, then he or she must specify "who or what" causes it. The revised sentence might read, "Long-term and concentrated use of the eyes on small figures and movements can cause eyestrain." And depending on the writer's intent, another revision might be equally valid: "A recent Medical College of Virginia report suggests that long-term and concentrated use of the eyes on small figures and movements can cause eyestrain." In both revisions of sentence 1, we clearly specified a subject (actor) for the verb (action) and eliminated the ambiguity for the reader.

A similar ambiguity appears in sentence 2. If we listen carefully to the sentence, we can hear its ineffectiveness, sense its missing element. Sentence 2 lacks an appropriate subject for its verb or action. Do Hispanics, Blacks, and Anglos "show" something, or do they "work together"? The sentence yields at least two interpretations or revisions, the first emphasizing "showing," the second, "working together":

1. [Successful television programs] show Hispanics, Blacks, Anglos, along with other minorities, working together on common causes.

   or

2. Hispanics, Blacks, and Anglos, along with other minorities, work together on common causes.

Exercises

Revise each of the following sentences, eliminating the ambiguities caused by the ineffective subjects and verbs. Explain the rationale for your revision.

1. Children are often frightened by television.

2. The runway is currently used as a dragstrip and place to hold parties since it is nonfunctional for air traffic.

3. When the Soviets are considered to be the enemy, they are no longer considered as people, just enemies—the bad guys, the robbers.

4. In "Transfixed" Chris Burden was literally crucified to the back of a Volkswagen that was backed out of a garage for a few minutes, its engine roaring at full throttle.

5. In reading the book by John Hersey called *Hiroshima* the author talks of shadows of people being burned into the walls of buildings, of how the fire ripped through people's homes ten miles away from the initial bombing, and of how the effects of being closer to the center of the explosion might have been better than the effects of being farther away because of less suffering.

6. In striving for perfection the status quo can never be good enough, nor can governments afford a policy of no deviation. Tolerance must be the policy.

Revising Verbs Since subjects and verbs are inextricably intertwined, the revision of one often necessitates revision of the other. After you have explored some options for the subjects of ineffective sentences, you can reduce further ambiguities by fine-tuning your verbs.

Active Verbs Verbs grab attention and hold sentences together. Active verbs tell readers the action the subject performs; they focus our minds on the actor and the action, and involve us in the motion and energy of the sentence. Active verbs show movement, whether mental activity such as "thinking" or physical activity such as "racing."

If we glance back over the preceding paragraph, we can find six active verbs: *grab, hold, tell, focus, involve,* and *show*. Each of these verbs depicts an action which "something" or "somebody" must perform, thereby directing our attention to both actor and action.

Being Verbs Other kinds of verbs exist, but they carry less impact than active ones. Static verbs, those derived from the verb "to be" and its synonyms—*grow, seem, appear, look, become, feel*—serve necessary functions in our dialogues. They function as equal marks in an arithmetical equation: $2 + 2 = 4$; Jack is my brother (Jack = brother) or Jack is tall (Jack = tall). Static or "being" verbs often appear in factual statements and contribute greatly to our notion of "dry facts." Used judiciously in moderation, static verbs offer us important flat statements, but used in sustained conversation with readers, static verbs turn our sentences into lifeless, dull dialogues.

Passive Verbs "Passive" verbs may breathe life, but they send readers ambiguous messages by concealing the actors of the sentences. Usually a passive verb tells what action was done to a subject, not what action the subject actually does. Notice the differences between these sentences:

1. Mark was robbed last night.

2. A mugger robbed Mark last night.

Sentence 1 tells us what happened to Mark, but it fails to specify an actor for the action, "robbed." When we read "Mark" and recognize him as the subject of the sentence, we expect him to "do something." In this instance, the passive verb fails to meet our expectations, and although we probably have a vague idea what the writer means, we really cannot be sure of it. Sentence 2, on the other hand, uses an active verb and clearly specifies the actor–action relationship for us. This sentence creates a sense of closure and satisfies our need to know what happened to whom.

Exercises

Revise each of the following sentences, providing subjects and verbs and reducing ambiguity and lifelessness wherever possible.

1. The effects of their divorce on their offspring are overlooked too often by the parents, who find themselves preoccupied with the formalities of divorce: personal property division, alimony settlements, and legal fees.

2. Unintentionally, the pressure, anxiety, and stress of a marital termination is passed on to the child, who is most undeserving of this treatment.

3. A "pretty picture" is formed in the young adult's mind, but unfortunately the paint begins to crumble after their first mid-terms when the real picture is then revealed.

4. If the signals are reached by loved ones, then the suicidal victim has a relatively high chance of alleviating his pressure.

5. On the morning of January 28, 1969, at Union Platform A, the normal process of extracting oil was aborted when a vital pipeline was disconnected causing oil and mud to shoot some 90 feet above the deck.

6. Furthermore, the most dangerous criminals are rarely the ones executed. Some examples are the Charles Manson gang convicted in the late sixties of murdering actress Sharon Tate and her three house guests. Another is the Son of Sam, killer of eight people in New York, who is still alive and well. The most notorious is Ted Bundy, a confessed killer of over thirty college students in several states and who is being supported by the taxpayers which include the victims' families.

Revising Sentences   After you have revised your subjects and verbs to specify actors and actions for each sentence, you can reshape your sentences for greater interest, emphasis, and clarity by varying their lengths and listening to their rhythms. Like speech, writing can be monotonous when its rhythms and sounds become repetitive and predictable. Through an awareness of sentence structure and its effect on your readers, you can create a clear, readable style that persuades your audience to listen closely to you.

Varying Sentence Lengths   No one can tell you how long a sentence should be. But when you hear a sentence in context and have difficulty understanding what it means or locating its subject and verb, you can assume it is edging toward marathon length. Short sentences are not intrinsically better than medium or long sentences. But often in the context of a paragraph or an essay, a sentence that sounded fine by itself suddenly sounds out of beat with the rhythm of its context. By shortening or lengthening the sentence, you can restore the flow and harmony of the work. Although reestablishing a consistent beat can easily take priority in revision, you should not sacrifice meaning for sound; keep in mind that the key to communication is clarity. Choose the right words, but put them in the best order.

Exercise

Combine each of the following groups of sentences into as few sentences as you can, and write them into stylistically effective paragraphs. Vary the lengths of your sentences to achieve the flow and rhythms you desire. Read your finished paragraphs aloud to two or three peers and ask them to note arrhythmical passages if they appear.

Before you begin, here is an example of how to proceed:

- There is a very old covered bridge near the town. It has been there for sixty years. The bridge is in a state of bad disrepair. It spans the Onawaga River. It is wide enough for only one car. It is the property of the state. The state historical trust wants to get it back to full use.

- A sixty-year-old covered bridge, wide enough for only one car and in a bad state of disrepair, spans the Onawaga River near the town. The bridge is the property of the state, and the state historical true: wants to buy it and repair it in order to get it back into full use.

1. Thousands of travelers go each year to Europe from America. Most travelers prefer Western Europe. Britain is a popular spot. There are no language problems in Britain. France is a favorite for its good food and wine and marvelous cathedrals. People like Spain for the sun and old castles. The Greek Islands are famous for their beaches and unspoiled terrain. Italian cities are hectic but stimulating. There are many wonderful buildings and museums in Italy. There are fairy-tale castles in Germany. Swiss scenery is charming. The Dutch people are very friendly.

2. John Sullivan is an American journalist. This is a true story. Sullivan is missing in El Salvador. Sullivan disappeared in December 1980. Eight foreign journalists have died covering the civil war in El Salvador. Sullivan is the only American journalist missing. His relatives think that he is probably dead. Two people have said that they saw Sullivan interrogated by the military.

3. There were many large family-owned book publishers in New York and Boston. Many giant corporations have taken over these publishing houses. Many independent booksellers are going out of business. Computers analyze sales and profits and determine what the large chains should carry. Book production costs have risen enormously. First-book authors have little chance of getting published. The IRS will not allow publishers to take a tax write-off for unsold books. Some publishers refuse to allow booksellers to return books. Booksellers must buy fewer books. Few books by an unknown author are bought. The trend is to best-selling mass-market material.

4. We are obsessed with the idea of genius. We want intellectual and artistic heroes. The idea is a Romantic one. The Romantic Movement was a revolt of the individual. Geniuses are those apart from the bland, ordinary masses. Geniuses are indifferent to what the public thinks. Many modern artists would rather be geniuses than craftsmen. Craftsmen just make things. Geniuses blaze new trails. Do we have any real artistic geniuses today? Geniuses are made by their contexts and environments, not by themselves. Geniuses are just super versions of the norm.

Varying Sentence Structure   As you probably inferred from our discussion of subjects and verbs, one key to clarity resides in the common sentence structure, subject–verb (S–V). Nearly all of our revisions thus far have stressed the importance of the subject–verb relationship and its role in achieving clarity in writing. We can manipulate the stylistic effect of a sentence in numerous ways as long as we preserve the S–V order of a sentence. We can make changes in our openers, interrupters, or closers, but if we do decide to change the S–V order, we should have a good reason for it.

We can begin sentences by placing *openers*—details and description—before the subject–verb, near the beginning of the sentence. The following examples demonstrate how we can add a single word, a phrase, or a dependent clause (a non-sentence containing a S–V) before the main S–V, which forms either a sentence or a sentence base for additional information.

1. The *Titanic* sank on April 15, 1912.   *(base)*

2. The unsinkable *Titanic* sank on April 15, 1912.   *(word)*

3. Proclaimed "unsinkable," the *Titanic* sank on April 15, 1912.   *(phrase)*

4. Although the press labeled it "unsinkable," the *Titanic* sank on April 15, 1912.   *(clause)*

Openers create new rhythms and textures for sentences. By adjusting the lengths and kinds of the openers, we control the time it takes for our readers to reach the main idea conveyed by the S–V base.

When we insert information between the S–V base, we "interrupt" the base and momentarily delay the connection between the subject and verb. Unlike the opener, which sounds appropriate most of the time, the *interrupter* can be used only in certain contexts. As we see below, the information that appeared as an opener may not be suitable as an interrupter. Notice what happens when we retain the same S–V base and change the openers to interrupters.

1. The *Titanic*, unsinkable, sank on April 15, 1912.   *(word)*

2. The *Titanic*, proclaimed "unsinkable," sank on April 15, 1912.   *(phrase)*

3. The *Titanic*, although the press labeled it "unsinkable," sank on April 15, 1912.   *(clause)*

Sentences 1 and 3 probably sound odd to you, even without the larger context of a paragraph. By listening to the sound and sense of a sentence as you revise, you can usually find an effective place for interrupters.

We can end a sentence or reach closure on an idea by placing details and information after the S–V base. And as with interrupters, indiscriminate placement of the *closer* yields odd and even non-English–sounding sentences.

1. The *Titanic* sank on April 15, 1912, unsinkable. *(word)*

2. The *Titanic* sank on April 15, 1912, proclaimed "unsinkable." *(phrase)*

3. The *Titanic* sank on April 15, 1912, although the press labeled it "unsinkable." *(clause)*

An analysis of these sentences explains why they affect readers as they do. Sentences 1 and 2 separate the details "unsinkable" and "proclaimed 'unsinkable'" from the word they describe, *Titanic*. The greater the separation between the detail and its noun, the greater the chance of ineffectiveness. Sentence 3 is clearer because the closer contains the word "it," which unmistakably links the closer to the word *Titanic*.

In most instances your decisions to use an opener, interrupter, or closer will be simple: If the revision sounds good to you, retain it. But in other cases—particularly with openers and closers—a pleasant-sounding sentence revision can be ambiguous, even humorously illogical. Notice how the information added to the following bases creates ambiguity.

1. Slowly descending the mountain, he saw two elk.

2. Flying high overhead, the hawk's shadow terrified the rabbit.

Because the opener in sentence 1 can describe either the movements of the subject (he) or the elk, it presents readers with an ambiguity. In this instance, since no context exists, readers assume "he" saw the animals as he came down the mountain. As readers, we take our signals from the placement of the details. We expect the descriptive information to be close to the word it describes or defines, in this case, the actor of the sentence. Another interpretation occurs when we transform the opener into a closer and revise the sentence to "He saw two elk slowly descending the mountain." By shifting the information to various places in the sentence, we can see where the details should go and ultimately reduce ambiguity for our readers.

Sentence 2 demonstrates another problem in clarity. According to its placement, the opener describes the actor of the S–V. This sentence tells us that the "shadow," not the hawk, is flying overhead. Unfortunately, simply moving the addition and transforming it into an interrupter or closer will not clarify this sentence. The S–V base is illogical. If the writer specifies the appropriate actor for the action, then the sentence, along with its opener, will make sense. A revision that preserves the S–V order of the sentence and places the opener beside the word it describes will yield a clear sentence: "Flying high overhead, the hawk terrified the rabbit with his shadow."

Exercises

1. Combine each of the following groups of sentences, converting one into a sentence with the main S–V and the others into openers, interrupters, closers, or combinations. The first pair provide an example.

   The Nez Perce were a peaceful tribe.
   The Nez Perce raised Appaloosa horses.

   - A peaceful tribe, the Nez Perce raised Appaloosa horses.

   - The Nez Perce, a peaceful tribe, raised Appaloosa horses.

   (a) The President was tired and ill.
   He flew to the disaster.
   (b) The Stinkos made their first American tour in 1980.
   They are a punk rock band from London's East End.
   (c) They played in several small clubs in Los Angeles, Chicago, and New York.
   They tore the stage apart with their raucous music.
   Their guitars cranked out discordant notes.
   Their notes had never before been combined in modern pop music.
   (d) The reporter leaned against the window.
   She had missed the interview for the third time.
   She was dejected.

2. The following passage is a "dewritten" version of the opening of John Updike's short story "A & P." Rewrite the following paragraph for

stylistic effectiveness and clarity. Use active verbs, additional details, sentence variety, and appropriate vocabulary to achieve the tone, voice, and effect you want your readers to have.

> In walked three girls in nothing but bathing suits. From my cash register I couldn't see them until they reached the bread. The one that caught my eye first wore a two-piece. She was a chunky kid. She had a good tan. I held a box of HiHo crackers. I rang it up again. The customer started giving me hell. She's one of those cash register watchers. It made her day. She's been watching cash registers for fifty years.

ANALYZING STYLE

A clear and interesting style is the product of careful revision. When we read a published document, we read the end result of extensive revision, crafted to produce a special effect on us as readers. Writers achieve effective styles when their words, phrases, and sentences clearly convey their ideas and their feelings about those ideas to us.

Below is an excerpt from Joan Didion's *Salvador*, an American writer's interpretation of a country's political upheaval. Record your reactions to her account of her trip and then write a brief paper explaining how she made you feel and react as you did.

Salvador
Joan Didion

That the texture of life in such a situation is essentially untranslatable became clear to me only recently, when I tried to describe to a friend in Los Angeles an incident that occurred some days before I left El Salvador. I had gone with my husband and another American to the San Salvador morgue, which, unlike most morgues in the United States, is easily accessible, through an open door on the ground floor around the back of the court building. We had been too late that morning to see the day's bodies (there is not much emphasis on embalming in El Salvador, or for that matter on identification, and bodies are dispatched fast for disposal), but the man in charge had opened his log to show us the morning's entries, seven bodies, all male, none identified, none believed older than twenty-five. Six had been certified dead by *arma de fuego*, firearms, and the seventh, who had also been shot, of shock. The slab on which the bodies had been received had already been washed down, and water stood on the floor. There were many flies, and an electric fan.

The other American with whom my husband and I had gone to the morgue that morning was a newspaper reporter, and since only seven unidentified bodies bearing evidence of *arma de fuego* did not in San Salvador in the summer of 1982 constitute a newspaper story worth pursuing, we left. Outside in the parking lot there were a number of wrecked or impounded cars, many of them shot up, upholstery chewed by bullets, windshield shattered, thick pastes of congealed blood on pearlized hoods, but this was also unremarkable, and it was not until we walked back around the building to the reporter's rented car that each of us began to sense the potentially remarkable.

Surrounding the car were three men in uniform, two on the sidewalk and the third, who was very young, sitting on his motorcycle in such a way as to block our leaving. A second motorcycle had been pulled up directly behind the car, and the space in front was occupied. The three had been joking among themselves, but the laughter stopped as we got into the car. The reporter turned the ignition on, and waited. No one moved. The two men on the sidewalk did not meet our eyes. The boy on the motorcycle stared directly, and caressed the G-3 propped between his thighs. The reporter asked in Spanish if one of the motorcycles could be moved so that we could get out. The men on the sidewalk said nothing, but smiled enigmatically. The boy only continued staring, and began twirling the flash suppressor on the barrel of his G-3.

This was a kind of impasse. It seemed clear that if we tried to leave and scraped either motorcycle the situation would deteriorate. It also seemed clear that if we did not try to leave the situation would deteriorate. I studied my hands. The reporter gunned the motor, forced the car up onto the curb far enough to provide a minimum space in which to maneuver, and managed to back out clean.

Nothing more happened, and what did happen had been a common enough kind of incident in El Salvador, a pointless confrontation with aimless authority, but I have heard of no *solución* that precisely addresses this local vocation for terror.

Any situation can turn to terror. The most ordinary errand can go bad. Among Americans in El Salvador there is an endemic apprehension of danger in the apparently benign. I recall being told by a network anchor man that one night in his hotel room (it was at the time of the election, and because the Camino Real was full he had been put up at the Sheraton) he took the mattress off the bed and shoved it against the window. He happened to have with him several bulletproof vests that he had brought from New York for the camera crew, and before going to the Sheraton lobby he put one on. Managers of American companies in El Salvador (Texas Instruments is still there, and Cargill, and some others) are replaced every several months, and their presence is kept secret. Some companies bury their managers in a number-two or number-three post. American embassy officers are driven in armored and unmarked vans (no eagle, no seal, no CD plates) by Salvadoran drivers and Salvadoran guards, because, I was told, "if someone gets blown away, obviously the State Department would prefer it done by a local security man, then you don't get headlines saying 'American Shoots Salvadoran Citizen.'" These local security men carry automatic weapons on their laps.

In such a climate the fact of being in El Salvador comes to seem a sentence of indeterminate length, and the prospect of leaving doubtful. On the night before I was due to leave I did not sleep, lay awake and listened to the music drifting up from a party at the Camino Real pool, heard the band play "Malaguena" at three and at four and again at five A.M., when the party seemed to end and light broke and I could get up. I was picked up to go to the airport that morning by one of the embassy vans, and a few blocks from the hotel I was seized by the conviction that this was not the most direct way to the airport, that this was not an embassy guard sitting in front with the Remington on his lap; that this was someone else. That the van turned out in fact to be the embassy van, detouring into San Benito to pick up an AID official, failed to relax me: once at the airport I sat without moving and averted my eyes from the soldiers patrolling the empty departure lounges. □

Didion makes us feel frightened when we read her work. She uses words, images, and details to convey her apprehensiveness toward her topic, but she also conveys a voice to us, an earnestness that makes us listen to her. For her, El Salvador is so filled with fear and terror that it permeates every aspect of daily life, even a simple ride to the airport. The fear she describes reflects her own sense of disbelief and her own sense of injustice. She casts a net of details and examples around us and inexorably tightens it as she brings us to her vision of the horrors surrounding her. By the time we complete her passage, we have faced the subjective reality she has confronted, and we have entered the terrible and unfamiliar world she describes.

How, then, does Didion involve us? What does she do to make us believe or disbelieve her, to make us respond to what she describes? A quick glance at elements of her writing style reveals an emotional as well as an intellectual intention. Didion wants us to feel as well as to understand.

By writing in the first person, Didion underscores her personal involvement with the events she discusses. Her details do not reflect the abstract language of political debates, but rather the graphic language of everyday experience, the casual matter-of-fact glimpses of life: flies, an electric fan, water standing on the floor, congealed blood on pearlized hoods, and a boy soldier twirling "the flash suppressor on the barrel of his G-3." And by delaying these details until the end of her paragraphs, Didion emphasizes the utter entrenchment of Salvadoran terror.

Didion sculpts her sentences to reflect the mounting danger she feels. Sentence after sentence begins with the subject and verb, a technique that establishes a predictable cadence. Each sentence moves us forward and directs our attention to the soldiers surrounding her car. She emphasizes the tension and the potential explosiveness of the situation with the short sentences "No one moved" and "I studied my hands." The soldiers stand as motionless as she sits, but there the resemblance ends. They are in control while she is powerless, and for the first time she feels the helplessness of a Salvadoran.

By carefully selecting the episodes she describes, she demonstrates her attitude toward her subject matter. Surely, something good or even remotely pleasant must happen to many people every day in El Salvador. But Didion chooses not to discuss any of the positive elements of quotidian life because such examples would seriously diminish the emotional impact of her point. Instead, she writes about the nameless, aimless terror that pervades the air and landscape.

Through Didion's eyes we see El Salvador as a country so terror-ridden that only catastrophes and events of major proportion can be considered newsworthy to outsiders. For Didion, herself a journalist, even seven dead men do not constitute the basis for news. It seems at first glance that to the citizens of El Salvador small things no longer matter, no longer penetrate the consciousness of those trying to lead normal lives. But she also depicts for us the fear of simple, everyday activities, the terror and paranoia of starting a parked car, of riding in an embassy van to the airport. Didion ultimately shows us citizens of fear who can no longer distinguish harmless events from harmful ones.

Didion "persuades" us to believe that terror exists in El Salvador largely through her careful selection and arrangement of detail, partly through her careful positioning of her most vivid images, and partly through her use of very short sentences that explode with tension. We understand and we feel her fear as we see nightmarish terror surface in daytime. And from the safety of our well-lit desks, we become convinced of its possible reality.

Exercise

Carefully analyze Didion's style in the passage above. You may use the same questions you used in your self-analysis in Exercise 2 in the first section of this chapter, "What Is Style?" or refer to the revision guide at the end of this chapter.

When we revise our work, we listen to the sounds of our language, see the shapes of our sentences, and consider the reactions of our readers. Our writing invites our readers into a personal dialogue and our styles keep them interested in us and in our ideas. A clear style reflects not only clear thinking, but also an intellectual openness and an eagerness to communicate with others.

Exercise

Analyze the following works, and explain how the writers' sentence sense (use of length and variety), vocabulary, tone, and voice contribute to the overall effect of each work.

Man's Search for Meaning
Victor Frankl

The attempt to develop a sense of humor and to see things in a humorous light is some kind of a trick learned while mastering the art of living. Yet it is possible to practice the art of living even in a concentration camp, although suffering is omnipresent. To draw an analogy: a man's suffering is similar to the behavior of gas. If a certain quantity of gas is pumped into an empty chamber, it will fill the chamber completely and evenly, no matter how big the chamber. Thus suffering completely fills the human soul and conscious mind, no matter whether the suffering is great or little. Therefore the "size" of human suffering is absolutely relative.

It also follows that a very trifling thing can cause the greatest of joys. Take as an example something that happened on our journey from Auschwitz to the camp affiliated with Dachau. We had all been afraid that our transport was heading for the Mauthausen camp. We became more and more tense as we approached a certain bridge over the Danube which the train would have to cross to reach Mauthausen, according to the statement of experienced traveling companions. Those who have never seen anything similar cannot possibly imagine the dance of joy performed in the carriage by the prisoners when they saw that our transport was not crossing the bridge and was instead heading "only" for Dachau.

And again, what happened on our arrival in that camp, after a journey lasting two days and three nights? There had not been enough room for everybody to crouch on the floor of the carriage at the same time. The majority of us had to stand all the way, while a few took turns at squatting on the scanty straw which was soaked with human urine. When we arrived the first important news that we heard from older prisoners was that this comparatively small camp (its population was 2,500) had no "oven," no crematorium, no gas! That meant that a person who had become a "Moslem" could not be taken straight to the gas chamber, but would have to wait until a so-called "sick convoy" had been arranged to return to Auschwitz. This joyful surprise put us all in a good mood. The wish of the senior warden of our hut in Auschwitz had come true: we had come, as quickly as possible, to a camp which did not have a "chimney"—unlike Auschwitz. We laughed and cracked jokes in spite of, and during, all we had to go through in the next few hours. □

My Speech to the Graduates
Woody Allen

More than any other time in history, mankind faces a crossroads. One path leads to despair and utter hopelessness. The other, to total extinction. Let us pray we have the wisdom to choose correctly. I speak, by the way, not with any sense of futility, but with a panicky conviction of the absolute meaninglessness of existence which could easily be misinterpreted as pessimism. It is not. It is merely a healthy concern for the predicament of modern man. (Modern man is here defined as any person born after Nietzche's edict that "God is dead," but before the hit recording "I Wanna Hold Your Hand.") This "predicament" can be stated in one of two ways, though certain linguistic philosophers prefer to reduce it to a mathematical equation where it can be easily solved and even carried around in the wallet.

Put in its simplest form, the problem is: How is it possible to find meaning in a finite world given my waist and shirt size? This is a very difficult question when we realize that science has failed us. True, it has conquered many diseases, broken the genetic code, and even placed human beings on the moon, and yet when a man of 80 is left in a room with two 18-year-old cocktail waitresses nothing happens. Because the real problems never change. After all, can the human soul be glimpsed through a microscope? Maybe—but you'd definitely need one of those very good ones with two eyepieces. We know that the most advanced computer in the world does not have a brain as sophisticated as that of an ant. True, we could say that of many of our relatives but we only have to put up with them at weddings or special occasions. Science is something we depend on all the time. If I develop a pain in the chest I must take an X-ray. But what if the radiation from the X-ray causes me deeper problems? Before I know it, I'm in for surgery. Naturally, while they're giving me oxygen an intern decides to light up a cigarette. The next thing you know I'm rocketing over the World Trade Center in bedclothes. Is this science? True, science has taught us how to pasteurize cheese. And true, this can be fun in mixed company—but what of the H-bomb? Have you ever seen what happens when one of those things falls off a desk accidentally? And where is science when one ponders the eternal riddles? How did the cosmos originate? How long has it been around? Did matter begin with an explosion or by the word of God? And if by the latter, could He not have begun it just two weeks earlier to take advantage of some of the warmer weather? Exactly what do we mean when we say man is mortal? Obviously it's not a compliment.

Religion, too, has unfortunately let us down. Miguel de Unamuno writes blithely of the "eternal persistence of consciousness," but that is no easy feat. Particularly when reading Thackeray. I often think how comforting life must have been for early man because he believed in a powerful, benevolent Creator who looked after all things. Imagine his disappointment when he saw his wife putting on weight. Contemporary man, of course, has no such peace of mind. He finds himself in the midst of a crisis of faith. He is what we fashionably call "alienated." He has seen the ravages of war, he has known natural catastrophes, he has been to singles bars. My good friend Jacques Monod spoke often of the randomness of the cosmos. He believed everything in existence occurred by pure chance with the possible exception of his breakfast, which he felt certain was made by his housekeeper. Naturally belief in a divine intelligence inspires tranquillity. But this does not free us from our human responsibilities. Am I my brother's keeper? Yes. Interestingly, in my case I share that honor with the Prospect Park Zoo. Feeling godless then, what we have done is made technology God. And yet can technology really be the answer when a brand new Buick, driven by my close associate, Nat Persky, winds up in the window of Chicken Delight causing hundreds of customers to scatter? My toaster has never once worked properly in four years. I follow the instructions and push two slices of bread down in the slots and seconds later they rifle upward. Once they broke the nose of a woman I loved very dearly. Are we counting on nuts and bolts and electricity to solve our problems? Yes, the telephone is a good thing—and the refrigerator—and the air conditioner. But not every air conditioner. Not my sister Henny's, for instance. Hers makes a loud noise and still doesn't cool. When the man comes over to fix it, it gets worse. Either that or he tells her she needs a new one. When she complains, he says not to bother him. This man is truly alienated. Not only is he alienated but he can't stop smiling.

The trouble is, our leaders have not adequately prepared us for a mechanized society. Unfortunately our politicians are either incompetent or corrupt. Sometimes both on the same day. The Government is unresponsive to the needs of the little man. Under five-seven, it is impossible to get your Congressman on the phone. I am not denying that democracy is still the finest form of government. In a democracy at least, civil liberties are upheld. No citizen can be wantonly tortured, imprisoned, or made to sit through certain Broadway shows. And yet this is a far cry from what goes on in the Soviet Union. Under their form of totalitarianism, a person merely caught whistling is sentenced to 30 years in a labor camp. If, after 15 years, he still will not stop whistling they shoot him. Along with this brutal fascism we find its handmaiden, terrorism. At no other time in history has man been so afraid to cut into his veal chop for fear that it will explode. Violence breeds more violence and it is predicted that by 1990 kidnapping will be the dominant mode of social interaction. Overpopulation will exacerbate problems to the breaking point. Figures tell us there are already more people on earth than we need to move even the heaviest piano. If we do not call a halt to breeding, by the year 2000 there will be no room to serve dinner unless one is willing to set the table on the heads of strangers. Then they must not move for an hour while we eat. Of course energy will be in short supply and each car owner will be allowed only enough gasoline to back up a few inches.

Instead of facing these challenges we turn to distractions like drugs and sex. We live in far too permissive a society. Never before has pornography been this rampant. And those films are lit so badly! We are a people who lack defined goals. We have never learned to love. We lack leaders and coherent programs. We have no spiritual center. We are adrift in the cosmos wreaking monstrous violence on one another out of frustration and pain. Fortunately, we have not lost our sense of proportion. Summing up, it is clear the future holds great opportunities. It also hold pitfalls. The trick will be to avoid the pitfalls, seize the opportunities, and get back home by six o'clock. ☐

REVISION CHECKLIST

1. Vocabulary

- Have you selected the most effective details?
- If you used technical terms, did you define them for your readers?
- Is your vocabulary suitable for the tone and voice in your work?

2. Sentences

- Does each sentence have a clearly specified *actor?*
- Does each sentence have a clearly specified *action?*
- Did you use *action* verbs whenever possible?
- Can your reader clearly see the subject–verb in each sentence?
- Did you vary the lengths of your sentences?
- Are your openers, interrupters, and closers clearly attached to the word they describe?
- Did you achieve sentence variety by using different kinds of openers, interrupters, and closers?

3. Tone

- Does your tone reflect your attitude toward your topic?
- Is your tone appropriate for your topic?
- Is your tone consistent?
- How intimate are you with your audience?
- Can you see a pattern of words that reinforces your tone?

4.   Voice

- Is your voice appropriate for your readers?
- Is your voice appropriate for your topic?
- Is your voice consistent throughout your work?
- Is your voice appropriate for your tone?

Acknowledgments

CHAPTER 1

Bernard Slade, excerpts from *Same Time, Next Year*. Reprinted by permission of the author.

Harold Pinter, from *No Man's Land*. Reprinted by permission of Grove Press, a division of Wheatland Corporation. Copyright © 1975 by Harold Pinter Ltd.

John Gardner, from *The Art of Fiction: Notes on Craft for Young Writers*. Copyright © 1984 by the Estate of John Gardner. Reprinted by permission of Alfred A. Knopf, Inc.

"Jane Martin," from *Twirler*. Copyright © 1981. Used by permission of Alexander Speer, Trustee for Jane Martin. All rights reserved. Caution: Professionals and amateurs are hereby warned that "Twirler," being fully protected under the Copyright Laws of the United States of America, the British Commonwealth, including the Dominion of Canada, and all other countries of the International Copyright Union and the Universal Copyright Convention, is subject to royalty. All rights, including professional, amateur, motion picture, recitation, lecturing, public reading, radio and television broadcasting, and the rights of translation into foreign languages, are strictly reserved. Particular emphasis is laid on the question of readings, permission for which must be secured from the author's agent in writing. All inquiries concerning rights should be addressed to the author's representative: Samuel French, Inc., 45 West 25th Street, New York, New York 10010.

Ed Bullins, from "The Taking of Miss Janie," in *Famous American Plays of the 70s*. Copyright © 1974 by Ed Bullins. Reprinted with permission.

Dick Jackman, "Light," from "Two Visions of America," in *Harper's*, March 1985. Copyright © 1985 by *Harper's Magazine*. All rights reserved. Reprinted from the March issue by special permission.

"Dark," from "Two Visions of America," in *Harpers*, March 1985. Copyright © 1985 by *Harper's Magazine*. All rights reserved. Reprinted from the March issue by special permission.

Walter Karp, "Only the Fearful Know Television," in *Harper's*, September 1984. Copyright © 1984 by *Harper's Magazine*. All rights reserved. Reprinted from the September issue by special permission.

Index

About the Authors

Eric Gould, Professor of English at the University of Denver, Colorado, received his Ph.D. from the University of London, England. He has directed the Freshman Writing Program at the University of Denver and is currently Dean of Graduate Studies. He teaches courses in modern literature and literary theory, interdisciplinary humanities, and freshman writing. Professor Gould is the author of *Mythical Intentions in Modern Literature* (Princeton), *The Sin of the Book: Edmond Jabès* (Nebraska), *Reading into Writing* (Houghton-Mifflin), and *Making Meaning* (Wadsworth). His reviews and articles have appeared in a number of journals including the London *Times Literary Supplement* and *The New York Times Book Review.*

Robert DiYanni is Professor of English at Pace University, Pleasantville, New York, where he is also Director of Interdisciplinary Studies. He received his B.A. from Rutgers University and his Ph.D. from the City University of New York. He has published articles and reviews on various aspects of English and American literature and on rhetoric and composition. Included also are a number of textbooks: *Prose Pieces, Modern American Prose, Literature,* and *Modern American Poets: Their Voices and Visions* (all published by Random House). He is currently working on a humanities textbook.

William Smith is Associate Professor of English and Director of Rhetoric and Composition at Virginia Commonwealth University, where he teaches undergraduate and graduate composition courses. He received his Ph.D. from the University of Utah. He is co-author with Robert DiYanni of a forthcoming text, *Reading, Writing, and Culture* (Random House).

Eric Gould, Robert DiYanni, and William Smith previously collaborated on *The Art of Reading,* also published by Random House.